When we grow up experiencing indifference, rejection and abuse, we make choices which are addictive and self-destructive. When self-love enters your life through changes brought on by the wisdom contained in this book, you will be reparented and reborn into a healthy life and diet of self-love.

—Bernie Siegel, MD
author of *A Book of Miracles* and *101 Exercises For The Soul*

Rather than promoting the deprivation that is typical of modern day diet mentality, Michelle Minero graciously invites us to imagine how our lives and our world might be different if, instead, we fed ourselves a consistent diet of loving thoughts and kind behaviors. She offers up surprisingly easy-to-follow, practical steps for doing so, skillfully demonstrating how following the path of self-love can lead to freedom from body-hatred and eating difficulties. This book is a gift for anyone struggling with eating, weight, and negative body image!

—Anita Johnston, PhD
author of *Eating in the Light of the Moon*

This book is a must read. It is especially helpful for anyone with an eating disorder or chronic dieting and the people who love them. What a wonderful world it would be if women loved and accepted themselves and their bodies unconditionally. Ms. Minero helps the reader along that path. She helps us to see the ways that our society and we ourselves perpetuate self-criticism. She then presents ways in which we can change that critical self-talk into self-love. At the end of each chapter Ms. Minero gives practical action points that help the reader incorporate the key concepts into their life. I will definitely be recommending *Self-Love Diet: The Only Diet That Works* to my patients and their families.

—Pamela Carlton, MD
Director, The Carlton Clinic for Eating-Related Disorders
author of *Take Charge of Your Child's Eating Disorder*

Michelle Minero is all about hope. And her book, *Self-Love Diet: The Only Diet That Works*, is too. You are sure to be inspired!

—Jenni Schaefer
author of *Life Without Ed* and *Goodbye Ed, Hello Me*

This book presents in a creative and accessible style a basic premise of self-help and wellbeing: self-love. Michelle Minero has been able to encapsulate and present in an easy to understand practice and put into action this difficult to grasp and even more difficult to internalize principle. *Self-Love Diet: The Only Diet That Works* will help many with eating disorders, and I recommend it to every clinician working with individuals struggling with self-acceptance. Kudos to Michelle for putting forth this valuable tool.

—Ovidio Bermudez, MD
Medical Director, Eating Recovery Center, Adolescent Services,
Denver, Colorado

Self-Love Diet

The Only Diet That Works

Discover the 7 Paths to Self-Love

Love Yourself, Love Your Body, Love the World

by Michelle E. Minero

Phoenix Century Press
P.O. Box 1792
Sausalito, CA 94966

www.phoenixcenturypress.com

Neither the author nor the publisher is engaged in rendering professional advice or services to the individual reader. The ideas, procedures, and suggestions contained in this book are not intended as a substitute for consulting with your physician or psychotherapist. All matters regarding your health require medical supervision. Neither the author nor the publisher shall be liable for any loss or damage allegedly arising from any information or suggestion in this book.

Self-Love Diet
The Only Diet That Works
by Michelle E. Minero

ISBN-10: 0615743803
ISBN-13: 9780615743806
LCCN: 2013930800

Editor: Emelina Minero
www.communitybucketlist.com/work-with-me

Cover Design: Gary Newman
Gary Newman Design, www.newmango.com

Cover Photography: Victoria Webb
Looking Glass Images, lgimages.biz/about.html

selflovewarrior.com
www.theselflovediet.com
www.lovewarriorcommunity.com

Printed in the United States of America

About the Author

Michelle E. Minero is a Licensed Marriage, Family Therapist who has dedicated her work to helping people recover from eating disorders and body-hatred. Michelle graduated from the University of San Francisco with a B.A. in psychology in 1976 and a master in counseling in 1988. She created the Quest Program, an intensive outpatient eating disorder program for Psych-Strategies Inc. in 2000. She brought the ANAD support group to Petaluma and founded Eating Disorders Recovery Support Inc. in 2005. She has four grown children, one granddaughter, and another granddaughter on the way. She is happily married to Al Minero and lives in Sonoma County, California.

love YOURSELF

Dear Adrienne,

Blessings to you on your Self-Love Diet !

Michelle

YOURSELF

Contents

Body Path of the Self-Love Diet

Introduction

If you have ever hated your body, ever wanted to lose weight or believed that if you lost weight you would feel better about yourself, you have mistakenly thought that your problem was your body. It is not. Changing your outsides has never been the solution. The problem has been your inability, up to this point, to understand that you are not your body, to know without a doubt that you are good enough, precious and lovable exactly as you are in this moment.

Any problems you may have with accepting yourself and your body is a reflection of hurtful experiences and faulty beliefs that can be reversed through the process of living the Self-Love Diet.

In the Self-Love Diet, diet is redefined as "regularly offering yourself love." How would your life be different if you regularly offered yourself love? This is what you will explore in this book, a guided practice on being more loving to yourself.

The Self-Love Diet exposes the lies and broken promises of the two-prong food and exercise diets of the past. The seven paths of the Self-Love Diet explore your relationship with your spirit, your body, your thoughts and feelings, your relationships with others, your culture and the world.

Working with my eating disordered clients and my own recovery from compulsive overeating and dieting motivated me to write *Self-Love Diet: The Only Diet that Works*. Helping people let go of their body-hatred, and bring in acceptance, care and love, witnessing my clients being able to wake up free from the obsession with their bodies and knowing that people can have a full life filled with passion—this is what motivated me to write this book. I believe everyone has everything they need inside of themselves to heal. The focus of this book is using love as the foundational component of healing.

This book is divided into five parts. Part one shows you a glimpse of what your life can look like when you love yourself and the connection between loving yourself and the world. Part two defines the Self-Love Diet and shows you steps to take to begin loving yourself. Part three increases understanding of the different eating disorders and reduces the stigma surrounding them through client stories, case examples and journal entries. Part four describes the seven paths of the Self-Love Diet, and part five is a call to action, a guide for continuing your self-love practice in your life after you have finished reading this book.

The examples I use in this book come from my work as a psychotherapist with my courageous, beautiful clients who have suffered from eating disorders. I have been protective of the confidentiality of my clients by changing their names and identifying information, and by sometimes creating composites of several clients into one.

To get the most out of this book, incorporate the action steps at the end of each chapter into your life, and write your responses in your journal or in the spaces provided throughout the book as you go along. You may also purchase a Self-Love Diet Journal at http://www.lovewarriorcommunity.com/store. You can bring what you've written to your therapist, support group or friends and family as prompts for discussion. You may decide to start a Self-Love Diet book club where you can discuss the questions with others who are on the same self-love journey, or invite others to begin a writing group based on the action steps at the end of each chapter.

Another invitation is to use the Love Warrior Community (LWC) as a companion online site to this book. The LWC is an online community that uses creativity for healing and exploration. Through writing, art, music, videos and imagery, the LWC provides motivation, inspiration and encouragement for you to further cultivate your self-love practice (www.lovewarriorcommunity.com).

Although my work with people struggling with eating disorders inspired me to write this book, they unfortunately are not the only ones who struggle with body image or self-esteem. If you do not have an eating disorder, you can still get help from this book. Love is a healing energy that can benefit the healthiest person, to the most terminal. Love can benefit the most confident person, to the most insecure. Treating yourself with more kindness and love can only benefit you.

There is no right or wrong way to utilize the information in this book. There may be chapters or action steps that do not fit for you. Take what you like and use it, and leave the rest. Begin the practice of loving yourself in your own timing and pacing, however it fits for you, and see where it takes you.

By bringing the concepts of this book into your daily life practices, my hope is that you will create a life filled with love, acceptance, forgiveness, passion, peace and joy. As you live a life focused on consciously bringing more love into your life, I trust that you will touch the lives of others in such a way as to bring healing and love into their lives. This book will not only help you to discover how loving yourself will be the only diet that you will ever need, but it will show you how loving your body will lead to loving yourself, and how loving yourself will lead to a better world.

I invite you to join me and the others who have already begun this endeavor to create a new culture devoted to love. How would your life be different if you loved yourself and your body? Walk down the seven paths of the Self-Love Diet with me, and others who have already joined the LWC, and find out.

Part One

*Do you want me to tell you something
really subversive?
Love is everything it's cracked up to be.
That's why people are so cynical about it …
It really is worth fighting for, being brave for,
risking everything for. And the trouble is,
If you don't risk anything, you're risking
even more.*

—Erica Jong

Love Yourself, Love Your Body, Love the World:
A Glimpse into Recovery

Part One of *Self-Love Diet: The Only Diet That Works* begins with my personal story of how I struggled with my body and the journey that led me towards self-love, self-acceptance and body acceptance. I began my journey with my body when I was five years old. That journey first led me to yo-yo dieting and compulsive overeating. I used food to cope with the stresses in my life, and as I began a new journey to explore my relationship with myself outside of my body, I slowly realized that the answers that I sought in life had always been inside of me. Through my recovery, through regularly offering myself love, how I viewed myself, my body and the world began to shift.

I started to understand the messages that my food cravings were trying to tell me. I began journaling about my food thoughts. Writing in a journal helped me to understand how I was using food to fill a deeper need that went beyond my body and food, and writing helped me to uncover what it was that I really craved.

I started to become aware of my self-critical thoughts, which empowered me to change them. It was a slow process, but one morning, while I was lying in bed, still waking up, I noticed that I was happy. I realized that I wasn't thinking about what I was or was not going to eat, and I wasn't thinking about weighing myself, or a number on the scale. Now, I wake up thinking about what I'm grateful for.

On February 7, 2011, I wrote a self-love blog post on my group self-love blog (selflovewarrior.com) called "Mini Miracles." This was the fifth mini miracle that I noticed during my daily self-love writings for the year:

> While drying myself off after a shower last week, I looked at my
> belly, and the following words slipped out of my mouth, "You're
> beautiful." I don't know how or why I said those words to my
> stomach. I wasn't consciously working with body acceptance
> or body love in that moment. I just was noticing how the soft
> shadow beneath my tummy made a beautiful curve, and my
> beauty struck me.

My belly has been the one part of my body that I have always been most critical of. I still remember the love, joy and excitement that I felt when "you're beautiful" slipped from my mouth, and when I realized that I was talking to my belly. When I had realized what I said, my eyes began to tear with joy.

Part one will introduce you to how my journey towards self-love began, and as you continue the book, you will also be introduced to an array of client stories and their exploration through recovery and self-love. Part one shows you a glimpse into the rest of the book and how the Self-Love Diet can impact you on a personal, cultural and global level.

1

¡Qué Lástima!
What a shame, she has such a pretty face!

*"We can never obtain peace in the outer world
until we make peace with ourselves."*

—Dalai Lama XIV

"¡Qué Lástima!" (What a Shame!) I hear my grandmother cry in Spanish.

"Michelle has such a pretty face, but she is too fat. You have to do something about it!"

My mother counters, "It's just baby fat; she will grow out of it."

At five years old, I overheard this argument between my mother and my grandmother.

Being fat is bad. That is what my grandmother's tone of voice taught me. Even though my mom defended me, from that day forward, I believed something was wrong with me. I wasn't good enough. Even though I was told I had a pretty face, it never made up for the fact that I was fat.

This memory of my mother and grandmother arguing over my appearance took root and started me on a lifelong battle with my body and issues with food. Compulsive overeating became my main way of dealing with life's challenges. If I was upset, food calmed me, distracted me and brought me instant pleasure.

The seed that was planted back then paradoxically led me on a road toward self-love and acceptance. This journey has had many twists and turns, leading me instinctively to my current profession as a marriage and family therapist, specializing in helping people recover from eating disorders. I've been working with women and their issues with their bodies and food as a licensed marriage and family therapist since 1994, and I began leading support groups for compulsive overeaters as an intern counselor in 1992.

In the sanctuary of my office, I sit with talented, gifted, creative, caring and beautiful women. I have worked with girls as young as ten, up to women in their sixties, and recently, I have been working with more men. They share with me the intimate details of their self-hatred, condemnation and disgust of their bodies. There is an alternative to this self-degradation: living life with joy, deep love and devotion.

Through my recovery, I've learned that each day is an opportunity to be conscious and mindful of the miracles in each moment. Others may mistake these miracles as mundane occurrences. I do not. I used to wake up thinking about what I was going to eat or not eat. I'd get out of bed and step on the scale in order to know if it was going to be a good day. My first thoughts when I wake up now are about what I'm grateful for: my love for my husband and his love for me, my family, spending time with my granddaughter, the sun coming through the window on a sunny morning and having a career that I love that allows me to help others. My life is now filled with miracles, wonder, grace and love.

These experiences are what led me to write this book, and these experiences are what led me to create the Self-Love Diet.

In Elizabeth Gilbert's book, *Eat, Pray, Love,* a young man named Giovanni teaches Elizabeth how to speak Italian. When she becomes frustrated by not being able to think of a word in Italian, Giovanni tells her, "Liz, you must be very polite with yourself when you are learning something new." I pass Giovanni's advice on to you. When reading *Self-Love Diet: the Only Diet That Works* you may be learning something new.

Depending on where you are in the process of loving yourself and your body, you may find yourself resisting the suggestions in the action steps at the end of each chapter, or you may find yourself ready to jump in. Give yourself permission to just notice where you are in the process of loving yourself and your body, and let it be your starting point.

My minimum prayer is that you will become more polite to yourself from reading this book, which will lead you to increased self-acceptance. My maximum prayer is that you will begin each day, from this day forward, with the intention and action of loving yourself, which will extend healing into our world.

How would your life be different if you experienced frequent moments of self-acceptance and love?

>> Action Steps <<

A) Take a moment to pause wherever you are right now in this moment. Become aware of your breath and your heartbeat, and find one thing that you can appreciate about your body. Once you've found what you appreciate, focus on it and let that appreciation expand throughout your body.

B) If you cannot find something that you appreciate about your body, bring your attention to what your body does for you rather than what it looks like. Perhaps you can appreciate your ability to breath deeply.

C) Write about the one thing you appreciate and why. Read it out loud, and if you're willing, read it out loud a second time while smiling. Notice how you feel.

2

Dancing in the Light of the Moon

Women's bodies are accepted and honored

"If one is lucky, a solitary fantasy can totally transform one million realities."

—Maya Angelou

Dancing in the Light of the Moon, by Michelle E. Minero

Dancing in the Light of the Moon is a story I wrote about a long ago culture that honored the female body and taught self-love and acceptance to their young girls.

When I read this story to my clients and then ask them what the world would be like if people accepted and valued their bodies, I usually get a blank stare. Either they can't imagine a world where they could accept their bodies as they are, or they have already lost the desire to even want to try. It's my job to educate, support and help my clients begin to remember that they are more than their bodies and that their bodies are magnificent miracles.

Other responses I get sound something like this, "It's not like that now. There's no way to get back to that culture and begin loving and accepting our bodies."

I disagree. *We* are the culture. What we can dream about, desire, feel and visualize, we can create. All that you do, say and think, along with all the things you read and buy, create our culture. If you look in the right places, you will find a critical mass of people, all speaking along similar lines. Jennifer Siebel Newsom talks about it in her documentary *Miss Representation*. Wisconsin news anchor of WKBT-TV, Jennifer Livingston, addressed it on air. Ashley Judd sparked The Conversation about it. The message is clear. We can change how our culture views and talks about our bodies. We can transform our culture into one that judges a person's worth by their character, and not by how they look, and we must. We must create the culture that we want to live in.

Can you imagine a world where people accept their bodies as they are?

In the world I created in *Dancing in the Light of the Moon*, you understand that you are not your body. In this world, you recognize that your body's function is to house your spirit. You appreciate your body as an instrument that helps you be of service in the world. Your body is not a target to merchandise the latest beauty products or to finance the billion-dollar diet industry, and you do not confuse the shape or size of your body with your worth.

When I think about women loving their bodies, my mind floats back to a time before the media was used to encourage us to be consumers of products. The *Earth's Children* series by Jean M. Auel and a conversation I had with Anita Johnston Ph.D., the author of *Eating in the Light of the Moon*, along with the work of Marija Gimbuta, guided my imagination towards writing the short story *Dancing in the Light of the Moon*.

Marija was a world-renowned archaeologist. According to Belili Productions, a production company that focuses on raising awareness on issues that impact women and the earth, Marija interpreted the artifacts she found as representing a culture that lived in the Neolithic period spanning the time frame from 6,500 to 3,500 B.C. as follows, "This was a long-lasting period of remarkable creativity and stability, an age free of strife. Their culture was a culture of art."

Marija theorized a peaceful, matriarchal, Goddess worshipping society, honoring and respectful of women, and void of war. She used her background in mythology and folklore to infer from the found artifacts a people who associated sacredness to the earth. She supposes that this culture honored the power of life, death and rebirth through the seasons and cycles of nature. I imagine the women of this time accepting and loving their bodies.

Sometimes going backwards and remembering our past can lead us forward to positive possibilities for ourselves, and others. I hope this story will plant the seed of yearning for self-love and acceptance within you and take root for our future generations.

Dancing in the Light of the Moon

Once upon a time, women were honored by all. These women had bodies that were supple and curvy. Their bellies were rounded, their hips were wide and curved in and out and their breasts were many different sizes. These women were taught as young girls to love their bodies. Their hips, buttocks and abdomens were considered the center of their creativity, fertility and power. Men honored and respected women and recognized their softness and curves as symbols of fertility.

All the women would gather under the moon when a maturing girl began her first menstrual cycle to initiate her into womanhood. Stories would begin about the wonders of her body and the honor being female had in their culture.

The women would drum and dance with the initiates in the light of the moon until sleep took them over or until the rapturous state was broken by the beckoning of the morning sun. During this celebration, the women would pass on the knowledge and wonders of womanhood and sexual union to the next generation of women.

Younger girls looked longingly at their budding friends and yearned for the day when their hips and stomach would fill out. They knew the prestige and desirability these changes in their bodies carried in their culture. They understood that it was the signal of the mysteries beginning within their friends and impatiently waited for their moonlight initiation with the women of the village.

Girls were taught from the very beginning to value themselves and their friends. Their special gifts were recognized and encouraged. Their identity and value was not confused with their appearance. This was a time of power that came from collaboration, instead of competition.

The villagers were taught to listen to their inner wisdom and to speak their truth. Differences were addressed assertively. Aggressive and passive communication was discouraged, and if it occurred, it was confronted with respect. Creativity abounded. People approached life with a mindset of abundance, vision and the ability to solve problems collectively.

They understood that their bodies were the temples for their souls. They were good stewards of their bodies, thoughts, emotions, words and actions.

Each person was revered and sought quiet, solitude and communion with their higher self. Each individual continually sought after their purpose and did their best to follow the will of their higher power.

The community encouraged individuals to find their unique place within the village. They lived together peacefully, with joy, respect, creativity and love.

I invite you to use this story to help you begin to imagine a world where women love their bodies and feel safe and comfortable enough to dance naked in the light of the moon. At the beginning of this chapter, there is an image of my painting, also titled *Dancing in the Light of the Moon*. The intention of that painting is to show women of different sizes and shapes who are comfortable in their skin. The women dancing together, naked in the light of the moon, represents their connection with themselves, each other and the world. Use that image of the different shaped bodies to help you accept, admire and love the diversity of sizes and shapes that women have.

Can you begin to visualize yourself feeling joy and freedom in your naked body? If not, do you wish that one day you could? You can.

It starts with self-love. It starts with small steps. It starts with deciding and committing to take action. It starts with you, and it starts today.

I dream of a day when all women will inhabit their bodies with joy and feel secure and free enough to dance naked in the light of the moon. Until then, I look at this painting and short story as a glimpse into our future.

How would your life be different if dancing naked in the light of the moon with your friends was comfortable and commonplace?

>> Action Steps <<

A) Begin by imagining yourself being comfortable in your body. Notice what thoughts or visuals come up.

B) Share your daydreams with friends you know who would also like to feel more comfortable with their bodies. Brainstorm ideas of how you can be supportive of one another to be more accepting of your bodies.

C) Commit to taking a step in the right direction. For example, perhaps you and your friends will go swimming in your bathing suits if you have not done so before.

3

Our Bodies as Mirrors
to Our World

The Ocean is our bloodstream, the earth our bones, the wind is our
breath, and fire creates the chemical reactions in our bodies

*This we know: All things are connected like the
blood that unites us. We did not weave the web of
life; we are merely a strand in it. Whatever we do
to the web, we do to ourselves.*

—Chief Seattle

Love's Healing Energy by Michelle E. Minero

While writing *Self-Love Diet: The Only Diet That Works*, I read Jean
Shinoda Bolen's compelling book, *Urgent Message from Mother, Gather the
Women, Save the World*. In this book Jean spoke of the Gaia Hypothesis:

In the mid 1960s, James Lovelock, an atmospheric scientist, and Lynn Margulis, a microbiologist, formulated the Gaia Hypothesis, which proposes that the Earth is alive and that it functions much as our bodies do to maintain homeostasis. To be alive and healthy requires very sensitive interaction among many systems—circulation, respiration, digestion, elimination, hormonal, and neurological systems, and so forth. Gaia—the planet Earth—maintains equally complex interactive systems involving the atmosphere, oceans, soil, and biosphere that also maintain an optimal physical and chemical environment for life.

Not only do our bodies function similarly to our earth to sustain life, but the two are connected and dependent on each other. For example we depend on our planet for life. Our world provides us with the air we breathe, the water we drink, and the food we eat. It depends on us as well. And we have not been doing a good job of caring for it. In fact we have been abusing it.

The reason why I think eating disorders are so prevalent today is because people are mirroring the dysfunction of the world. We've created a disordered world through our lack of stewardship, at the same time that people are abusing their bodies and eating disorders are rampant.

The world is out of balance, and people are also out of balance with the basics, like eating.

If we compare the behavior of disordered eating, and the way we interact with our bodies to the way we interact with our world, we may begin to see a comparison. Is it possible that how humans have been treating the earth is manifesting in how humans are now treating their bodies?

Bulimia

We have individuals bingeing on food then vomiting it into toilets, at the same time we see people "eating" up all of earth's natural resources. Companies are throwing up our waste into our planets' waterways, dumping our refuse into her earth and releasing billowing toxins into our atmosphere. There's a growing consciousness and anger toward corporations who are irresponsible with how they deal with their waste.

Antoinette's family was angry and resentful toward their daughter by the time they brought her to me. Her mother was furious when she came in for the first appointment with Antoinette, a lanky dark haired 16-year-old. "Our bathroom is horrendous. Toni does not clean up after she purges. Our bathroom smells like vomit!" Her mother's reaction is a common one.

We may also feel angered by corporations who do not clean up after their messes. Look at the latest oil spill. Many were angered by BP's inadequate response to the oil spill that devastated country after country as the tides brought the oil from shoreline to shoreline. The feeling of helplessness we all felt during this natural disaster is not dissimilar to the helplessness my clients feel.

Binge Eating

Mr. Smith called me and left a message on my voice mail. He was angry, and confused. His message stated, "Amy is ransacking our pantry, refrigerator and freezer! We buy food for the week for our family. I come home to cook our dinner and find that a week's measure of food is gone! She's like the locust cleaning out our entire crop!"

If current human behavior is mirroring the state of our world, the comparison of our deforestation and our consumption of oil can be made to Amy's eating all the food in the pantry. Looking at the problems of our world today, we can feel out of control and helpless to make changes.

Binge eaters have reported feeling out of control and helpless, unable to stop overeating, even in the face of severe medical diagnoses such as diabetes, high blood pressure, high cholesterol and heart conditions.

Anorexia

I have witnessed a continuous stream of clients refusing to eat from the abundance available to them, unable to give themselves the nutrition their bodies need.

Sally spends countless hours going through recipe books, shopping, preparing and cooking wonderful meals for her family. She sets a beautiful table, and then sits and watches her family eat. Her stomach aches from hunger, while her mind tells her that she cannot eat a bite because she cannot get fat.

Can this be similar to our refusal to look at the abundance of solar power available to the whole world, or the multitude of renewable, sustainable energy supplies available to us, while being stuck in the mindset of using our diminishing natural oil as our main energy resource?

I attended a conference where Carolyn Costin, MFT, was presenting. She showed a photo of an anorexic woman. This photo was difficult to look at because of the skeletal nature of her body, viewing her ribs sticking out from under her skin made me gasp. Carolyn suggested that eating disorder sufferers are like the canaries that were used in mines. Miners in the past would bring canaries with them into the mines. If the canaries died, they knew there was not enough oxygen. It was their message to get out of there fast.

Could these women, and a growing number of men and children who are suffering from anorexia, be our canaries, telling us that our culture and our world are toxic?

We must change the culture that puts so much emphasis on outward appearance to the detriment of our bodies and souls, in order for these more vulnerable beings to survive. By appreciating what our bodies do for us, and allow us to do for others, vs. what they look like, we can change our world as we know it for our coming generations.

How would your life be different if you believed there was a connection between how you treat yourself, and how the world is treated?

>> Action Steps <<

A) Each time you catch yourself being critical or judgmental of yourself, stop, apologize, and appreciate something about yourself. To make the connection to the world, you might stop listening to negative news, reporting violent, hurtful acts, and spend some time creating more joy in the world. A deceivingly simple small step would be to smile at a stranger, and say hello.

B) If you want to help the world, you could start in small ways to make a difference. Perhaps you may change one light bulb a week, or a month to an energy efficient type. To make a connection to the personal, you might start small by committing to take 3 slow deep breaths before you answer the phone as a practice in energetic self-soothing.

C) As a treat, you can take yourself out on dates to walk around a lake, to an art gallery, or simply sit quietly in your garden. To make a connection to the world, you might consider spending time helping an organization that supports the health of our world.

Part Two

If you asked yourself, and acted on this question:

"What is the most loving thing I can do
in this moment?"

How would this day be different?

—Michelle E. Minero

Redefining Diet

Part Two of *Self-Love Diet: The Only Diet That Works* redefines the word diet to regularly offering yourself love, and equips you with Self-Love Diet tools to get you started on your self-love journey.

In Part Two, I also explore how my relationship with my body evolved and how that led to the Self-Love Diet. At different stages of my journey, before I had created the Self-Love Diet, I was not ready or willing to adopt certain practices that I do today. Allow yourself to incorporate the tools that work for you. In Chapter 7, "Recovery vs. Cure," I give examples of how my clients chose to incorporate the Self-Love Diet tools that worked for them into their healing process. I also introduce the concept of conscious body-based eating and provide you with the Self-Love Diet Food and Eating Guidelines.

As you make a conscious effort to put these tools into practice, these actions will become easier, and the easier they become, the more you will want to practice them. It's a beautiful cycle that builds upon the loving thoughts and actions that you bring into your life.

As you continue exploring the Self-Love Diet, you will reach a point where implementing the Self-Love Diet tools becomes an unconscious habit, and followed by that, so will loving yourself.

4

The "D" Word

Diets are ousted and the word diet is redefined

The second day of a diet is always easier than the first. By the second day you're off it.

—Jackie Gleason

I still remember my mother's shock when Bobby Sauer said the F-word to my first grade teacher, Mrs. Best. My father was visually upset when my mother told him about it. My parents did not swear. It was considered scandalous. I don't even remember Bobby Sauer saying the F-word, but I remember my parents' reaction.

Professionals who specialize in the field of eating disorders are similarly shocked when we are contacted by parents who bring in their 10-, 9-, 8- and even 7-year-old children who have started dieting and are afraid of getting fat. The word diet has become our F-word.

According to the Huffington Post, 1,500 youth ranging from seven to 18 years old were surveyed about dieting. For those under 10 years old, over 40 percent said they worried about gaining weight, and one-fourth of all surveyed said they had dieted within the last year.

According to the Agency for Healthcare Research and Quality, "hospitalizations for eating disorders in children under 12 increased by 119% between 1999 and 2006." Professionals in the field of eating disorders are clear that diets do not create eating disorders, but the majority of my clients who find themselves in the midst of an eating disorder began by dieting. A diet can be a gateway towards an eating disorder. When you go on a diet and focus on weight loss, even if it never becomes an eating disorder, you are likely to choose a path of deprivation and obsession with weight, food and your body.

In my past life I was a connoisseur of diets. I started off in junior high school with the Weight Watchers diet. I did lose weight, and got my picture taken, and was a success story. I stopped going to meetings, didn't follow my maintenance phase for life and gained my weight back again. After that first success and failure with Weight Watchers my mother and I continued our search for the perfect diet.

I followed the grapefruit and hardboiled egg diet, then the Hollywood Diet; what teen wouldn't want to be on the glamorous *Hollywood* diet? I watched with interest as my mother and my Aunty Phyllis went to the diet doctor and got their injections of pregnant cow urine. I watched with curiosity while they put plastic gloves on their hands before cutting up the chicken for dinner one night. When I asked why they were wearing plastic gloves, my mother told me that their doctor instructed them to wear the plastic gloves while preparing chicken in order to keep the fat of the chicken from penetrating their skin. He warned them that if they touched the fat, it would reverse the effectiveness of the injections.

Thank goodness the doctor said I was too young for that diet.

My diet stories are probably familiar to many of you. The problem with all of these diets is that they keep the dieter constantly focused on food and losing weight. Traditional diets focus on counting calories, decreasing portion sizes and limiting certain foods, which invites an obsession with food. These aspects of diets can lead to a sense of deprivation. Dieters begin to experience trouble when they feel deprived, and they then rebel against all of the restrictions of the diet. Many people give up before they attain their goal. This creates feelings of inadequacy and failure from not being able to meet their weight loss goal. Self-hatred ensues from believing that they are the problem and not the diet. Others become adept at the rules of dieting and continue to raise the ante until their food rules create fewer and fewer allowable foods that they give themselves permission to eat; this is like playing roulette with anorexia.

One client told me, "I started getting compliments once people started noticing that I was losing weight. Friends and family would say, 'Boy you have such will power; I could never stay away from sweets. The less I ate, the more powerful and stronger I felt; it was like an addiction. I kept pushing my goal weight to lower and lower numbers. Soon after, I knew I had crossed a line. Anorexia had me, and I would never be happy until I died."

Another client described that her lure to bulimia started with her diet of skipping breakfast and lunch. This diet resulted in her being ravenous at night. She would binge at night until she could not take another bite and then experience the relief of vomiting it all away. She reported that when she started this behavior, "It seemed like I had hit the jackpot! I could eat whatever I wanted and not have to worry because I wasn't going to keep it."

The relief however was short lived. Before she knew it, the bingeing and purging were taking over her days and nights. Soon she had no time for studying, going out with friends or hanging out with her family. Her diet began with the promise of paradise, but ended with an eating disorder that became a living hell. The guilt associated with her bingeing and purging left her feeling powerless, discouraged and disgusted with herself.

If diets can be dangerous, you may be wondering why I have the word diet in my title.

According to the Pocket Oxford Dictionary edition 1992, the definitions for the word diet are:

1) Range of foods habitually eaten by a person or an animal.

2) Limited range of foods to which a person is restricted.

3) Things regularly offered.

I will not be using definitions one or two. Instead, I use the third definition, *things regularly offered*, to help define the Self-Love Diet.

Have you, or anyone you know, gone on a diet?

>> Action Steps <<

A) If you have dieted before, what diets have you gone on?

B) What did you notice about your thoughts, emotions or behaviors while on the diet and when you went off the diet?

C) Write about what you noticed about the process of dieting in your journal.

5

Diet Redefined: A Diet of Regularly Offering Yourself Love

Daily servings of self-love are described

You can search throughout the entire universe for someone who is more deserving of your love and affection than you are yourself, and that person is not to be found anywhere. You, yourself, as much as anybody in the entire universe, deserve your love and affection.

—Siddhārtha Gautama

The Self-Love Diet turns the word diet upside down. When you think of the word diet, you will replace the old diet mentality of deprivation and food and body obsession with a radically different concept. I'm asking you to connect the word diet to thoughts of *regularly offering yourself love*.

In this chapter, I highlight the differences between the Self-Love Diet and the antiquated diet mentality by offering examples of actions, thoughts and perspectives that differ from any previous diets you've been on. You will get a flavor of what regularly offering yourself love will sound like and a taste of what your actions will look like when you begin to put the Self-Love Diet into practice. I will also highlight the difference between focusing on weight loss versus focusing on loving yourself.

When I ask my clients to imagine offering themselves loving thoughts, feelings and actions every day, instead of focusing on what they will or will not eat, I get a common response.

"Michelle, this is fine in theory, but I don't love myself. So how can I offer myself something that I don't believe is true?"

My answer is this: act as if you do. Yes, *act* as if you do love yourself. As long as you understand that you are just acting for now, it really is not as hard as it sounds. It's okay if you don't believe it, but if you don't, it is important to act as if you do so you can begin the Self-Love Diet.

The Self-Love Diet is not a quick fix approach to life. It is a process that takes time. Your current beliefs about yourself were developed through a series of experiences and repeated thoughts and actions that fed those beliefs. This means you can change how you feel about yourself by choosing actions and thoughts that reflect how you want to feel about yourself.

Over time, you began to believe that there was something wrong with you and that you needed to change your body into a certain size or shape to be acceptable. You were not born believing you were unlovable. This happened because you mistakenly believed that you were to blame for the hurtful experiences that happened to you, and like a broken record, you told yourself that you were not deserving of love.

In the Self-Love Diet, you will be using the same process of using your thoughts and experiences to develop a belief system over time, but this time you will consciously choose loving actions and thoughts in order to reverse your negative beliefs about yourself and your body. You are choosing to transform yourself through regularly offering yourself love.

If you know how to religiously follow a diet, if you consistently think about your body, food or exercise, then you have the tools in place for the Self-Love Diet, focus and commitment. The difference is I am asking you to focus and commit to loving yourself instead.

When you wake up in the morning tell yourself that you love yourself. When you look at your body in the mirror say, "I choose to love my body today." While brushing your teeth, stop and look into your eyes kiss your reflection and tell yourself how lovely, tantalizing and juicy you are. Throughout the day, and every day, continue to give yourself healthy servings of self-love. Everything you do, say, feel or think will all be a reflection of loving yourself.

Does this sound silly, inauthentic or too simplistic? Let's take a moment to stop and look at what you are doing instead.

When you wake up in the morning, what is the first thing you tell yourself?

When you look in the mirror before or after a shower, what do you say to yourself about your body? While brushing your teeth, if you stopped to look at yourself, what would you notice about your face? What might you say to yourself about what you see? If you looked into your eyes, which would you see: a person of infinite value or a person who has a pimple, wrinkles or a double chin? Pay attention to the way you see yourself these next few days. I hope you will notice a loving dialogue, but if you don't, you will unfortunately be in the majority.

Many of my clients have used these concepts to their benefit. Others have complained that they would feel childish if they were to tell themselves how wonderful they are. You may feel childish at first when you begin to tell yourself how much you love yourself. However, you may find that childish can feel really good. In fact, it feels much better than criticizing yourself each morning.

This notion of self-love is simplistic. However, simple does not mean easy. If you have a history of being criticized or a history of abuse, it may take some time before these new thoughts begin to take hold. If you start out the Self-Love Diet acting *as if* you loved yourself, even though you don't, with time this acting will turn into a reality. In chapters five and six, the concept of acting *as if* is explored in more depth.

What about those of you who are thinking, "Fine, Michelle. I can love myself, but I still want to lose weight."

I would suggest that you ask yourself this question: Is my weight creating complications to my health?

One of my clients answered, "No" to this question and said, "But I'll be more comfortable in my body with some of this excess weight off. I can't

run or play tennis at this larger size, and these things are important to me."
I agreed that those activities were important to her, and I asked her if she
could work her way up to running and playing tennis by walking or hitting
the tennis ball against a wall first. She looked at me in surprise and said, "I
can run and play tennis. I'm just not comfortable doing it at this weight."

She noticed that her discomfort came from her self-criticism about how
she looked in her tennis outfit and while running. She projected her own fat
talk onto how others would see her and believed that she had to lose weight
before she could enjoy running and playing tennis again. She believed that
she wouldn't feel comfortable or confident in her body until she lost weight,
but focusing on weight loss fostered more self criticism and stopped her from
doing what she loved.

What she needed was a change of focus. Instead of focusing on losing
weight, I asked her what it would be like to focus on loving herself and doing the things she loved to do. Once she began focusing on what she loved,
her motivation changed from weight loss and what others thought of her to
how she felt in her body and the fun she had connecting with her friends.

Things go wrong when you start focusing on losing weight from a
stance of body-hatred. Negative self-talk is not empowering: it strengthens
thoughts of fear and shame that hold you back from what you really want.

If you have children, imagine the following scene. If you don't have a
child, pretend along with the following scenario.

Imagine your child waking up in the morning, and you greet him or
her by saying, "Oh my gosh, you are so fat. You have to lose weight! Look at
your stomach! It is too big! Look at your arms. They are so fat!"

If you said this to your child each and every morning, do you think this
would help him or her to lose weight? More importantly, how would your
child feel about him or herself? This type of fat talk would not help your
child, and it does not help you.

If your weight is actually having a negative impact on your health,
then you may indeed need to focus on regaining your health. The Self-Love
Diet offers an alternative to the traditional diet approach. On the Self-Love

Diet, you will consistently offer yourself daily servings of self-love rather than focusing on weight loss. Over time, as you make self-love your focus, your body will find its natural set point, which is the weight that your body maintains naturally.

You can begin the Self-Love Diet this very moment. You only have one life. Why wait for happiness until the number on the scale tells you that you are OK the way you are? The scale cannot measure your value as a person. If that's how you're using it, you will never find happiness.

If you wait for self-love to fall into your lap, you'll be waiting forever, but if you start working towards self-love right now, then moment-by-moment, day-by-day, you'll be closer to self-acceptance, self-confidence and self-love. What have you got to lose?

If you decide to embark on this diet of self-love, it may actually be the hardest thing you have ever attempted. The rewards may also be the most important you have earned.

How would your life be different if you let yourself be curious about the Self-Love Diet?

>> Action Steps <<

A) Be aware of your thoughts in the morning. What self-talk do you notice?

B) Practice giving yourself compliments on your inner qualities.

C) When you find yourself struggling with a decision, ask yourself, "What would love you do?" Use this question as a guide throughout the day.

6

How Do You Begin to Love Yourself?

Beginning steps towards self-love are described

You expect for me to love you when you hate
yourself. When I tell you I love you, you can't
believe that it's true.

—Stephen Stills and Neil Young
"Everybody I Love You"

The Self-Love Diet does not focus on weight loss or food. So where do you begin? How do you go about regularly offering yourself love? In this chapter, I will highlight Self-Love Diet tools previously mentioned and introduce you to some of the tools that you will explore in more detail later in the book. You can begin to consciously build your Self-Love Diet toolbox today and call upon any of these tools when you want to practice offering yourself love.

In the previous chapter, "Diet Redefined: A Diet of Regularly Offering Yourself Love," I described the tool of acting as if. Acting as if is a wonderful tool to put into practice when beginning the Self-Love Diet because you don't have to love yourself to act as if you do. In the previous chapter you were given examples of ways you could speak to yourself when using the tool of acting as if. In this chapter examples are given of actions you can take when using the tool of acting as if. Below are examples of beginning steps my clients have taken to act as if they loved themselves.

+ Not working through your lunchtime. Use all of your lunch hour, even if you are finished eating before it's time to go back to work. If you have extra time, go for a short walk or meditate. Make sure to leave your desk or office to eat in a pleasant environment.

+ Stop work when your day is over. Do not bring work home or stay overtime, especially if you do not get paid for it.

+ Get monthly massages, manicures, pedicures or facials. If you don't have the budget for it, meet with a friend to give each other manicures.

+ If you have children, make sure to take time for yourself. Hire a babysitter so you can take yourself out on a self-love date in nature, to a movie, to an art gallery or to do something you enjoy.

+ Give yourself permission to say no to friends if they ask you for help when you are sick or in need of rest. Put yourself as high on your priority list as the people you support.

These examples were vital steps for my clients towards their goals of self-love. They were evidence that they were beginning to believe that they were worth the time and effort to be nurtured.

When my clients began adding the above list of nurturing behaviors into their lives, their body-hatred and self-loathing thoughts didn't vanish overnight. For many of them, their critical thoughts were still ever-present. What my clients soon learned was that they were able to use their negative thoughts to their benefit. The ever-present negative chatter provided them with opportunities to become aware of their thoughts, which enabled them to combat their negative self-talk. This leads to the next two Self-Love Diet tools: paying attention and confronting and challenging your thoughts and beliefs.

Paying Attention and Challenging Your Thoughts

Another Self-Love Diet tool is to be conscious of any negative thoughts you may have toward yourself. You can only challenge the thoughts and beliefs you are aware of. "I'm stupid!" "I'm so fat!" "Who would want to be with me?" "I've tried that before and it didn't work, I will never … lose that weight, get that job, find love, finish school, and earn enough money." The list goes on and on, often under your awareness. Working on regularly offering yourself love will help you to increase your self-awareness, and paying attention to your thoughts will become easier. Once you become aware of your thoughts you can choose to confront and challenge them.

Many of my clients can pinpoint a definitive moment in childhood when the negative beliefs began and where a decision was made which laid the groundwork for their subsequent self-hatred. Looking at the source of these thoughts can give perspective. These defeating beliefs can be understood in context. Today a choice can be made to keep the belief, or to let it go. Robin made the choice to let hers go.

Robin clearly remembered being called Thunder Thighs at her sixth grade graduation swim party. From that day forward, she began restricting her food, which led to anorexia, and later bulimia, which took control of her life.

When Robin came into my office with a photo of herself at the sixth grade graduation party she saw an average sized girl in a bathing suit. Looking at the photo, she noticed the boy who called her Thunder Thighs was overweight. With an adult's perspective she guessed that he was projecting his own issues onto her. She confronted her belief that her thighs were too big and decided that it had never been true.

Robin's work was to love her thighs and to remember it was only a story about her thighs being too big. In order to challenge this long held belief, I suggested that she write a new story. The story she wrote started with the opening scene of her sixth grade swim party. In this story when he called her thunder thighs she was splashing with her friends in the pool and couldn't hear him clearly. She heard him say Wonder Eyes and for the rest of her life believed that her wonderful eyes were her most beautiful feature. Robin rewrote her life story. You can too.

Paying attention and confronting and challenging your thoughts and beliefs will be explored in more detail in chapter 24, "How Do I Change My Negative Body Image?"

Externalization

Another Self-Love Diet tool I use when I'm working with someone with an eating disorder is externalization. We will oftentimes call their disordered thoughts ED, which is short for eating disorder. By externalizing the voice that tells them they are disgusting, and personalizing it, my clients are better able to distinguish the thoughts from themselves. They can begin to tell when ED is talking versus their authentic loving self. Differentiating your negative voice from your higher self becomes an important tool in the Self-Love Diet.

The inner voice of one of my clients constantly told him he wasn't doing enough. He couldn't go to bed because he had not worked hard enough or accomplished enough that day. He named that part of himself the Critical Achiever. I asked him to draw this part of himself and to speak the thoughts out loud. He chose a British accent and drew a large scowling man pointing a finger. This process helped him to put the image and sound of the voice to his thoughts. Personalizing the thoughts he labeled as his Critical Achiever helped him to observe his thoughts as separate from himself, which made it easier for him to confront them and go to bed.

Another client was anxious about her excess weight. She was bothered by her Worrier voice. She drew her Worrier as an older woman with big worry lines across her forehead. When she spoke from this part of herself she used a high-pitched tone. Her Worrier told her that she was going to die at night because her fat would put pressure on her lungs and wouldn't allow her to breathe. Her Worrier also admonished her, telling her she couldn't make love to her husband because she was too fat and would crush him. When we explored these fear together, she was able to see them for what they were, fear, and not reality.

As you begin the process of self-love, it's important to identify and drag your shadows out of the closet and into the light of day in order to recognize how you are being controlled. These voices, thoughts or parts of you can seem evil or harmful with no positive attributes. On closer look, you will find that they usually have the job of protecting you from imagined harm or pain. The previous example of the woman who was afraid that she would crush her husband if she made love to him discovered that this thought protected her from possible rejection by her husband.

When you begin paying attention to your thoughts, you may identify your thoughts as obsessions that are intrusive, untrue and relentless. Many of my clients who have come for help with an eating disorder have also discovered that they suffer from obsessive-compulsive disorder. By changing your thoughts you change your neuropathways, which creates new and more comfortable feelings and increased self-esteem, as well as decreases the compulsions brought on by the obsessive thoughts.

Photographs of peoples' brain scans before and after mindfully confronting and changing their obsessions show actual changes in their brains. Obsessions do have a negative effect on self-worth and have been connected to the development of depression. Medication can also help people resolve the negative impact of OCD or mood disorders in their lives. If you want to find out more about OCD, there are some good books in the bibliography at the back of this book.

The Five-Step Process

Another Self-Love Diet tool is easily remembered by counting the number of digits on your hand (as long as you have five). The Five-Step Process is based on Cognitive Behavioral Therapy, CBT. Using your growing awareness of your critical thoughts, you can:

#1. Catch your thought.

#2. Confront your thought by asking, "Who says?"

#3. Replace the thought.

#4. Apologize to yourself.

#5. Commit to change.

Here's an example of how to use the Five-Step Process. If you have discovered that you have a running negative commentary in your mind about your body or yourself, you can:

Catch the Thought

I noticed that I just told myself, "My hips are too big to wear these pants. I look disgusting."

Confront the Thought

"Who says my hips are too big? The advertising agencies who are selling these pants? A group of unknown people sitting around a conference table who deemed that lean was in and curvy was out?"

Replace the Thought

"My worth does not depend on the size of my hips. I am a good person and a good friend, and I do my best to leave each place I visit a little better. My inner qualities are more important than the dimensions of my body."

Apologize to Yourself

"I'm sorry for calling myself disgusting."

Commit to Change

"Each time I catch myself criticizing my body, I will confront, replace and apologize to myself until I no longer criticize myself."

This five-step process is a good tool to use to begin establishing the ability to regularly offer yourself loving thoughts.

Just Noticing

Just noticing is another Self-Love Diet tool that helps you become mindful of your thoughts. Becoming mindful of your thoughts invites you to be aware of the "you" who is thinking those thoughts. By just noticing your thoughts you allow them to be like clouds that pass through your mind. You hear them and have a detached stance of observing them as they come in and go out.

A practice of sitting quietly can enhance this ability to be mindful, and it is quite different from catching, confronting, replacing, apologizing and committing to change. If you already have a meditation practice, you will be aware of the gazillion thoughts that can pass through your mind in a matter of 5 minutes.

Here is a personal example of using mindfulness. When I was about half finished with writing this book I went through the process of writing a book proposal. Part of the proposal required that I write an analysis of the competition. As I was looking at other authors' books in the same genre as mine, I noticed thoughts like, "Her book is awesome. Why should I even write my book?"

"What do I have to say that hasn't already been said, and said better?"

"My book won't be as good as her book."

I noticed all of these thoughts come and go. At first I let the thoughts get to me. I noticed I was anxious during the analysis of the competition. I realized the word competition made me think that I had to win or lose. Then I realized that I was giving these thoughts more energy. So I remembered to just notice them flow in and out of my consciousness. The next time I noticed a thought suggesting my book would not be good, I pictured it floating through my brain and out again, just like clouds on a fast motion time lapse video. See if you can use the just noticing Self-Love Diet tool the next time a negative thought comes to mind.

Lastly, I will share Judy's story with you. Judy is an example of how accepting her emotions without criticism lead to self-acceptance and finally to self-love.

Judy was in her early 50s and came to see me for problems in her male dominated career. When I first met Judy she described herself as, "fat, overworked and undervalued." She told me that she was a hard worker with good ideas that were not respected or listened to by the men in authority. The action that prompted Judy to come in was a confrontation she had with one of her superiors. She had a legitimate complaint. When she brought it up to the captain, he minimized her concern and suggested it was her fault that her supervisor had acted in the manner he did. She was so angry that she cried during their meeting.

"Crying takes all of my credibility away when I'm talking to my male supervisors. They see me as the emotional woman. I need help handling my emotions better." Judy told me.

Judy had a big job. She was in charge of a staff of 50 women. When Judy asked her staff to cover shifts they would tell her about their hardships and the reasons why they couldn't come in. Her compassion for her subordinates made it hard for her to ask them to put in overtime. Judy had been scheduling herself for the extra hours instead of her staff. Since she was salaried, she did not get paid overtime and was working 60-70 hours a week. Judy was angry because she felt that her staff took advantage of her.

"I don't get the respect I deserve from my superiors or my staff. I'm thinking of just quitting even though I only have a few more years till retirement," Judy told me.

As Judy began her personal growth work, she realized that she was angry a lot, and that she did not believe it was acceptable to be angry. When she told me about her childhood she described a mother whose anger was out of control when she drank, which was often. Judy was the target for her mother's anger, which led to repeated bruises on her face and a trip to the hospital to cast her arm. She discovered that she had chosen to avoid the emotion all together. As Judy began to view the assertive, angry part of her as acceptable, she began to own her anger and express it clearly and respectfully.

After Judy had been in therapy for about a year, she realized she no longer felt guilty when she was angry and frustrated. She was able to acknowledge that it was important to learn what her anger was trying to tell her.

As Judy acknowledged that all of her emotions were valid, she was able to accept herself more fully. She no longer worked 60 or 70 hour weeks and was now able to delegate hours to her staff when overtime was needed. She realized she could still be a caring, supportive person while requiring her staff to put in overtime. She noticed she was also becoming much more supportive and caring of herself.

At staff meetings Judy began to repeat herself until she was acknowledged, because she believed that her perspective was a valuable and necessary compliment to the men's perspective. As Judy accepted and respected all the parts that made her who she was, she increased her ability to love herself more fully.

In this chapter you have been given a number of Self-Love Diet tools to begin your journey. If you noticed that I have not mentioned food or exercise tools this is because the foundation of the Self-Love Diet is an inside job. By changing your self-defeating thoughts and behaviors into self-loving ones, you will be on the road to self-love.

How would your life be different if you practiced the Self-Love Diet tools provided in this chapter?

>> Action Steps <<

A) Give a name or an image to a repeating negative thought pattern that is common for you. This will help you to recognize it when you think of it.

B) Write in your journal with the intention of chronicling or discovering emotions that are more difficult for you than others. See what you discover.

C) Choose one Self-Love Diet tool from this chapter to incorporate into your life.

7

Recovery vs. Cure

What's the difference?

Real hope combined with real action has always pulled me through difficult times. Real hope combined with doing nothing has never pulled me through.

—Jenni Schaefer

What's the difference between recovery from an eating disorder and being cured of an eating disorder? And where does the Self-Love Diet fit in?

The word *cure* comes from the medical model. If you have an infection and take the necessary medications, then the infection can be cured. It's gone, and you don't have to think about it ever again. The concept of cure is very inviting. Who wouldn't want to ever think about their eating disorder or negative body image again?

Over and over, I have been witness to young women successfully abstaining from their disordered behaviors. Their families are overjoyed; "Our daughter is cured!" they will shout!

When a person is cured from the disordered behaviors, it is a huge accomplishment. However, abstaining from eating disordered behaviors does not necessarily mean they are cured. The word cure suggests a black and white, now you have it, now you don't approach. Kim's story is a good example of the difference between the concept of cure and recovery.

Kim had the diagnosis of anorexia and had recently regained her period, returned to a stable weight and had consistent healthy vitals for two months. It was cause for celebration. Her family and friends saw her as cured.

Kim's reality was different. She was still suffering. She reported to me that each meal was a battleground. Her eating-disordered self told her she was disgusting for eating the food on her plate. This voice did not let up, even as she ate her meals with her family.

Kim was still filled with body-hatred and disgust, which colored everything she did and thought about herself. In this scenario, the eating disordered behaviors had diminished or stopped, but the eating disorder mindset was still active, keeping her a prisoner of self-hatred. Kim knew she was not cured. At the point where everyone thought we were done, our work had just begun.

The word recovery comes from the substance abuse, addiction field. This approach requires that a person abstain from alcohol or drugs in order to heal from their addiction.

You'll also find the term recovery in the Overeaters Anonymous (OA) 12-step program. The twelve steps and traditions of the OA program are not food-based, but are spiritually based. There is no official food plan in OA. However, there is a culture within some OA meetings that views certain foods as addictive, such as white flour and sugar. There are others in OA who don't view food as addictive and who say they can eat whatever they want, but it's the behaviors they are addicted to, such as compulsive overeating, bingeing and purging or restricting food.

The difference between addiction to alcohol and drugs is that people can stop using these substances and live a healthy life, whereas in the OA program, people must continue to eat; they cannot abstain from all food.

Many people have benefited from OA, and similar programs, and have used the spiritual component to regain their health and sense of control with eating.

One difference between the 12-step model and the Self-Love Diet is that many O.A. members focus on weight, mostly weight loss. Instead of focusing on weight, Self-Love Diet followers focus on regularly offering themselves love, and trust that by doing the most loving thing in each moment, their body will find it's natural set point when given the chance.

Another difference between the 12-Step model and the Self-Love Diet is the concept of addiction. O.A. believes that their members will always be compulsive overeaters, even if their behaviors have been in check for years. The Self-Love Diet proposes that your eating disordered behaviors can be a thing of the past and that all food can be neutralized and eaten in moderation.

I didn't always believe that food could just be food, or that I could eat in moderation. I remember laughing about the concept that food could be eaten in moderation when I joined OA in the early 90s. I would have never let go of my program of abstaining from foods with sugar because the thought of losing the control I had gained over my relationship with food terrified me. I believed that I was addicted to sugar, and if I ate it, I would relapse back into my compulsive overeating and not only lose control over the food, but of my life as well. This program offered me a spiritual base, a support system and a substantial improvement in my quality of life compared to the years that I struggled with compulsive overeating.

Through my personal journey of experimenting with and continuously molding the addiction model to see if it would continue to work for me, alongside my work with people in recovery from eating disorders, I have come to learn that I am not addicted to sugar or the behavior of compulsive overeating. I learned that when I shifted my focus from weight loss and abstinence to loving myself healing happened at a deeper level.

The Self-Love Diet is the result of my personal and professional work that takes the concept of healing to the core of our ability to believe without a doubt that we are lovable, worthwhile and valuable human beings, and that our spiritual essence is what makes us so, not our bodies.

Fully inhabiting the Self-Love Diet takes time. If you are in a 12-step program and it is working well for you, you do not have to throw it away. You can incorporate tools from the Self-Love Diet into your existing program. Donna is a good example of someone who incorporated the Self-Love Diet into her 12-step program.

I worked with Donna on issues of grief for a while before she shared with me her success story with the OA program. "This program saved my life. I was close to using insulin for diabetes and now I am active and healthy. I have a strong program," Donna stated. Donna called her sponsor each morning and reported her planned meals for the day, and then later called her sponsor in the evening to report how well she had followed her plan. She read inspirational readings, wrote in her journal each morning and went to three meetings a week. Donna thrived on the structure she had created and believed the addiction model was a fit for her. I offered Donna information about other ways people had recovered and dealt with food and eating. We incorporated those concepts from the Self-Love Diet that made sense to her. Although the 12-step program worked well for Donna, it does not work well for everyone. If you've tried it and it has not worked for you, remember that you did not fail. It was just not the right fit for you. This was the experience for Kathy.

Kathy had been in the OA program, but she told me it didn't work for her. She told me that in her meetings she heard the same story from people week after week, and she was not losing weight, which was her reason for joining. She didn't see any changes in herself or others. She left OA and joined a group called Food Addicts Anonymous (FA). This program shares OA's spiritual principals and the addiction model, but has a more rigid structure. FA believes that overeating is caused by a biochemical disease of food addiction. In this program, members are required to abstain from sugar, white flour and wheat, and are required to follow a strict food plan.

Kathy had been in the FA program for 18 months when she came to see me. She told me that she had lost almost 50 pounds in that time and was the FA poster child. What she and others saw as success early in her program turned into a dangerous back slide into an eating disorder. With each ensuing pound lost, her food choices became more and more rigid. Kathy came to see me after she had been bingeing and purging for 3 months. Before this, she had not been actively bulimic for over 15 years. Kathy's sponsor didn't know how to help her, and suggested she seek therapy. As we worked together, Kathy stopped blaming herself and discovered how the structure of the program was a trigger for her disordered thoughts and behaviors.

The culture of restricting certain foods created a diet mentality of good foods versus bad foods, which led her into the trap of black and white thinking. She would say she was *good* when she ate according to her plan and was *bad* if she ate something that was not on her food plan. If she was bad, she could not speak in the meetings; this kept her diligent. Her ability to stay on her food plan became her only measure of personal success. Soon foods she believed she could not eat created feelings of deprivation, which led to her bingeing behaviors and compensatory purges. "I put my tiger in its cage at every meal," Kathy told me. This metaphor reflected the out of control feeling Kathy felt concerning food.

The above examples showcase the addiction model. In both instances, Donna and Kathy were encouraged to have a black and white approach to certain food categories. The implication was that if they slipped, their old behaviors would come back in full swing. Donna was able to stay within the bounds of the program, but Kathy was not. Recovery for both of these women implied an addiction lurking in the background, waiting to pounce on them at any moment, like Kathy's tiger metaphor.

Kathy and I began the process of shifting her perspective to self-love and acceptance, instead of weight loss. As a checkpoint before making decisions for her self-care, she began using the mantra, "What would love do?"

Kathy was a fast learner. She quickly made the connections between how she had been living a fear-based, scarcity model with food and how this translated to her approach to life in general. She learned to listen to her body and decipher when she was physically hungry and when she was satisfied. She could tell the difference between her stomach being empty and her emotional emptiness. Kathy was able to legalize all foods, and she learned to eat in moderation without the black and white, deprivation, fear-based relationship she had experienced with food in her FA program.

I offer a warning to people about the FA and 12-step programs. There are certain meetings where you will find the belief that medications for mood disorders are not necessary. This is dangerous territory. Nobody can decide that for you besides you and your doctor.

I know two people who are followers of the FA program, and they believe it has made all the difference in positively influencing their health. The structure, which is dangerous for some people, is experienced as a container for them. The difference between them and Kathy is that they did not have a history with eating disorders, and they found sponsors within the program who were willing to change the rules to make it work for them. They instinctively knew what worked for them, and what didn't. They had the ability to look within themselves, instead of looking outward to an authority for answers on understanding their own needs. The concept of looking inward, instead of outward is described in more detail in Chapter 34. These qualities of looking within and being able to change the rules of the program to make them work for you are vital for these programs.

Recovery in a 12-step program focuses on abstinence. There is no abstinence in the Self-Love Diet. Recovery in the Self-Love Diet asks you to regularly offer yourself love for the rest of your life.

This ongoing practice of consciously thinking loving, affirming thoughts goes beyond food and body; it includes your spiritual, mental, emotional and relational health, as well as the interconnectedness of your culture and your planet.

Recovery in the Self-Love Diet does not mean you will never think about eating when you are not physically hungry or never have a critical thought about your body again, but this is not necessarily bad news.

In my own recovery, I have come to see my infrequent cravings to eat when I'm not physically hungry as one of my greatest gifts. I use these cravings, or food thoughts, as clues that something is up. I used to write about these cravings to gain clarity. Now I can easily figure out what's going on. Sometimes it's as simple as wanting to procrastinate with a job that I find challenging. Other times I get these cravings because I'm tired or stressed, and my mind is incorrectly interpreting these cues as hunger. Today, it comes as second nature to use these fleeting food thoughts to correctly assess if I am physically hungry or not. I have enough experience to know what my body is requesting and to know that if I eat when I'm not hungry it is not the most loving thing to do.

Today, I am committed to treating myself in the most loving way I can. If I'm tired, I'll rest or go to bed. I listen to my tiredness and figure out what it's trying to tell me. It's usually telling me to slow down my pace of life.

If I'm stressed, I'll stop and figure out what's going on in my life that is stressful. If I can't do anything to change my life circumstances, or even if I can, I take deep breaths, stop and meditate, stretch or go for a walk. I find getting out in nature, praying, calling a friend, asking for a hug or giving myself permission to say "No" to myself, when I want to do everything, are loving behaviors. I have also written my concerns down on slips of paper and put them in my God box, which is a box where I put my written concerns and trust they will work out. When I am not physically hungry all of these actions address much closer what I need in the moment more than food does. Ultimately, these behaviors help me to love myself by experiencing that I can care for myself in an appropriate manner, instead of looking for comfort or distraction in food.

There are still occasional times when I will eat because I'm tired rather than hungry, but they are infrequent, and I quickly become conscious of my actions. The Self-Love Diet is about progress, not perfection.

Recovery vs. Recovered

Carolyn Costin, MFT, defined *recovered* in her book, *100 Questions and Answers About Eating Disorders*, as:

> Being recovered is when the person can accept his or her natural body size and shape and no longer has a self-destructive relationship with food or exercise. When you are recovered, food and weight take a proper perspective in your life, and what you weigh is not more important than who you are; in fact, actual numbers are of little importance at all. When recovered, you will not compromise your health or betray your soul to look a

certain way, wear a certain size, or reach a certain number on the scale. When you are recovered, you do not use eating disordered behaviors to deal with, distract from, or cope with other problems.

I agree with Carolyn's definition of recovered. You can be recovered from an eating disorder. Nevertheless, in the Self-Love Diet, the term recovery is used instead of recovered. The word recovery in the Self-Love Diet refers to a continual process, not one of struggling with your eating disorder, but a continual process of offering yourself love.

I have met many people who are the happy recipients of the unexpected gifts that recovery in the Self-Love Diet brings into their lives. Imagine these gifts being yours.

- You wake up in the morning with a clear mind and positive expectations for the day. Food thoughts are no longer your clingy companions.

- You enjoy food as an integral part of life without unwarranted emphasis.

- You look in the mirror and see a person of value and innate beauty, and it's you!

- You experience harmonious, reciprocal relationships where you are free to speak your truth and be respected for it, even if you are not agreed with.

- You are clear about your purpose in life and experience the joy of living a life with passion.

You have a choice in every moment to choose the most loving behavior or thought. The Self-Love Diet views your non-loving behaviors as opportunities to offer yourself compassion and to learn from the experience. The Self-Love Diet shows how a daily loving practice, starting with yourself, is a wonderful lifestyle that not only heals you, but that also has the potential to heal our world.

How would your life be different if recovery meant you would offer yourself love from this day forward?

>> Action Steps <<

A) Write out loving actions you can take each day in your journal. For ideas, refer to Self-Love Practices and Self-Love Commitments in the Appendix at the back of the book.

B) Consider asking someone you trust to be your self-love partner. The two of you can commit to your self-love intentions and check in as desired to encourage one another.

C) Explore in your journal your beliefs regarding recovery in the Self-Love Diet vs. recovery in the 12-step model.

8

Is Healing Possible?

Healing happens daily, if you know where to look

> *Reach across the isolation of the human*
> *experience, and hold another person's legend. In*
> *doing so, we build a bridge that may heal us both.*
>
> —Tracy Walton

The answer is yes. Healing is possible. It happens in small, sometimes invisible ways every day. Bringing your awareness to the healing process and realizing that the ability to heal lives inside of you are foundational components to the Self-Love Diet. If you are struggling with an eating disorder, it's important that you recognize the everyday healing that's occurring so you can make your invisible successes visible. Be on the lookout for success, and give yourself credit for all the times you have abstained from an unhealthy behavior or noticed your inner dialogue changing from eating disordered thoughts to self-affirming ones. Below are examples of healing you may not have been aware of.

For every person suffering with bulimia who is struggling to abstain from a binge and a purge, there is the knowledge that she has battled and won many challenges, even though she still may be bingeing and purging. Each time she successfully avoids a binge purge cycle, there has been healing. Unfortunately, her family and loved ones are unable to know of the countless battles won; they can only see evidence of the battles lost.

If you struggle with bulimia, give yourself credit for every binge purge cycle you have stopped. Find a friend, family member or a therapist who can see the invisible healing process and who recognizes the effort you have been putting in and the progress you have made. Recovery does not happen overnight, and each success is important and healing to recognize.

Another example of invisible healing is when a person struggling with body-hatred goes out into the world, even though she'd rather stay hidden because of her imagined flawed appearance.

When a disordered eater begins to focus attention on self-love instead of on the disordered thoughts and behaviors of an eating disorder, healing is beginning. Each time we bring the spotlight on our inner qualities, leaving diets and preoccupation with body in the darkness, there is healing.

I witness visible evidence of healing all the time. I see miracles materialize in the lives of my clients. People are able to heal from the most horrific trauma, abuse, neglect, ridicule, and yes, people heal from eating disorders. They and their families can resume or create full, vibrant and passionate lives.

The Self-Love Diet's foundational premise is that you have an inherent ability to heal. If you think about how your body heals, you will have evidence of this capability. When you get a scratch, your body sends white blood cells directly to that area. These cells begin the healing process by eating up the bacteria, cleaning up the debris and preventing infection. A scab begins to form over the scratch, and you can feel the pull on your skin as the new skin forms. The scab may begin to itch, and it eventually falls off, revealing fresh, pink skin where the scratch once was. Soon your skin returns to its natural state with no sign of the scratch. All of these events, the healing process of your body, happen just under your awareness.

Let's bring your awareness into the healing process. Just as your body can heal itself, your spiritual nature, in combination with your mind, can heal your body and soothe your emotions.

Your mind has a tremendous capacity for healing. When you remember a peaceful evening watching the stars out in nature, your mind does not differentiate between the feelings evoked from remembering that experience and the emotions evoked from the actual experience. Just like your body will flinch when it remembers hearing a nail being scratched across a black board, your body also reacts by relaxing when you bring to mind the peaceful sensations in your body from watching the stars. You have the ability to elicit and even create more healing in your life, and your body, by consciously seeking a memory that brings you a sense of well-being.

Not only can your mind initiate healing by calling upon calming memories, but you can also initiate healing by consciously focusing on your breath. Research into the parasympathetic nervous system has discovered the vagus nerve, which when activated through deep breathing brings on the relaxation response. Through deep breathing, you can reduce your levels of cortisol, which is part of the sympathetic nervous system, which is connected to the flight or fight or freeze response.

As you activate the vagus nerve through deep diaphragmatic breathing, your anxiety lessens, your muscles relax and more oxygen enters your body. This process supplies more oxygen to your cells, which produces more endorphins. Endorphins signal the brain to create feelings of euphoria and help cultivate a greater sense of well-being. Endorphins also lessen pain, working as natural painkillers. According to Medicalium, "Tibetan monks have been practicing this to modulate the effects of stress for decades. They don't practice these ancient techniques to improve their memory, fight depression, lower blood pressure, or heart rate, or boost their immune systems, although all of those happen."

By understanding the healing power in your thoughts and breath, you can then harness those abilities to heal yourself. You can practice visualization and deep breathing by themselves, or together, and you can build upon these healing tools to create new healing practices.

Knowing the power in calming memories, you can repeatedly focus on soothing memories to enhance the healing of your body and to soothe your mind, emotions and spirit. This action of repeating positive and relaxing memories is similar to the repetitive instant replay process that referees use in the NFL. They repeat a play over and over again to make sure they make the right call. Instead of ruminating over past hurts or traumas, you can make the right call by using the instant replay process to continually repeat loving, healing memories.

Guided visualization is another tool that you can call upon to initiate healing. Through guided visualization, I teach my clients how to create a safe place in their minds. This practice of visiting your safe place is a lifelong practice you can benefit from. This healing work comes from my training in Affect Management Skills Training, AMST, and Affect Centered Therapy, ACT, from John Omaha, PhD. The safe place practice uses bilateral stimulation, which was developed by Francine Shapiro in her Eye Movement Desensitization Reprocessing (EMDR) protocol.

Bilateral stimulation is the process of moving your eyes from left to right, or holding Thera-Tappers, one in each hand, which provides a low level of electrical stimulation. When the right hand is stimulated, the left hemisphere of the brain is stimulated. When the left hand is stimulated, the right hemisphere of the brain is stimulated. This process allows the neuropathways in your brain to be activated while remembering or imagining your safe place, which fortifies the feelings associated with your safe place in your brain, and when called upon, throughout your body.

Chapter 45, "Safe Place Visualization Script," will offer instructions on how to create your own safe place and how to adapt the bilateral stimulation when not working with a therapist. If you have trauma in your background, or are suffering from anxiety or depression, I encourage you to work with a therapist who has been trained in AMST and ACT.

Opening up your awareness to the present moment is another way that you can cultivate healing. Just like your mind can remember a past event that brought you love and a sense of well-being, like the memory of watching the stars out in nature, you can use the present moment in the same way. By choosing to be mindful of your environment, you can consciously bring healing to yourself.

The next time you are outside on a grey day, if you notice the sun beginning to shine, stop and pay attention to the way the sun comes out from behind the clouds and the way it transforms the grey, muted light into a warm luminosity. Beautiful and breathtaking events are happening all around you. Being in the moment and paying attention to these soulful, healing moments allows an expanded sense of well-being.

Slow down and bring these experiences into your senses. Use your sight to notice the nuances of color and shifting light in the sky. When you close your eyes, what do you hear? Do you hear the wind blowing through the trees or the sound of kids playing at the nearby park, accompanied by the low squeak of the swings as they move back and forth? Notice what smells accompany the scene. Do you smell the fresh, sweet aroma of the pine trees nearby?

What do you taste? Can you taste hints of pepper from the mint bush on the side of your house? Notice what you feel in your body. Can you feel openness in your chest or the warmth in your hands?

Opening yourself up to the present moment allows you to become aware of and experience the beauty that constantly surrounds you. By experiencing your surroundings with all of your senses, you're learning to align your awareness with your body. You may feel a sense of calm by visiting your favorite nature spot, but when you take the time to fully inhabit the present moment through all of your senses your mind awakens to how your environment impacts your body and emotions. This awareness of how your body relaxes in a calming environment enables you to create that same calming process throughout your body at any moment. This awareness also allows you to heighten the soothing sensations you experience when visiting your favorite nature spot or when appreciating the everyday beauty that's waiting to be unveiled by you. Practice awareness of the present moment through all of your senses, and cultivate the healing process within you to foster a heightened sense of well-being.

When you are beginning the practice of cultivating self-awareness and healing, it can help to practice in an environment that you naturally find calming. Time spent in nature has measurable positive physiological and spiritual effects.

In Japan, from 2005 to 2006, research coined as Shinrin-yoku was conducted, which translates to forest bathing or taking in the forest atmosphere. Twelve subjects were relocated from a city to a forest, and their vitals were contrasted between the two environments. According to the U.S. National Institutes of Health's National Library of Medicine, "The results show that forest environments promote lower concentrations of cortisol, lower pulse rate, lower blood pressure, greater parasympathetic nerve activity, and lower sympathetic nerve activity than do city environments."

Spiritual experiences when in nature are common human occurrences. Sylvie Shaw, PhD states in the International Community for Ecopsychology journal, "Being in wild nature engenders a sense of mystery about the world; a sense of awe or wonderment about the earth or particular naturescape; a sense of connectedness or oneness with the natural world; a profound feeling of transcendence (within and without); a belief in a power greater than oneself; and an appreciation of the beauty in nature. It sparks feelings of inner peace, hope, joy and empowerment; promotes physical and emotional well-being, and brings about 'significant' changes in attitude and behaviour."

Healing is possible, and the ability to heal is already inside of you. This ability is at the core of the Self-Love Diet. Through *regularly offering yourself love* you will activate and strengthen the healer within you. It may be hard to imagine a future where you love yourself and your body, but you don't need to have that belief right now to begin healing or to begin your journey through the seven paths of self-love.

Getting out of bed today, going out with friends when your mind berates you with fat talk or abstaining from a binge and a purge, these are all examples of healing. When you made the choice to read this book today you made the choice to bring healing into your life. This is a visible success that you can acknowledge and celebrate.

**How would your life be different if you believed
healing was possible?**

>> Action Steps <<

A) Tell a safe, supportive person your intentions for healing.

B) Remember those small, almost invisible, healing moments. Keep a journal and write them out so you will have evidence of your progress. Put stickers on your calendar for each day you offer yourself love.

C) Spend time in nature, breathing deeply, and consciously being in the moment.

9

I Can't Eat Love, So What Do I Eat?

Conscious body-based eating:
Self-Love Diet Food and Eating Guidelines

*Eventually you will come to understand that love
heals everything, and love is all there is.*

—Gary Zukav

If you've lived life from a diet mentality, how are you supposed to magically become a conscious, body-based eater? Here are the Self-Love Diet Guidelines.

#1: Eat when you are physically hungry

Offer your body attention. It will tell you when it's hungry. Have you ever fed an infant? They are great examples of Self-Love Diet body-based eating. Babies cry when they're hungry. Even without words they let you know when they need food. They have no diet plan. They depend on the sensations in their body to tell them when they are hungry. Some of you reading this book may have temporarily lost your ability to understand your body's signals. Here are some physical signals your body gives you to tell you when you are hungry.

Early Stage Signs of Hunger

In the early stages of hunger your body's signals are subtle. You need to pay attention to the following:

- You will feel a slight drop in energy.
- You will feel a subtle empty feeling in your stomach.
- Thoughts of food come and easily go.
- You may hear a teeny grumble in your stomach.
- If you see or smell food, you notice it and continue with what you're doing.

Mid Stage Signs of Hunger

- Your energy level drops to low; you may feel tired or sluggish.
- You notice a little more emptiness in your stomach.
- Your thoughts of food increase.
- Growling of your stomach increases.
- Your ability to focus and concentrate is lessened.
- When you see or smell food, your senses are heightened. Food looks and smells appetizing.

Signs of Starvation

- You feel exhausted, tired and realize you need more energy.
- Your stomach may hurt because it's so empty.
- You can think of little else but food.
- Your stomach is growling loud enough for others to hear.
- You find it difficult to concentrate or make decisions.
- You become more irritable.
- You get light headed or dizzy.
- You become stressed out and anxious more easily.
- Your senses have intensified and you become less picky about your food choice. Anything looks good now.
- Your vision will be distorted; you'll think you need more food than you need.
- You will eat more quickly; there will be a frenetic quality to your eating.

If you have been starving yourself or overeating, you may have lost the ability to recognize or feel hunger. If you find you are not able to tell when you are hungry or are unable to eat even when you know you are hungry, it will take a while for you to develop these skills. Depending on how long you've been ignoring your body's signals, the time it takes to learn these skills will vary. Be patient with yourself. It's a process. It's not a habit that you learn immediately after reading about it. It takes time to learn how to read your body's hunger signals.

If you always feel hungry and think, "If I eat when I'm hungry, I'll always be eating," then wait for #3 and you will get help for distinguishing body hunger from emotional hunger.

#2: Stop eating when you are satisfied

Offer you body attention. It will tell you when you are satisfied. In order to pay attention to your body's signals you need to have an environment that cultivates self-reflection. If you are watching TV, on the computer, reading a book or driving your car while eating, you are not creating the environment for learning your body's satiation signals. Choose a quiet, calm environment whenever you can. It's easier for you to hear your body telling you when it's satisfied.

Here are some physical signs of satiety:

+ You can feel the food in your stomach and notice if you have more room or not.

+ The food begins to lose its visual appeal.

+ The food doesn't smell as good as it did at first.

+ The food is not as tasty as the first bites.

+ You begin to think about not eating any more.

+ You feel full and know if you eat more you will be uncomfortable.

If you have been overeating or bingeing, you may have gotten real good at turning off your body's satiety signals. By regularly offering your body the attention it deserves, you will be able to reclaim your ability to recognize the signals your body gives you to let you know it is satisfied.

If you have been restricting your food and are working on refeeding yourself, this is not the time for body-based eating. You will need to eat according to a schedule and with the help of a registered dietitian and a therapist who specializes in working with people with eating disorders until you can learn to interpret your body's signals correctly. When you restrict your food over a period of time your body slows down your digestion. You will experience constipation, bloating and an exaggerated sense of fullness. If you're used to having an empty stomach or have only allowed yourself a minimally full feeling, then you can expect the following:

+ When you begin to eat a little more food, but not a full meal, you will feel uncomfortable psychologically and emotionally, resulting in distorted physical sensations of fullness.

+ When you begin to increase your food portions even more, but are still not eating a full meal, the same mental and emotional discomfort interferes with your ability to discern satiety.

+ As you build your ability to trust and interpret your body's signals and once you're consistently eating nutritionally complete meals, your body will regain its capacity to work as intended.

Karin Kratina, PhD, RD, LD/N created the Hunger Satiety Scale in her book Moving Away From Diets: Healing Eating Problems and Exercise Resistance. I use this scale with my clients to help them put a number to their hunger and satiety levels. You can find this scale in the appendix at the end of the book. Use it daily to assess where you are along the scale and you will soon be able to know when it's time to eat and when it's time to stop without any outside help.

#3: Neutralize foods and choose foods that you enjoy

Offer your body colorful, aromatic, tasty, satisfying foods. Have you developed a relationship with food where you have categorized food as good or bad, healthy or non-healthy, scary or safe, heavenly or sinful? Neutralizing your food will allow your food to just be food.

+ Notice if you have food categories.

+ Notice if you have food rules.

+ Let go of your categories and rules.
+ Try new foods. Experiment with foods that have been in your negative categories.
+ Choose tasty satisfying foods by:
  + Asking your body what it wants.
  + Test-driving your food choice before deciding.

Here are some examples of how to take action on the above guidelines.

Notice if you have food categories: Write Good/Bad, (or Healthy/Unhealthy, Scary/Safe and Heavenly/Sinful) in your Self-Love Diet journal. Write the foods that you have put in those categories under their titles. Continue to add to the columns as you discover the categories you have created.

Notice if you have food rules: Write them out in your journal. Here are some examples to get you started.

+ I can't eat after 8 pm.
+ I can't eat anything after dinner.
+ I must drink water before each meal.
+ I can't eat cooked vegetables and raw vegetable together.
+ It's ok to eat dessert as long as I work out the following day.

Let go of your food categories and rules: This is a difficult task. It requires concerted, consistent awareness of your categories and rules, and then it requires you to confront them and to change your behavior. Be gentle with yourself and hold the intention to make progress on letting go of your rigid rules rather than expecting perfection from yourself. The previous act of writing out your categories and rules will help you be conscious when they pop up. Once you are aware of when you are thinking of your rules you have the opportunity to work with letting them go. This is a process. It takes time. Give yourself permission to have this be an ongoing challenge. Perhaps a better way of thinking of it is an opportunity to regularly offer yourself the freedom from food categories and rules.

Try foods that have been in your negative categories: This can be a very scary experience if you are beginning to eat foods that you have not allowed yourself to eat before. Be gentle with yourself, and be aware of your thoughts and emotions. In chapter 31, "Thoughts, Feelings, Actions Loop," you will get help with a common thought pattern: "I shouldn't have eaten this cookie (or any other food on your bad list). I messed up, so I might as well eat the whole bag." Or, "I shouldn't have eaten this cookie (or any other food on your bad list). I messed up, so I better eat less to make up for it."

Many of my clients have shared that they feel bad, guilty, discouraged, hopeless or scared when they begin to eat the foods on their bad list. Chapter 29, "Treasure Chest of Emotions," will give you tools to handle the emotions that will come up for you as you practice this guideline. Once you are aware that your food and eating rules are present you have the opportunity to do something different.

Do your best to take foods out of their negative category prison, and give them a chance to offer you the nutrition, taste and enjoyment that they can offer. Remember this is a process. You are looking for progress, not perfection.

Choose satisfying foods: This is a two-step process. First, your mind will offer suggestions, and then your body will test-drive your choice before eating it.

Ask yourself what you want to eat

Does your mind think of something warm and substantial, like beef stew or a cheeseburger? Or does your mind think of something cool and refreshing, like yogurt and fresh fruit? Perhaps your mind thinks of something sweet and creamy, like chocolate pudding? Or something salty and crunchy, like nuts or chips? Give yourself permission to let your imagination offer you complete meals. Allow whatever comes to mind in whatever portion comes to mind. Remember, this is an imaginary meal.

Take this food on a test-drive

Visualize this food on a plate in front of you. What does it look like? Take your time to smell it. See if you can sense its temperature. Now imagine yourself bringing the food to your mouth. If it is finger food, pay attention to how it feels in your hand. If you are using a spoon or a fork, pay attention to the anticipation and sensation of the food in your mouth. Notice the texture of this food, the taste of it and the temperature, and take your time chewing it. Bring your attention to the feeling of swallowing this food. Continue imagining eating this food in this deliberate, mindful manner until you decide to stop. Write down the food and the quantity that your mind chose.

_____

_____

_____

Now imagine yourself 20 minutes into the future after your body has digested this food. What energy has this food provided your body? Are you energetic and renewed, or do you feel tired and lethargic? Is the food comfortable in your stomach? Discern if your body is nurtured by the portion your mind chose. Write down your body's experience of the food that your mind offered it below.

_____

_____

_____

If your mind and body are in sync, you will feel satisfied, not stuffed, and you will feel physically nurtured by the foods you've eaten. If on the other hand, you discovered that you felt uncomfortable after taking these food choices on your test-drive, you can learn from the experience and make different choices of foods or quantities.

If you notice just imagining food is overwhelming for you, it may be an indicator that you need more support in this process from a registered dietitian or a therapist who specializes in working with people with eating disorders and disordered eating.

#4: Mindfully bring gratitude to all of the people who grew, packaged, delivered, sold and perhaps cooked this food to you

Offer yourself moments of reflection. Cultivate gratitude at each meal. When I was a little girl, we started all of our meals with grace. Soon the practice of saying grace became a meaningless rote litany before we could eat. I remember saying it as fast as I could so we could start our meal. The Self-Love Diet invites you to regularly offer yourself pauses in your day, moments of self-reflection and invitations to bring in gratitude. Each meal time is a sacred moment when you are offering your body nourishment in gratitude for all it does for you. This gratitude can be expanded along with your awareness of the multitude of people who have provided you with the food for each meal. By blessing them and the food, you are blessing yourself. This process also allows you to be more present with yourself, and your food. Being in the moment is another gift you can regularly offer yourself.

#5: Set the table for your meals; treat yourself like an important guest

Offer yourself the gift of treating yourself like an important guest. Think of someone who you hold in high regard. Imagine the opportunity to share a meal with this person. Perhaps a political person comes to mind, a movie star, your favorite entertainer or a respected athlete. Allow yourself to imagine a person in your current life that you want to make a positive impression on. You might even imagine a historical, religious or spiritual figure.

If I had Hillary Clinton or Michelle Obama as my lunch guests, I would not drive through a fast-food restaurant and eat our lunch in my car. I would want to spend quality time with them.

I know I would definitely clean my kitchen, actually the whole house. I would set my table with flowers, put candles on the table and use colorful place mats. I wouldn't use paper plates or plastic silverware. I would use my pretty dishes and my best glassware.

Visualize how you would set your table for your person. In the Self-Love Diet, the concept is to treat yourself as well as you would a person you look up to. Having your meals be relaxed and in a beautiful setting is one way to practice the Self-Love Diet, and it creates an environment to practice the above tools. If you do not already, I hope you will soon treat yourself as well as you would others that you admire and love.

#6: Distinguish between body hunger and emotional hunger

Offer yourself the time to stop, slow down and ask the following questions. Ask if your body is telling you it's hungry. If you can't tell, offer your body attention by reviewing the guidelines in #1 to discern if you are hungry. If you can tell that your body is not hungry, check in with your emotions. I adapted the following acronym from Alcoholics Anonymous.

H = Am I hungry or hurt?

A = Am I anxious or angry?

L = Am I lonely (or sad)?

T = Am I tired or thirsty?

B4 = Halt *before* you eat.

B = Breathe. Slow down. Make time to take five deep full breaths. This allows you to physiologically soothe your body and emotions. By bringing oxygen into your brain, you are telling it that everything is okay and that you're safe. Your brain knows that if you were in danger you would not be breathing fully and slowly, so it stops the production of adrenalin in your body and offers you a reprieve from anxiety in which to make a loving choice.

4 = Four actions to take after breathing.

1. Tell yourself, "Calm down, I'm safe in this moment." (Or another statement that fits better for you to soothe yourself.)

2. Review the emotion you realized was masquerading as hunger.

3. Decide the best action to address this emotion's message.

4. Take the action that better addresses your emotion than eating.

Once you are able to notice the difference between your body's hunger and your emotional hunger, you are in a better place to make a loving decision in that moment. If you use the HALT B4 acronym and discover that you have hurt feelings, your rational mind understands that food will not help the hurt. The most loving thing to offer you in that moment may be to let yourself feel the emotion of hurt, knowing it will pass. You may also decide to write about your hurt or perhaps call a trusted friend and talk to them about the situation. You may decide to tell the person who hurt you that you were hurt by his or her actions. You can also decide to let it go. All of these actions better address your hurt feelings than food.

Thirst and tiredness in the T of HALT are commonly mistaken for hunger. When your body is dehydrated it is more difficult to discern physical hunger. When your body is tired it is searching for energy. This request for energy can be mistakenly perceived as a request for food. Ask yourself if you are hungry. If you say No, double check by asking yourself how long ago you ate. If you just ate and there is still food in your stomach and you are not thirsty, your body may be needing energy through rest.

#7: Learn the symbolic message of your food cravings when your body is not physically hungry and take non-food action steps that fill your symbolic cravings

Foods have different qualities and offer different energies to our body. Coffee offers stimulation and can rev up the body. For many people, comfort foods, such as macaroni and cheese, mashed potatoes or French bread and butter, may offer the body a soothing, numbing quality and can slow the body down. Ice cream, without other ingredients, offers a cool, smooth texture. Nuts offer a hard crunchy experience. Chocolate can offer a sweet or bittersweet taste; it may melt in your mouth, or it can be a chewy sensation. The qualities and symbolic meanings of food are as varied as the people who crave them. Here are three basic ideas to get you started.

1. **Notice what food you are craving when your body is not hungry.**
   Perhaps you notice you crave ice cream at the end of the night when you realize your body is not hungry

2. **Pay attention to the quality of that food.**
   You become aware of the cold, smooth and sweet taste and texture of the ice cream.

3. **Explore the symbolic message that food offers.**
   Barbara Birsinger, RD, created a system for this concept that she calls the Behavior Decoding Method or BDM. Following is an example of how to use the short version of her work called the Quick Decoding Process™ when you are having a craving.

Once you find yourself on the not hungry or full side of the hunger continuum, and you still want to eat, you can begin the Quick Decoding Process as follows. I filled in the exercise with example answers.

- **Name the feeling you have at the time of the craving, and describe what happened just before you noticed the craving.** I noticed I felt angry as I thought about what to say to my co-worker, Suzanne, the next day at work.

- **Name the feeling that you would like to have. This is the feeling you are reaching for with food.** I noticed that I wanted to feel appreciated by her for what I do at work.

- **Name the physical qualities of the food you crave. Be specific and detailed.** The ice cream is cool, smooth and sweet. I like the way it changes from hard to soft as I eat it. I enjoy the way it melts and the cool softness of it as it goes down my throat.

- **What does the word(s) represent that you want, or what you are attempting to work out?** I suppose cool represents my need to cool down. Smooth represents how I wish I could smooth things out between us. Sweet is how our work relationship used to be and how I wish it were again. Hard represents how it is between us now, and soft is how I wish it were. I wish we could melt our anger and be cool with each other again.

- **When you have this trigger feeling and food craving, if you could shout out, "What I really need right now, is…" What would that be?** I want to be friends again!

- **List the deeper need that is trying to get met here.** Love and Connection.

- **List as many activities or experiences that you know, now or in your past, that helps satisfy that need and the desired feeling.** Going out with friends. Laughing at YouTube videos at work when we're supposed to be working. Going to our weekly work meetings and hearing what a good job I'm doing. Talking with friends on the phone, or going on Facebook and checking in with people. Walking along the lake with Suzanne during our lunch break.

- **What do these activities do for you that fill your need better than food?** These activities help me feel connected, appreciated and loved. They help me feel competent and needed.

With these strategies, food no longer has the role of an emotional coping tool. Food becomes the source of proper nourishment and savory satisfaction, with the body determining the what, when and how much to eat.

Use the concepts of regularly offering yourself love to continue searching for ways to get your feelings and needs met more directly. Once you become aware of the emotional need your food cravings have been trying to address, you open the door to more loving ways of fulfilling your needs.

As you continue to learn how to separate physical hunger from emotional/symbolic hunger, you will choose the most loving actions for yourself. This is a great example of the Self-Love Diet's instruction to regularly offer yourself love.

The seven Self-Love Diet food and eating guidelines are listed in bullet form in the appendix of the book for your convenience.

How would your life be different if you were able to correctly interpret your bodies' signals and eat accordingly?

>> Action Steps <<

A) Review the Seven Self-Love Diet food and eating guidelines and pick one to work on.

B) Choose a second guideline once you feel competent with your first one.

C) Write in your journal as you go along so you can go back and see your progress.

Part Three

*If you can get up the courage to begin, you have
the courage to succeed. It's the job you never start
that takes the longest to finish. Don't worry about
what lies dimly at the distance but do what lies
clearly ahead.*

—Bill Greer

Reducing Stigma by
Understanding the Disorders

I hear many uninformed comments about eating disorders in the media, in my day-to-day interactions and from some of the family members of my clients. Unaware and frustrated, parents and loved ones have said things such as, "It's not that complicated. She just needs to eat."

"It's just a phase. She'll grow out of it."

"She just wants attention."

The information in the following chapters will help you if you are caring for someone with an eating disorder or if one of your family members, your partner or your friend has an eating disorder and you want to understand what they are going through. Through the descriptions of each eating disorder, you will get an inside look of the struggle that someone goes through and how their eating disorder affects them. In the chapter, Family Affair, you will also see how your loved one's eating disorder can affect you, how it's beneficial for the whole family to take part in the recovery process and how it's important for you to focus on your own self-care while you're supporting your loved one's recovery.

If you are struggling with an eating disorder, this section will offer you hope by showing you that you are not alone in what you are going through. Through client examples, you will see how others were affected by their eating disorders and how they were able to recover.

For people who don't struggle with eating disorders, by understanding them you will help end the judgment and stigma assigned to these struggles and the people who are besieged by them.

In the following section, I will go over the four main eating disorders: anorexia, bulimia, eating disorder not otherwise specified, and binge eating. I will also compare and contrast binge eating from compulsive overeating, and I will offer a framework for normal eaters who eat for non-hunger reasons and suggest that normal is not to be confused with healthy eating.

For the specific criteria of each disorder, refer to the Diagnostic and Statistical Manual of Mental Disorders, DSM-IV. The DSM-IV is the manual used by professionals to diagnosis mental health issues. The DMS-V is expected to be released in 2013. To learn more about each disorder, look through the reference page or the suggested resources in the bibliography at the back of the book. I bring your attention in particular to Ancel Keys' Minnesota [Semi] Starvation Study to understand more in depth the physical, psychological and emotional effects of eating disorders.

Lastly, you will learn about the factors that contribute to the development of an eating disorder, the role that genetics plays in the development of eating disorders and the importance of increasing awareness about eating disorders. As more people realize that eating disorders are a serious, life-threatening disease, and that they are largely genetic, we can help reduce the stigma associated with eating disorders, help eliminate the blame that loved ones or people struggling with eating disorders carry and help the general public to see eating disorders as a legitimate disease that needs attention and more funding for research, education, prevention and treatment.

10

Anorexia

Fear of food, emotions and life

Loving can cost a lot but not loving always costs more and those who fear to love often find that want of love is an emptiness that robs the joy from life.

—Merle Shain

Anorexia is a serious, life-threatening disorder. Its victims are unable to eat without intense fear of uncontrolled weight gain. Sufferers fear becoming fat with symptoms of panic and high levels of anxiety that overrule the body's hunger signals.

Obsessive interest in diets, recipes, coupons, food labels, cooking for others, odd food choices and ritualistic eating behaviors are aspects of anorexia. A change in personality from carefree and fun to depressed and austere is a common by-product and indicator of anorexia. Body distortion, increased exercise, restlessness, irritability, moodiness and isolating behaviors are other indicators of anorexia.

Unchecked, anorexia overrides the body's basic needs for food and rest and takes over the ability to correctly assess body size and shape. The ultimate goal of anorexia is to starve its victims to death by causing their hearts to stop.

As the brain becomes malnourished from starvation, its ability to discern incoming stimuli is distorted, similar to how words appear backwards in a mirror's reflection. A positive statement from a loving, supportive person such as, "You look great. You are looking much healthier!" will be heard as, "You've gained weight and are now fat and disgusting!" The eating disorder will say, "You must stop eating immediately or you will continue to get fatter and fatter."

Remember Kim from Chapter 7? Kim is a good example of how the mindset of the malnourished brain continues to persist even after restricting behaviors have ceased.

Kim was 17 years old when she came to see me after her insurance would no longer cover her stay at a residential treatment program where she had been in treatment for 60 days. Kim had gained weight and was capable of eating foods that had been on her *bad* list. Her father stated, "We've got our daughter back! She's eating breakfast, lunch and dinner. She's following her food plan to a T. She no longer looks like the skeleton we dropped off at the program only 60 days ago."

Once her parents left the room, Kim confided in me that each meal was torture. Each bite she took was confronted by the voice of her anorexia screaming at her, "You are a fat pig! How can you eat all of that food?"

Kim's parents had no idea how entrenched Kim still was in the anorexia mindset because they could not hear her internal struggle now that her outward behaviors had changed. Kim was uncertain how much longer she would be able to follow her food plan now that she was out of the structure of the residential treatment program.

Patricia was in a residential program similar to Kim when she wrote the following poem about her struggle to let go of anorexia.

Bare Bones

Bare Bones
No meat on "them" bones,
that's what people say,
Eat, eat, eat, just for today.

Foods all around me,
I just can't escape,
What's really a nightmare,
Is what's on my plate.

Don't eat that don't eat that,
The voices will say.
You'll get fatter and fatter,
Back to Layne Bryant someday

Stop the voices, stop,
I cry out in pain.
I'm falling, I'm falling,
Becoming insane.

I get on that scale daily,
Which determines my mood.
Will I be anxious, depressed or happy,
I brood.

It's numbers, those numbers,
That race in my head.
Get them down, get them down,
You will never be dead.

My bones from my hips,
Stick out from my skin.
I'm so happy, so happy,
I will definitely win.

Win what? Win What?
A race towards death?
My healthy part says,
"I want another breath!"

I want to have a life,
Free from despair.
However, there's a part of me,
That's deeply scared.

For peace and relief from Anorexia,
This is what I pray.
God responds, "Take it slowly,
One small step each day."

Below I focus on each stanza of the poem, using Patricia's words to let you inside her thought process as she battles anorexia.

Bare Bones
No meat on "them" bones,
that's what people say,
Eat, eat, eat, just for today.

The first part of this poem reflects the time when Patricia's family was confronting her. Her family members and loved ones were able to see her bones, and told her to eat. It seems like the logical response. They are right, that is the answer. Unfortunately, it is not that simple for someone with anorexia. This disease is very difficult for loved ones. They have no understanding of the complexities that interfere with their daughter's difficulty with eating. It seems pretty clear cut to them; she needs to gain weight, so she needs to eat more. When this logic doesn't help their daughter, the frustration builds, along with the fear, anger and resentment. All of these emotions are valid, however, they usually only make the problem worse.

Foods all around me,
I just can't escape,
What's really a nightmare,
Is what's on my plate.

Take a moment, and see if you can think of something that is terrifying to you. Perhaps you have nightmares of Jason from *Friday the 13th* stalking you. Imagine the panic you would feel if Jason was standing at the foot of your bed when you opened your eyes. Or maybe you have a phobia of snakes. Picture how you would feel if you walked into your bathroom and stepped on hundreds of slithering snakes. Patricia has experienced similar panic at the thought of eating the food on her plate. Often family members have little to no insight into the intensity of the fear that a meal can present for their loved ones.

Don't eat that, don't eat that,
The voices will say
You'll get fatter and fatter
Back to Layne Bryant someday

Patricia is letting you hear the constant barrage of dialogue telling her "Don't eat that! You'll get fat!" You can tell that she has begun recovery from this stanza because she differentiated the voices from herself. Once a person can separate themselves from the "voices," the voice of anorexia, they have an opportunity to overpower the thoughts of the eating disorder.

> *Stop the voices, stop,*
> *I cry out in pain*
> *I'm falling I'm falling*
> *Becoming insane.*

Patricia finds herself in quite a dilemma. She knows the voices are not her healthy part, and yet they continue hounding her. She's stuck between the proverbial "rock and a hard place." She's making progress by eating the food in front of her, but the anorexia is escalating, and is getting louder and louder, telling her not to eat. At this part of her story, Patricia allows us to be aware of the feeling of insanity that an eating disorder creates in one's mind.

> *I get on that scale daily*
> *Which determines my mood*
> *Will I be anxious, depressed or happy*
> *I brood.*

This next part of her poem speaks to the compulsion of daily weighing. The scale has taken on the magical powers of determining how she will feel about herself. Anorexia tells her she cannot be happy unless she has lost weight or is under a certain number. This is a great example of how anorexia takes control of her emotional life. Her well-being depends on what the scale tells her each day.

> *It's numbers, those numbers*
> *That race in my head.*
> *Get them down, get them down*
> *You will never be dead.*

Now we are able to hear the eating disorder telling her that she must get those numbers down. We can read in these lines that she has been told that if she continues to restrict her food she will die. The reason we know this is because the disorder is confronting the truth with the lie, "You will never be dead." This level of denial is strong because she has a brain that is lacking nutrition, and therefore unable to see things clearly.

My bones from my hips,
Stick out from my skin,
I'm so happy, so happy,
I will definitely win.

We are not listening to Patricia in this stanza; anorexia is talking. The fact that her bones are sticking out from the skin of her hips makes the eating disorder happy because it believes it's winning the anorexia war. There is no fighting back in this stanza. This part of the poem shows us how anorexia has taken over, making it very difficult for Patricia to stay in contact with her authentic self.

Win what? Win What?
A race towards death?
My healthy part says
"I want another breath!"

By this part of her poem, the authentic Patricia is back and is confronting anorexia's thoughts. We are witnessing the constant battling between the healthy self and the eating disorder. She has given us front row seats in the battle between life and death.

I want to have a life,
Free from despair.
However, there's a part of me
That's deeply scared.

At this juncture, we are able to partake in her clarity and passion for life. She is tired of the battle and the daily despair. She wants freedom. She is also aware of the part of herself that doesn't know what life will be like without her anorexia. What is difficult for others to understand is the intimate relationship that develops with anorexia. There is some aspect of the disease that works; otherwise, it wouldn't be so hard to break away from it. Anorexia provides familiarity and a lifetime of knowing what to expect. Recovery is the unknown. It's like walking straight toward the fear of becoming fat that anorexia has been protecting her from. She is telling us that it scares her to not know what comes next.

> *For peace and relief from Anorexia,*
> *This is what I pray.*
> *God responds, "Take it slowly,*
> *One small step each day."*

We now hear her pray; she is connecting with her spirit. She is going inward for peace, rather than stepping on the scale for a sense of well-being. She is staying in the present moment by taking recovery slowly, taking one small step each day. When she is not in the past with anorexia or in the future with the fear of getting fat, she can practice being in the moment.

Reaching out to a power greater than you and realizing that you are more than your body is a corner stone of the Self-Love Diet, no matter how you define that greater power.

How might you lessen the stigma of anorexia?

>> Action Steps <<

A) When someone makes a negative comment about someone with anorexia, you can let them know that anorexia is complicated and not something that someone chooses to have.

B) Notice your own thoughts and beliefs about fat. If you have a fear of being or getting fat, reevaluate your beliefs.

C) Be conscious of what you say about your own or others' bodies. Remember that complimenting people on their inner qualities can be more empowering than complimenting them on their ability to lose or gain weight.

11

Bulimia

The hamster wheel of the binge/purge cycle

I count him braver who overcomes his desires than him who conquers his enemies; for the hardest victory is over self.

—Aristotle

Bulimia is a serious, life-threatening disorder. Its victims are unable to eat mindfully and stop when satisfied. Sufferers eat amounts of food way beyond their physical needs. This eating, or bingeing behavior, is done in a trancelike state, making the person suffering from bulimia feel like the behavior is out of their control. Victims of bulimia fear becoming fat after bingeing and report feelings of guilt, shame, remorse and high levels of anxiety, which compels them to purge. Once the binge is over, purging brings a feeling of release, relief and momentary euphoria. As this disorder progresses, the relief does not last as long and is followed by guilt, shame and remorse, similar to the feelings experienced after bingeing. Bulimia's victims get caught in the hamster wheel of the binge/purge cycle.

Purging is marked by a number of compensatory behaviors. Vomiting, exercising and restricting food are some examples. The following instance may help you to get a feel for the power that bulimia has over its victims.

Fiora was 16 years old. She was an averaged sized teen with auburn, shoulder length curly hair. Her pale, acne marked skin highlighted her emerald eyes. Her forehead was etched into a permanent scowl. She had been forced to see me by her mother, who had joined her in our first session. Fiora was not happy to be in my office.

Her mother was fuming. "Fiora refuses to stop throwing up! Her room is disgusting. I can't even walk by it without feeling nauseous from the smell. She won't clean her room when I tell her to, and I find quart size plastic baggies filled with vomit in her closet, under the clothes on her floor and under her bed."

Fiora's mother was certain that Fiora was doing this just to make her mad.

After her mother left the room, Fiora became quite animated and talkative. She told me that her bulimia had started when she was in sixth grade. She had complained to a friend that her stomach hurt because she had eaten too much pizza at a party. Her friend told her, "That's not a problem. You don't have to keep that in your stomach. Just put your finger down your throat. I do it all the time."

Fiora said that the first time she tried it she didn't like it, and she decided she wouldn't do it anymore. Later, during the summer between sixth and seventh grade, her parents told her and her older brother that they were getting divorced. Fiora remembers crying along with her mother, while noticing her father and brother seemed calm.

"I thought one set of us must be wrong," she said. "I was angry that I was acting like my mother. I felt weak, and couldn't understand why they weren't upset."

Fiora described her and her brother eating junk food and watching movies during that summer when her parents were at work. Her brother began to tease Fiora about getting fat. He told her not to eat so much, yet he continued to make cookies, popcorn, and pizza before putting movies on. Fiora said she tried, but she couldn't stop eating the food while they were watching movies.

Soon her mother and father both mentioned her added weight. Fiora began skipping breakfast and lunch. She would eat a "normal" dinner with whichever parent she was staying with at that time. Later, once she was alone, she began to eat the forbidden foods in the pantry that she deemed off limits or she would finish off the leftovers that were left on the counter. She felt out of control and remembered the advice from her friend in sixth grade.

"When I first purged again, after eating the leftovers in the refrigerator at my Mom's house, I felt so relieved. I thought I could use this as a backup plan. I told myself it wouldn't become a problem."

By the time Fiora walked into my office that day I first saw her, she was bingeing and purging daily, sometimes five times a day, desperately seeking the momentary sense of relief purging brought her.

"I'm so sick of this pit of depression spilling over with food," she said. "I hate lying on my bed feeling so gross and stuffed that I can't even drag myself to the nearest bathroom. Throwing up in those plastic baggies has been my solution." With tears flowing down her pale face, she told me this cycle of bingeing and purging had taken over her life to the point that she didn't want to live anymore.

What Fiora's mother didn't understand was that although Fiora did get a secondary benefit of pissing her off, Fiora desperately wanted to stop, but couldn't.

"It's like someone inside of me takes over and I have no control to stop myself," she said. "Sometimes, I feel like I'm not even in my body."

Fiora's backup plan had become as out of control as she felt in her life. Her father suffered from depression and was isolating himself at the very time Fiora needed to be reassured of his love. Fiora's mother was overwhelmed and was unable to manage her own emotions. She and Fiora both experienced frequent mood swings, which negatively affected their relationship. They would say spiteful things to each other, call each other names and slam the door on each other. Both of Fiora's parents had unresolved contempt for each other that created a toxic environment in their homes. When Fiora was at her mother's house, she described life as chaotic. When she stayed with her Dad, she felt alone, even when he was home.

Fiora's recovery was hard won. Mood disorders were part of her genetic pool. Beyond the diagnosis of bulimia, Fiora also suffered from bipolar disorder and PTSD from witnessing the accidental death of her grandfather. My first referral for her to a higher level of care was the intensive outpatient program I had recently developed. Fiora made progress in the intensive outpatient program and came back to individual sessions with me to continue her recovery. Fiora's full recovery took three more referrals for higher levels of care before she was able to get the relief from within herself that she had been seeking from the bulimia.

Many years later, I received a note from Fiora. She told me she had been married for two years and that they were creating a healthy relationship together. She had made peace with her diagnosis of bipolar disorder and was taking medication, which she said made a tremendous difference in her ability to handle her emotions. She visited her family infrequently, but described the state of their relationship as much improved.

How might you lessen the stigma of bulimia?

>> Action Steps <<

A) When someone makes a negative comment about someone with bulimia, you can let them know that bulimia is complicated and not something that someone chooses to have.

B) Notice your own behaviors or inclinations to exercise or eat less the following day when you think you have overeaten.

C) Be conscious of what you say about your own or others bodies. Remember that complimenting people on their inner qualities can be more empowering than complimenting them on their ability to lose or gain weight. Remember that weight gain is not the end of the world and that suggesting someone go on a diet may not be the solution to the problem.

12

Eating Disorder Not Otherwise Specified (EDNOS)

Life-threatening behaviors do not always fulfill diagnostic criteria for a specific eating disorder

Success is not measured by what you accomplish,
but by the opposition you have encountered, and
the courage with which you have maintained the
struggle against overwhelming odds.

—Orison Swett Marden

If you know of someone who has been given the diagnosis of Eating Disorder, not otherwise specified, or EDNOS, it does not mean that they are out of the woods. In fact, this diagnosis can be as life-threatening as the two previous disorders. *Not otherwise specified* means that the person does not fulfill all the specific criteria in the DSM-IV for anorexia or bulimia, but their life is still at risk.

A good example of someone with the diagnosis of EDNOS is Leah, a young woman who came to me for treatment at the demand of her employer. She worked as a home health aide for an elderly couple. She drove them to doctor appointments, helped with cooking and did light housekeeping. Leah also stayed with the husband to give the wife time off from her caregiving duties.

The intake call came from the wife. She told me she loved her young caregiver, but she couldn't keep her unless she sought treatment. She said Leah had blacked out during her last home visit and could tell that she was purging her food.

When Leah was confronted by her employer, she confessed that she had strenuously been restricting her food, and she agreed to go to counseling in order to keep her job.

When Leah first walked into my office, her ash blonde hair was in a French braid that hung down her back to her waist. She gave me a shy smile as she silently sat down on the antique brocade couch. Her skin was clear and rosy, her lips had natural color and she had an attractive, firm, curvy body. The only indication that Leah was not healthy was the dark circles under her beautiful blue eyes that were outlined by thick dark eyelashes.

Leah was 21 and was far from her home in the UK. After my initial assessment, I discovered that she was restricting her food intake as severely as I had ever encountered. She experienced constant dizziness, headaches and stomach pains. She was also blacking out, which put her life in danger each time she got behind the wheel of her car. She had all the behaviors of anorexia, but she did not qualify for the diagnosis because her current weight had not dropped to the levels required for that diagnosis, and although her periods were shorter and lighter, she still had her menses. Although she was purging, she was not bingeing, so she did not fulfill the criteria for bulimia either.

Leah wanted to continue to lose weight. She had restricted her food intake so strictly because she was not losing weight with her previous strategies of cutting back on certain foods. She was only in my office because she did not want to lose her job. Leah believed that if she lost weight and got the body she desperately desired, all would be well.

Leah's malnourished brain inhibited her from seeing the dire situation she was in and interfered with her ability to see herself clearly or make rational decisions for her health. EDNOS had taken over. Once she was under the care of a doctor and had agreed to let me contact her family, she was able to see that it was not safe for her to drive or to continue to care for the couple.

She needed a higher level of care than the three sessions a week in my office.

When Leah came out of the residential program, she stepped down to a 4 day a week outpatient program, and then came back to individual therapy with me. Leah had one more relapse and admittance into a day treatment program.

Leah worked on her relationships in her family while in the eating disorder programs. During her first program, her parents came from the UK to take part in the family week, and they participated by phone in her ensuing programs. She resolved a long-standing schism with her older sister and addressed the loss of a best friend that she had suppressed until later in treatment. Leah is now healthy. She decided to go back to college and is an active advocate for self-love and recovery on her campus.

How might you lessen the stigma of Eating Disorder NOS?

>> Action Steps <<

A) When someone makes a negative comment about someone with disordered eating behaviors, you can let them know that eating disorders are complicated and not something that someone chooses to have.

B) Notice your own thoughts and beliefs about the importance of losing weight. Reevaluate your beliefs.

C) Be conscious about how you talk about your body. Notice if diet mentality creeps into your conversations.

13

Binge Eating, Compulsive Overeating

Binge eating and compulsive overeating behaviors overlap

> *We don't want to EAT hot fudge sundaes as much*
> *as we want our lives to BE hot fudge sundaes. We*
> *want to come home to ourselves.*
>
> —Geneen Roth

Binge eating is currently being researched with the intention of adding it to the list of eating disorders. Binge eaters find themselves trapped in serious, life-threatening eating behaviors. Like people who suffer from bulimia, binge eaters eat larger amounts of food than most people would eat in a similar amount of time. Sufferers report feeling out of control and unable to limit the quantities of food they eat. Feelings of helplessness and hopelessness are common. Unlike their fellow sufferers of bulimia, binge eaters do not compensate through regular purging behaviors. Morbid obesity can often times be the result.

I have worked with many people who would not describe themselves as binge eaters, but instead call themselves compulsive overeaters. Although the clients share many of the same behaviors, the main difference between the two labels is that compulsive overeaters do not necessarily eat a large amount of food in one sitting that would be considered a binge. There are a number of different eating styles that reflect compulsive overeating.

People who eat compulsively can graze throughout the day, eating small, consistent amounts of food. All of the compulsive overeaters and binge eaters

I have worked with describe a long history of diets, weight loss programs and feelings of failure and inadequacy, even in the face of success in other areas of their lives.

The research criteria for binge eating disorder in the DSM-IV includes the following behaviors:

1. Eating much more rapidly than normal.
2. Eating until feeling uncomfortably full.
3. Eating large amounts of food when not feeling physically hungry.
4. Eating alone because of being embarrassed by how much one is eating.
5. Feeling disgusted with oneself, depressed or very guilty after overeating.

If I were to add to this list based on what I see in my client's behaviors, I would add the following information.

Eating Style Characterized by the Following:

+ Difficulty in assessing hunger and/or satiation or differentiating hunger from thirst.
+ Eating triggered by external stimuli.
+ Eating triggered by emotional stimuli.
+ Eating used as a soothing mechanism.
+ Tuning out or unconscious eating. For example, eating while watching TV, reading, working, doing homework, doing housework, watching a movie at the theater or driving a car.
+ Grazing style of eating with no delineated meal times.
+ Eating normally during the day. Overeating in the evening.

Emotions and Compensatory Behaviors:

+ Repeated diets used to compensate for weight gain.
+ Feelings of self-control and increased self-esteem while on a diet.
+ Inability to sustain weight loss.

- A cycle of compulsive overeating, weight gain, dieting, weight loss, compulsive overeating and weight gain repeated over a lifetime.

- Feelings of being out of control, helpless and hopeless and feelings of self-hatred, guilt and shame.

- Inability to recognize the futility of the dieting process. Excited to start new diet.

- Belief that a diet is the answer to their problem.

- Self-esteem is tied to body size, minimizing inner qualities as compared to appearance.

The following journal entry from a 61-year-old client of mine, Emma, will give you an inside look into the devastation binge eating inflicts on its sufferers.

I told Jim I didn't want to go to the wedding. At the church, I felt as if I took up the whole pew. I looked like a whale in my blue floral muumuu. I'm disgusting. I didn't want people to see me. I know my family loves me, but I don't love myself.

Sitting on the pew, I began to list off all of the life events I've stayed away from because of my weight. The last time I flew in an airplane I barely fit in the seat, and the stewardess was so lovely, telling me that they use seat belt extenders all the time, but I was humiliated. I will not fly again.

What's the matter with me? Why can't I eat like other people?

I missed my niece's wedding vows because I was in my head, beating myself up during the whole ceremony.

When we got to the reception, I was gripped with fear when I saw that I was seated at the table right in front of the wedding table, and next to my sister's table. I looked at the seats and wondered if mine would hold me. I plastered a smile on my face as my niece came over to give me a hug. Why does she even want me here? Doesn't she know

I'm an embarrassment?

The next horror was the banquet table, all that food. What was I going to do? I told myself I wouldn't eat, but everyone kept saying, "Emma, aren't you going to eat?" I thought to myself, "You're not fooling anyone. They all know you pig out. You might as well give yourself the one pleasure you can count on."

I went to the banquet table and started putting the food on my plate. As I walked down the length of the table, I started plopping the frittata squares into my mouth to make room for the chicken wings, and then the chicken wings were in my mouth to make room for the macaroni salad. I continued eating as I was going along, desperate to have enough, to not miss anything, to make sure I got it all. I felt like such a loser. "You're a loser, a big fat loser!" The refrain repeated in my head. I can't go on like this, but I don't know how to get out of this hell.

The self-loathing thoughts in this journal entry unfortunately are not unusual for people, regardless of their size. For Emma, it was a slow pace to recovery. Her negative image of herself and hopelessness had been ingrained for many years. The well-meaning directions from her doctor to lose weight and exercise actually pushed Emma in the opposite direction. Her motivation to seek help came from a conversation with her daughter. Her daughter had taken her out to lunch and told her that she was pregnant.

Emma's beautiful dimples were showing through her smile as she was telling me about her conversation with her daughter, but her deep brown eyes belied the sadness within.

"My daughter told me she was afraid I wouldn't be alive to see her child grow up. I want to get better, but I just don't know how."

She had been on many different diets over her lifetime and reported that she got bigger and bigger after each one. She believed there was nothing she could do about her problem.

We worked diligently on Emma catching and stopping the constant thoughts of self-hatred. We were like detectives looking for evidence of her value and worth. Slowly but surely, Emma was able to find positive attributes about herself, and she learned to replace her criticisms with positive statements we had developed that she believed true. The Self-Love Diet was different from anything she had ever done before. By her granddaughter's fifth birthday, Emma flew with her to Disneyland and reported the thrill of clipping the regular seat belt around her waist.

How might you lessen the stigma of binge eating and compulsive overeating?

>> Action Steps <<

A) When someone makes a negative comment about someone who is binge eating you can let them know that the behavior is complicated and not something that someone feels they're able to control.

B) Notice your own thoughts and beliefs about people who binge eat. Reevaluate your beliefs.

C) Be conscious of what you say about your own or others' bodies. The next time you catch your negative body talk stop to think about what you're saying and how it makes you feel.

14

"Normal" Eaters

Range of behaviors are explored in non-eating-disordered population

Normal is not something to aspire to; it's something to get away from.

—Jodie Foster

Being a normal eater does not necessarily mean you are a healthy eater. The parameters of healthy eating are ever changing. I remember growing up being told red meat was good for your blood. Eggs were later promoted as the better protein, soon after we were told to cut our egg intake to four a week. It's hard to know what healthy eating is. If you do not have an eating disorder, you are more than likely a normal eater. What does normal mean? If you are a normal eater you may still find yourself exhibiting eating disordered behaviors on occasion. Overeating is one example, and Thanksgiving is one occasion where many are likely to overeat. We all use food at some time in our lives for reasons other than physical nourishment. Food is used to celebrate, to distract, to numb, to soothe, and even to punish ourselves. Recognizing the commonality of these behaviors may help you to understand the disorders.

Celebrate

Celebrations almost always include food. I bet you've eaten a slice of cake at a birthday party, even though you weren't hungry. Perhaps you've had appetizers at a party even though you ate not long before arriving. Food is a way we connect with one another and celebrate special occasions.

Distract

If you are a student, it's likely you'll recognize getting something to eat to distract yourself from writing a paper for school. Food can be used as a distraction for anything: your emotions, cleaning the house to starting a project, and even cooking dinner.

Numb

People will use food when they are upset to deaden their emotions, either by eating or not eating. How many times have you or someone you've known said, "I can't eat now because I'm too upset"? Your body can also be anesthetized by food. I hear comments like, "I was in a food coma" being used as a joke by non-eating disordered eaters who overate a favorite food. Although they do not have an eating disorder, feeling like they were in a food coma may be a fair description of their experience.

Soothe

Have you seen mothers bring their babies to their breasts when they're crying, even if they've just eaten? Suckling is a soothing action. That's why pacifiers were invented. I remember my pediatrician offering suckers to me after each shot at my annual physical. Food can actually soothe our nervous system on a biological level.

Punish

Are you familiar with compensating for occasional overeating by restricting your food intake the following day or days? Eating celery, carrots or other diet foods to compensate for overeating, and not for the pleasure of the texture and taste, can be a form of punishment.

You may even find yourself starting and restarting diets or exercising more than usual to compensate for the additional calorie intake. All of these behaviors can be within the realm of normal. It's not until these behaviors go over the top that they may qualify as eating disordered behaviors.

If you are eating for non-food reasons or not eating when your body needs fuel, it's an invitation to discover what it is you truly need or want.

These food-related behaviors are invitations to open your eyes and heart to your emotions and needs.

On an individual scale, these behaviors are an invitation for us to take responsibility for ourselves by committing to self-love. On a larger scale, as a country we also need to take responsibility for these life-threatening disorders through education, prevention, assessment, diagnosis, treatment and research.

How might you lessen the stigma of eating disorders now that you understand the similarities between normal eaters and eating disordered individuals?

>> Action Steps <<

A) When someone makes a negative comment about someone who has an eating disorder, let that person know that normal eaters have similar behaviors as someone with an eating disorder, just on a smaller scale.

B) Have you used food to celebrate, distract, numb, soothe or punish? Write about occasions where you have used food for non-hunger reasons.

C) Notice your own thoughts and beliefs about people who have eating disorders. Think of the occasions when you ate for non-hunger reasons and the similarities in your eating behaviors to that of the eating disordered individual.

15

A Family Affair

An eating disorder invites all members of a family to get help

> *Call it a clan, call it a network, call it a tribe,*
> *call it a family.*
>
> *Whatever you call it, whoever you are,*
> *you need one.*
>
> —Jane Howard

Most people who are living with a person with an eating disorder are clear that their loved one needs help. What's not as apparent is that family members need assistance too. A helpful paradigm is to think of this as a family problem rather than an individual's problem.

If you substitute cancer for an eating disorder you can understand how each member of the family is affected. There are numerous appointments to attend and schedules to take into consideration. With the cost of treatment, money can become an issue, working with insurance companies adds stress and you begin to feel a sense of helplessness in the face of this disease. A loved one's life is at stake. You begin to let your self-care slip as your life takes on a new role of caring for your loved one.

If someone who you loved had cancer you would want to know what kind of cancer they had and what stage they were in, as well as the best course of treatment. You'd research everything you could about the type of cancer they had because you know that your loved one could die. The same holds true for people with eating disorders. If untreated, it can be a terminal disease. Education about eating disorders is important because it helps the family to understand what is happening to their loved one and what they could do to help.

When a family member is diagnosed with an eating disorder, all the members of the family have an opportunity to recover together. Each family member will have one or more lessons to learn from the eating disorder. A family can be of more support to their family member with the eating disorder if they do their personal work of wading through feelings of guilt, helplessness, anger, fear and confusion that affect their relationship with all of the members of the family. The person struggling with the eating disorder does better when their family is getting their own support.

Here is one mother's experience of going through the process of both of her daughters' recoveries and coming to the realization that she needed to care for herself.

> I knew I would be fine…as long as my children were fine. But somehow both of my children ended up not being fine. They struggled. A lot. How could I ever be able to be fine or happy or joyful, if they were not? Somehow I let my life become so intertwined with that of my daughters'—their happiness was my happiness; their sadness, mine; their struggles, mine also. I was riding their roller coaster and I didn't know how to get off. It was a terrifying ride, one in which I had no control.

> I was so afraid I was going to lose my girls, but it was me who got lost. I lost who I was, what I wanted for my life, put my needs behind theirs. I couldn't even remember what my needs were. It was such a slow process. I didn't even see its progression. My life was one of anxiously standing guard, waiting to take care of whatever need or crisis presented itself. I stopped going out, stopped having fun. Just stopped. It didn't look like it from the outside, but it felt that way on the inside.

> I suffered from guilt. It was deep and it was painful. What was my

part? I was their mom. Wasn't I supposed to be my daughters' mentor for learning self- love? I think now that perhaps one of the greatest ways in which I can mentor my daughters is to choose to love myself and to choose to grant myself forgiveness. I choose not to regret the past. I choose only to learn from it and move forward. For whatever my part, I let guilt pass. I give myself the gift of forgiveness, just as I hope my girls will give themselves that gift. To silence the critical voice each and every time it tries to speak.

Gratefully, I am someone who reaches out for help, who knows that seeking support is a strength, not a weakness. So I did reach out; found support not for my daughters, not for my family—just for me. I found a safe place to find me, with a therapist I trusted, where I could feel lost and terrified and ashamed and understood, And reclaim my life.

Family Recovery

It is the whole family that needs recovery. This is a process our family has worked on long and hard. It has been difficult. Family therapy was often very messy-sadness, anger, shame, tears, frustration, denial. We would walk into family therapy sessions appearing as lambs to slaughter. We quietly shot blame like arrows in all different directions and defensiveness shielded our pain.

Therapists would help us find the glimmers of light, of love for each other, but it was a very long, very slow process. Lots of starts, lots of stops, lots of therapists, lots of telling a painful story over and over again. When our younger daughter was in a therapeutic boarding school, our "vacations" were seminars that focused on healing the family, 8:00 a.m. until midnight every day. It was exhausting, physically; exhausting mentally; exhausting emotionally. But we gained some tiny steps forward, and a deepened understanding of how important we are to each other and a chance to hug a daughter we had not seen for too many months.

People will say that family therapy doesn't work for them. That it makes things worse. Therapy can feel that way, especially family therapy. It brings up painful and difficult feelings that were thought to be over and done with. They are not. The pain is still there, just obscured. Anger. Shame. Guilt. So a family stops therapy without allowing the time it needs. Without allowing the unfolding. Without allowing the healing.

Confidentiality

What a family chooses to do about confidentiality when their children have a mental health diagnosis is an individual choice. For the most part, my husband and I decided to put our children's confidentiality in their own hands—to share their story with whom they chose. It is absolutely not out of shame that we do not openly share their story. We do not share it because it is theirs, and we respect that. With whom they do chose to share, I hope they speak with tremendous respect for their own courage, for they are both very courageous.

Faith in Our Children

When our younger daughter no longer wanted to see a therapist, it felt like I lost hope for her. But how would that feel for my daughter, that I had lost hope?

This too, became part of my work. My therapist helped me to reconnect with my feelings of faith and hope in my daughter's process. That my daughter could do it; she could take care of her life. Not only that, she deserved to take care of it; it was her right.

At difficult times in my life, my husband, my close friends and my therapist have expressed faith and hope in me. It has turned my struggles into challenges that can be welcomed and overcome. We need to give that gift of faith and the gift of hope to our children.

How can getting support for yourself support your loved one's recovery?

>> Action Steps <<

A) If you have a loved one with an eating disorder, understand that an eating disorder is too complicated to be your fault.

B) If you have a loved one with an eating disorder, take time to have fun, smell the roses, be with your friends or do things that are nurturing for you.

C) Write in your journal to reflect on how you're feeling, what you need and to help you clarify your feelings to your family members.

16

How Do You 'Catch' an Eating Disorder?

There's still a lot to learn

Genetics is the gun, society is the trigger.
—Craig Johnson, PhD

There is still much to learn about how and why eating disorders manifest. The honest answer is that we do not know. More research is necessary. What we do know is that there are a lot of contributing factors, but there is not one specifically that causes an eating disorder.

A lot of attention and blame is focused on the diet, fashion and media industries. Although these industries in our culture can be poisonous when it comes to self-love and body acceptance, these businesses alone do not create eating disorders.

Certain attitudes in families and cultures, whether it's a nationality, peer group or specific sport, can also encourage the development of eating disorders. The body requirements for ballet and gymnastics can pressure dancers and gymnasts to create the body necessary for their success, regardless of their natural body type. Although these environments can encourage an eating disorder, they alone are not the reason they develop.

Working with my clients who struggle with eating disorders, it's not uncommon to find a history of trauma and post-traumatic stress disorder in combination with their eating disorder. A history of trauma can be another factor in the causation of eating disorders, but it is not the sole cause.

There is growing evidence that genetics play a larger part in the etiology of eating disorders than was once thought. Eating disorders overlap with other categories of mental disorders that are recognized as hereditary, such as obsessive-compulsive disorder, anxiety and mood disorders. Carolyn Piver Dukarm, MD, Patricia Quinn, MD, as well as Kathleen Nadeau, PhD, make a link between eating disorders and ADD.

For the past couple of decades, we have known that eating disorders are more common among families. As of September 2006, Walter Kaye, MD of the University of Pittsburg Medical Center and The National Institute of Health surveyed 600 families with two or more members suffering from an eating disorder. They concluded that both anorexia and bulimia might be "as heritable as other psychiatric illnesses such as schizophrenia, depression, anxiety, and obsessive-compulsive disorder." Their research shows that chromosomes 1 and 10 have both been linked to anorexia and bulimia, and many other genes have been found that may indicate a predisposition to eating disorders.

Although we're learning that genetics is playing a bigger part in the etiology of eating disorders, it alone is not the cause. One of my clients who struggled with anorexia was a twin. Her and her sister were raised in the same family environment, they went to the same college and, as identical twins, they shared the same genes. However, my client had anorexia and her sister did not, but it is interesting to note that her sister was diagnosed with obsessive-compulsive disorder, which is one of the overlapping mental disorders mentioned above.

Researchers have also been looking at phenotypic traits as markers of susceptibility for eating disorders, which is an example of the age-old question of nature vs. nurture. Craig Johnson, PhD, chief clinical officer of Eating Recovery Center, has studied clusters of personality traits that seem to come together with specific eating disorders, which raises the question, do specific personality traits lend themselves to the development of specific eating disorders, or does the eating disorder create these specific personality traits?

Johnson's research suggests that people who succumb to bulimia and anorexia tend to have tense, anxious dispositions. Individuals with anorexia tend to be anxious and fearful of new experiences and of negative consequences relating to their actions, leading to a good girl perfectionistic, controlled life style. In contrast, individuals with bulimia tend to be open to new experiences and risk taking and have difficulty with impulse control.

Another question raised by this research, can the dynamics of a family contribute to the personality traits that put their members at risk for eating disorders, or are the personality traits putting them at risk genetically inherited?

Currently, these studies indicate genetics contribute 30 to 60 percent when looking at personality traits that may lend themselves to the development of an eating disorder. What about the other 40 to 70 percent?

Could an overly protective, achievement-focused family style contribute to the worrying, anxious and cautious tendencies in a person, leading them toward anorexia? Similarly, could an impulsive, chaotic family environment contribute to the anxious and impulsive use of food to self-soothe, leading to bulimia?

A note to families: these questions being researched must be depersonalized. It is not helpful to take on guilt, shame or responsibility for the development of an eating disorder in a member of your family. In my personal experience working with families, I have seen the most loving, supportive families have one or more members develop eating disorders. At the same time, I have worked with families who have had attitudes that have been toxic and unhealthy and their children did not develop eating disorders.

There are many factors in the establishment of an eating disorder, and we still have a lot to learn. The University of North Carolina conducted a study that looked at 31,0000 twins and concluded that genetics attribute to 56 percent of the development of an eating disorder. Although genetics are not the sole cause of eating disorders, we are discovering that it may be one of the leading factors.

How would your life be different if people understood that genetics play a part in developing an eating disorder?

>> Action Steps <<

A) Help yourself or others decrease blame by realizing that there is no easy answer to why or how eating disorders develop, and that a large part of it is genetics.

B) When you hear people blaming eating disorders on one specific cause, for example, the media, you can share that there are many factors that influence the development of an eating disorder.

C) Go to the reference section of this book and look up the research cited in this chapter to help you increase your understanding of what causes eating disorders.

17

These Numbers Are Really People

Statistics point to an unacceptable number of people suffering

> *It is not because things are difficult that we do not*
> *dare, it is because we do not dare that they are*
> *difficult.*
>
> —Seneca

There seems to be a "magical" number that reflects a significant problem. Before we hit that number, as a society, we may not notice. Eating disorders have reached the levels to be noticed, and taken seriously. Why then do the following statistics show us a lack of concern? Take a moment before reading the next information and keep in mind each number represents a person. Their suffering calls us to action.

In 2010, the National Institute of Health (NIHinfo@od.nih.gov) funded the following disorders accordingly:

Illness	Prevalence	NIH Research Funds
Schizophrenia	2.2 million	$259,000,000
Alzheimer's diseases	4.5 million	$428,000,000
Anorexia*	10 million	$7,000,000

According to Eating Recovery Center, four out of ten Americans either

---

* Reported research funds for anorexia only. No estimated funding is reported for bulimia, binge eating, or eating disorders not otherwise specified.

suffered or have known someone who has suffered from an eating disorder.

This discrepancy in research funding toward eating disorders is not acceptable. According to the National Eating Disorders Association, "only 1/3 of people with anorexia receive mental health care," and "only 6% of people with bulimia receive mental health care." Anorexia alone is responsible for more deaths compared to all the other mental disorders put together, and yet it is drastically underfunded.

Currently, in California, we have parity coverage offered by insurance companies. This means the insurance industry is recognizing that eating disorders are on par with physical diseases that require long-term treatment. Unfortunately, insurance coverage continues to be extremely limited. Ask any family that has mortgaged their house to provide residential treatment for their child. Craig Johnson, PhD, chief clinical officer of Eating Recovery Center advocates for more funding to research the role of genetics in eating disorders. "If eating disorders are discovered to be primarily genetic, the 'cap' or maximum amount an insurance company will pay for treatment of the disorder is greatly increased," said Johnson.

Why is there such a discrepancy of attention and money spent on researching anorexia and the other neglected, devastating and life-threatening eating disorders? Could it be because in our culture we are blaming our sufferers? Many of my clients who suffer from eating disorders have told me that they were once judgmental of people with eating disorders and blamed them for their disorder as if they chose it and could stop whenever they wanted to. Why would attention and money be spent on research for the cause of eating disorders if the general belief were that people choose these behaviors and could choose to stop them?

My clients have also told me that they viewed people with eating disorders as superficial and vain and saw them as people who were just concerned about appearances. What they discovered in treatment from their own eating disorder is that their issues go deeper than their body and food.

If my clients viewed eating disorders as a superficial disease that was nothing more than vanity, then what does that say about how we view eating disorders as a culture? We do not take eating disorders seriously. We don't view them as legitimate, life-threatening diseases and we believe that the issues are surface deep and should be easily fixed.

We live in a culture that fosters this belief. The pharmaceutical companies and the diet industry sell us an ideal body that we need to achieve to be healthy, successful and beautiful so that we'll buy their products. According to HCD Diet Direct case studies, only five percent of people dieting will be able to maintain their weight loss once their dieting program is complete. Conversely, 95 percent of dieters regain their weight, and usually gain more once they stop their diet. The diet industry wants us to believe that we're broken and need fixing, and when we fail diet after diet they want us to believe that it's our fault. They are also helping foster the belief that our problems lie in our appearance, and that once we have our ideal body image, all of our problems will magically be fixed. Our diet, body-obsessed culture is cementing the belief that issues related to our body are normal, easy to fix and not life-threatening.

Eating disorders need more research funding. My hope is if the genetic factors in eating disorders were given sufficient research dollars, it would validate to the general public that eating disorders are a serious and dangerous disease, it would require insurance companies to give more money for eating disorder treatment and it would equip us with more resources for eating disorder education and prevention. Another benefit of this genetic research is that it can help reduce the stigma associated with eating disorders. As people understand that eating disorders are genetic in nature, feelings of shame and embarrassment can be decreased and our cultural view towards eating disorders can begin to shift. People are not ashamed or judged when they get a diagnosis of cancer, instead people gather around and offer compassion and support. As we increase our understanding of these disorders we will begin to see love, compassion and support spreading throughout the world. Together, we can end eating disorders.

How would our world be different if we drew together in order to end eating disorders?

>> Action Steps <<

A) Let people know that eating disorders are serious. Share the fact that anorexia alone kills more people than all of the other mental disorders put together.

B) Donate your time and energy to increase attention and research for eating disorders. Share the information that you've learned from this book or outside research on your social media profiles.

C) Donate money to eating disorder research, education, prevention or treatment.

Part Four

*Love is the great miracle cure. Loving ourselves
works miracles in our lives.*

— Louise L. Hay

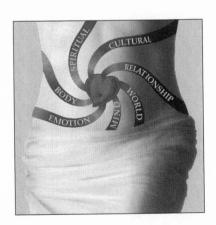

The Seven Paths of the Self-Love Diet

Each path of the Self-Love Diet introduces you to Self-Love Diet tools,
practices and exercises to help guide you on your journey of not only making
self-love a habit, but also a belief that you will fully embody. The end result
of the Self-Love Diet is that you will be motivated to regularly offer yourself
substantial servings of love each day.

Spiritual Path of the Self-Love Diet

While beginning the Self-Love Diet, you may not love yourself yet or believe that you are worthy of love. The Spiritual Path of the Self-Love Diet will help you to understand that your value exists within you and that you are more than your body. It reminds you there is a higher power guiding you if you slow down and listen. This understanding will build the foundation for your Self-Love Diet as you continue through the other paths and as you work on offering yourself love more and more each day.

Body Path of the Self-Love Diet

Even though your worth is not determined by the shape or size of your body, the Body Path of the Self-Love Diet helps you to love your body by seeing your body's value beyond its appearance.

If you think of your body as a million dollar gift, like an expensive racehorse, you can begin to understand how you need to treat your body, and when you realize that your body gives to you unconditionally from conception to death, you can begin to appreciate your body and be grateful for what it does for you and allows you to do in your life.

The Body Path of the Self-Love Diet attunes you with your body and helps you become fluent in its language so you can listen to its needs and know how to love it.

Mind Path of the Self-Love Diet

The Mind Path of the Self-Love Diet reminds you that the thoughts you think and the beliefs you hold have tremendous power over your health. You and you alone, have the power to create a life filled with self-love or a life filled with self-hatred. By being mindful of your thoughts and regularly offering yourself love you have the power to bring healing to yourself, others and the world in which you live in.

Emotional Path of the Self-Love Diet

Emotions have been given a bad rap. "She's so emotional" is used as a criticism. The truth is we are all emotional beings. It's part of our humanness.

If you were given a gift that had the power to make you feel exuberant, powerful and on top of the world, but this gift could also make you feel worthless, hopeless and suicidal, would you read the directions that came with the gift or just open up the box and see what happens? The Emotional Path of the Self-Love Diet is an instruction manual on how to confront, manage and learn from your emotions. The Emotional Path of the Self-Love Diet will help you to uncover the messages behind your emotions.

Relationship Path of the Self-Love Diet

The Relationship Path of the Self-Love Diet helps you to strengthen your relationship with yourself and your relationships with others. Your primary relationship is with yourself. Your job is to bring harmony between your spiritual self and your physical self. Your secondary relationship is between you and others.

Your relationships with others can be used as a mirror to see the condition of your relationship with yourself. If your relationships with others are troubled, it's a message to look inward. If your relationships are harmonious, it's a reflection of the harmony within yourself. When you become aware that your purpose is greater than an existence focused on your body, your relationships with others flourish and you open yourself to a passionate, purposeful life.

Cultural Path of the Self-Love Diet

The Cultural Path of the Self-Love Diet brings your attention to those aspects of our culture that diminish your ability to stay focused on self-love.

We are becoming more aware of the subtleties of advertising and media that foster body-hatred and self-loathing. Actresses, models and the general public are speaking out and confronting the practice of air brushing photographs. Slowly we are seeing a trend toward healing through confrontations of our current body obsessed culture.

We must remember that we are the culture. What we watch, buy and condone will be prevalent. As we become more conscious of our power to influence our culture, we have the key to changing it. We can create a self-love, body-loving culture that will support the healthy development of our coming generations, as well as the healing of our planet earth.

World Path of the Self-Love Diet

The World Path of the Self-Love Diet takes into account that you are intimately connected to our planet. She is your mother earth. Attunement to one another is essential in order to bring balance to you and to her. Just as your behaviors affect the health of our earth, all the life forms of our planet affect you.

We are already seeing the benefits of the World Path of the Self-Love Diet. Consciousness is growing about how our personal choices affect our world. Celebrities in the music world as well as movie stars have used their celebrity to bring awareness to different causes. Our world can be healed through a concerted effort of individuals working on healing themselves and living according to their passions and values. Just like viruses can cause epidemics of disease, using the seven paths of the Self-Love Diet can cause an epidemic of healing for our world.

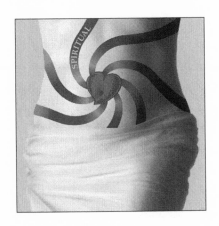

Spiritual Path

*Love is what we are born with. Fear is what we
have learned here. The spiritual journey is the
unlearning of fear and the acceptance of love back
into our hearts.*

—Marianne Williamson

Spiritual Path of the Self-Love Diet

2004 was the year I began to practice self-love in earnest. I wrote a Self-Love Prayer that I read to myself in the mirror every morning. It helped me to connect with my soul, which lessened the importance of the appearance of my body.

Spirituality is at the core of the ability to love yourself. Perhaps you've learned songs, stories, concepts and religious beliefs as a child. You may even be part of a religious community, and God may be present in your life. You may not believe in God. You may believe in a connection with nature or a connective energy among living beings, or you may not believe in anything outside of what you can prove and see.

The Self-Love Diet asks you to recognize that you have a purpose in this life that goes beyond your appearance. At its basic level, it's realizing that your thoughts, feelings, actions, desires, needs and passions are not connected to your body. It's realizing that your worth as a person does not stem from your appearance, but it comes from your spirit, which is the essence of who you are. It's realizing that your body is important, but only to the extent that it allows you to experience life, to follow your passions, to love and to see the beauty that lives inside of you that you have to offer to the world.

When you can separate your identity from your body, you can focus on what impassions you. Without being preoccupied with negative body talk, you can live in the present moment and see the opportunities around you with opens eyes and an open heart. When you realize that your value is not attached to your body, you can begin to fully inhabit your body and enjoy and appreciate what it does for you and allows you to do.

The spiritual path of the Self-Love Diet is not connected to any religion or dogma; rather, it's a practice of finding your center, your inner source of guidance and power. For you that guidance may be God, or it may be your inner wisdom and intuition.

When I am not connected to my spiritual self, I feel like an unfettered balloon. When I'm feeling anxious, down or have eaten more than is comfortable, I know something is off. That *something* is my spirit or inner self. In my pre-Self-Love Diet days, if anything caused me stress, I would go to food to try to soothe myself and to try to fix what wasn't feeling right. Understanding that I am more than my body, I now realize that food cannot fix my problems. Using food to soothe myself was a distraction from confronting what was making me feel anxious, down and off balance.

When I'm having difficulty with something that needs resolution, I immediately go inward and seek my part. I ask for guidance, wisdom and a path of action. These actions come easily when I am connected, centered and grounded. When I take the time to be with myself and God, I feel as if all is right in the world, even in the midst of news that would tell me differently. By being present and aware of my spiritual nature, life with all of its joys and tribulations flows more easily. I am able to let go of life the way I believe it should be and am more accepting of what is. This allows me a freedom I hadn't known before. I hope the spiritual aspect of the Self-Love Diet will bring abundant joy and peace into your life.

I ask that you stay open to reading the spiritual path of the Self-Love Diet, and decide for yourself what spirituality means for you. Discover who the "you" is inside of your body.

18

Self-Love Prayer, Letter and Manifesto

Daily spiritual reading and writing practice enhance self-love

Heaven on Earth is a choice you must make,
not a place you must find.

—Wayne Dyer

Reading inspirational quotes, articles, books and other writings that inspire you may help you to clarify what resonates with you, and from that, your beliefs. I offer you my first Self-Love Prayer as a jumping off place for you to begin your self-love journey. If the concept of God or prayer is uncomfortable for you, you can write a Self-Love Manifesto or a Self-Love Letter. When writing your letter, manifesto or prayer, follow your intuition and let the words flow from your pen or keyboard.

Writing a Self-Love Prayer, Letter or Manifesto is a great way to start connecting with the "you" that lives inside of your body. As you begin writing, you may realize that you enjoy the writing process. Making a habit out of self-love writing is a great way to incorporate more love into your life, as well as a great way to reflect on what you're going through as you continue your self-love journey. If you decide that you like writing, you can begin each morning by writing in your Self-Love Journal with a focus on your intentions for the day, or you can write each night, recapping the self-love actions you incorporated into the day and what you noticed.

If you find that you don't like writing, give yourself permission to read other people's writings that inspire you. The Love Warrior Community's group blog, Self-Love Warrior, is a place for people to share their writing, as well as a place for people to read others' self-love writing.

Below, you'll find my first Self-Love Prayer from when I started my Self-Love Diet, as well as the changes I've made to it over the years as my self-love practice has evolved. When I began my self-love practice, I read my Self-Love Prayer each morning to help set my intentions for the day with a focus on loving myself, and others.

I invite you to do the same. I invite you to use my Self-Love Prayer as is, or as a jumping off point for writing your own Self-Love Prayer, Letter or Manifesto. You may already have favorite quotes and writings that resonate with you. If so, then there is no need to fix what isn't broken. Take them out, dust them off and read them each morning to help focus your intentions on self-love throughout the day.

My First Self-Love Prayer

Today, I am a strong steady tree that is coming into a new season of growth and fruition. Self-Love is a journey I am beginning in a new comprehensive, conscious way. I'm peeling the proverbial onion to new depths as I come into contact with the lovable gifted person I was created to be before hurtful life experiences stunted my growth.

Today is a new day. I commit this day to Self-Love. I commit this day to the power of the mother in me who loves me without reserve. I stand in strength together with Love Warriors of all ages for positive spiritual influence. Self-Love is the answer and self-forgiveness is the path.

I forgive myself today for the part I had in my own demise. I can see the part of me that swallowed whole all of the negative comments, beliefs and messages I received.

It stops today.

I forgive myself today for any mistakes that have caused harm to me, or others.

I forgive myself today for any mistakes I may make in the future.

I have the understanding of humility, which teaches me that I am only human, and therefore perfection is no longer my path.

Humility helps me connect to the imperfection, and glory in everyone.

If I do not judge others, I offer others the opportunity to not judge me.

I understand that I have no control over what others think of me.

Today, I commit to being the best me I can be, letting go of my past need of approval from others.

By nurturing non-judgmental relationships, I create the climate for vulnerability.

Vulnerability offers the incredible healing power of emotional honesty.

Emotional honesty allows others to see me and invites them to accept me with all of my flaws and foibles.

The experience of another human being accepting me with my imperfections allows me to cultivate self-acceptance and self-love.

Today, I begin this process by being willing to love myself unconditionally.

I will not judge myself harshly.

I ask for divine assistance in remembering that "I AM ENOUGH;

I HAVE ENOUGH, AND I DO ENOUGH."

Please remind me to ask for guidance each day.

Help me to reach out to myself as you would have me reach out to others.

I understand that by reaching into myself and offering love, I am coming in closer contact with you.

Thank you for guiding me to take this time with you each morning. Help me to be a blessing to all I meet this day. Amen.

As I continued on my self-love journey, I noticed that I stopped reading my Self-Love Prayer daily. So I developed a shorter Self-Love Letter that would help me be more consistent in reading it to myself each morning.

Self-Love Letter

Good Morning Michelle,

I love you.

I commit to loving myself to the best of my ability today.

My value in this life is connected to my ability to be with myself, and others, in the most loving way I can.

My body houses my spirit. I will love my body and myself this day.

I will help others to love their bodies and themselves this day.

I promise to take time today to sit quietly and spend time with God and connect to my higher self.

I will slow down, take in each breath and bring the colors of the flowers into my soul.

I will love my body by stretching it, strengthening it, moving it and resting it.

Thank you body for all you do for me.

I commit this day to love you to the best of my ability.

If the above examples do not fit for you, perhaps you will consider writing a personal Manifesto. Below is an example of a manifesto that I wrote when clarifying what Love Warriors' beliefs are.

Love Warrior Manifesto

Our bodies were created to allow our spirit a house to live in while on this earth.

We were created to give our gifts to the world.

The size, color, shape or gender of our body is irrelevant to this mission.

We are all sharing this planet. We need to love ourselves, and each other, in order to solve the problems that are endangering our very existence.

As the years progressed I found that I had stopped reading my Self-Love Letter to myself each day, so I began the practice of taking a deep breath, looking deep into my eyes in the mirror and saying, "I love you." I talk more about the practice of looking in the mirror in Chapter 22, Mirror Image.

> **How would your life be different if you started each day with writing in your Self-Love Journal or with reading your Self-Love Prayer, Letter, Manifesto or inspired writings of others?**

>> Action Steps <<

A) Begin reading spiritual or inspirational books for a good spiritual start to your day.

B) Write your own Self-Love Prayer, Love letter or Manifesto. You may develop a daily writing practice. Decide if you will share it on the Love Warrior Community blog or writing sections. (selflovewarrior.com and lovewarriorcommunity.com/writing).

C) Read your self-love writing while looking into your eyes in the mirror each morning and/or night. Journal about your experience so you can compare how you feel after a month of this practice to before you started.

19

Spiritual Power Seekers

Eating disorders as a portal to spirituality

We are not human beings having a spiritual experience. We are spiritual beings having a human experience.

—Pierre Teilhard de Chardin

I have a sticker in my office from Beyond Hunger, an eating disorder recovery nonprofit based in Marin County, California. The sticker states, "It's not about food; it's about everything else."

When my clients read this bumper sticker, they intellectually understand that their struggles with food and their body are just a symptom of a larger issue unrelated to food. Even so, it is very difficult for them to break away from their obsessions with food.

Clients come in to see me seeking help to stop their eating disorders. Others I work with think losing weight will raise their self-esteem. My clients use the behaviors of dieting, eating disorders and body dissatisfaction to seek perfection, control, power, acceptance, self-love and ultimately, God.

For my clients who are unsure if there is a God, or who don't believe in God, I would say that they are in quest of their purpose in life and are trying to find out who they are. I view all of my clients as spiritual seekers.

I must admit, I've never had a client suffering from an eating disorder come into my office and say, "Michelle, I am seeking God. Can you help me?"

However, I have heard the following comments in the sanctuary of my office.

"There's a hole in the center of my being."

"It feels like there's an empty pit in my stomach".

"I feel an abyss inside."

"I know I'm not physically hungry, but I have an inner hunger that all the food in the world would not satisfy."

The people I am privileged to sit with in my office are desperately trying to fill that hole with food, a lack of food, shopping, alcohol, sex, drugs, gambling, computer time, work or busyness.

What is this hole? I believe it is the space within each person that yearns for the divine. This connection to spirit, however you define it, is missing for the majority of the people I work with. This disconnect with the spiritual aspect of themselves interferes with their ability to love themselves and others.

"You shall love your neighbor as yourself." This spiritual teaching from Jesus began bothering me due to my work with my clients with eating disorders. The self-condemnation and body-hatred I am witness to leads me to fear for our neighbors if my clients loved them as they love themselves. However, my clients love their neighbors with much more ease and frequency than they are capable of mustering for themselves.

They easily put others before themselves. They are the people who can be counted on. They will extend themselves and go over and beyond what is expected.

Unfortunately, the love they show others is forfeited from themselves. This focus on others holds the key to what they can do for themselves.

As a human race we have created exciting technology and have explored outer space, yet we have not learned the basics of non-judgmental self-love. Utilizing the seven paths that lead to self-love is not part of our public school curriculum. The fundamental human lessons of feeling our emotions, soothing ourselves, observing our thoughts, connecting with our spiritual self, speaking our truth, creating harmonious relationships and taking positive action to impact our culture and the planet we live on—these core life lessons go untaught. The power that comes from connection to our higher power is not exalted in our culture.

Power has been defined in our global consciousness as the Rambo model of power or the stereotypical masculine power of domination. The power of domination says whoever is the biggest, strongest and richest gets their way and wins. This kind of power comes from taking away the power of others. Might makes right is an antiquated and dangerous philosophy. This type of power has gotten our world into its present state.

The encouraging news is that another type of power is growing. This power comes from listening to your intuition and knowing your truth. It is a power of collaboration, creativity, cooperation and give and take. This alternative power is the power of dominion that stems from feminine power.

The qualities of the feminine model of empowerment are not connected to gender. There are women who operate from domination, just as there are men who collaborate, cooperate and look for consensus. The feminine model of empowerment is about connecting with and harnessing the power that's inside of you. It's about making that connection between you and your God or your higher self.

The power of domination stems from self-doubt, insecurity, fear and the belief that others' growth and success will take away from your own. The power of domination leads people to act from a place of fear, doubt and mistrust. This kind of power is temporary; as long as you have it, you fear that you can lose it at any moment.

The power of dominion refers to a power within, not over somebody else. It is about focusing on your needs, listening to your body and trusting your intuition. This kind of power stems from self-love, and it fosters trust and openness with yourself and those you interact with. Acting from the feminine model of empowerment, you support others in their success knowing that empowering and helping others to share their gifts with the world will help more people to see the value within themselves that they have to offer the world.

Feminine power is what is needed in the world. The feminine power of collaboration and cooperation bears the fruits of peace, joy, creativity and spiritual connection. This feminine power of cooperation is ultimately necessary if we as humans are to continue to share this world.

Our ability to communicate with people from all over the world through the internet is creating a more connected global community, and we are becoming more aware of our brothers and sisters sharing this planet with us. With the threat of global warming, and the endangered species list growing as we continue to squander earth's resources, we are now at a time in history where we must work together.

In order for us to work together, acting from a place of self-doubt and mistrust will not help us; we need to let go of the fear that holds us back from collaborating with others. We need to connect with God or the higher power within ourselves. We need to be able to tap into the potency of the power that comes from loving ourselves.

If, like my clients, you are better at caring and supporting others than yourself, your challenge is to channel the love within yourself towards you, and your eating disorder can help you. Your eating disorder can be used as a portal to connect you with your spirituality. Your eating disordered thoughts and behaviors are signals letting you know that everything is not alright, and they are opportunities for you to practice offering yourself love. By exploring the issues that go beyond your eating disorder, by focusing on healing and by incorporating the tools of the Self-Love Diet into your healing process, you can begin to form a strong relationship with yourself that is built on trust and self-love and you can begin to build a connection with yourself that goes deeper than your relationship with your body.

Channeling the love that you give to others towards yourself is trickier than it sounds. One way I help people channel the love they offer to others toward themselves is by helping them learn how to create boundaries by speaking respectfully and assertively. Feelings of personal power are developed when they use the following formula, "I feel ... because... and I want/wish..."

My clients have described themselves as "bitchy" or "mean" if they take a stand or say the "N" word ("No"). Setting boundaries and speaking up for themselves has gotten confused with being selfish or mean.

Many times there are past traumas that have resulted in their faulty belief systems, such as:

"I'm not worthy."

"I'm not valuable."

"I'm not lovable."

"There's something the matter with me."

"I'm repulsive."

"I should not have been born."

"I'm inherently bad or evil."

These mistaken beliefs are where we focus in therapy to find the truth of their inherent goodness. If we are compassionate with ourselves, we can see that we are all trying to cope. *Loving ourselves from the inside out* is the direction of healing that brings our attention to our spiritual nature.

It is time to stop looking at the reflection in your mirror for what is wrong and to start looking past the reflection into your soul. You will not solve your problems by focusing on your outsides. Putting the focus on your body distracts you from connecting with your spiritual nature and from connecting to the power that's already inside of you.

What makes you who you are? It is not your body. What qualities do you own that you want to develop? What qualities do you want to moderate?

You are a spiritual being encased in human flesh and bones. It is time to begin to love the body that allows you to be here on this beautiful planet. It is time to love yourself and to discover your divinity and purpose in life.

Through the process of learning to love yourself, you will grow your ability to love others, creating a climate of cooperation and collaboration. We all have the ability to channel the energy that was once wasted on self-hatred and denial of our difficulties and of our world's state of affairs towards creating a life of peace, joy, creativity, connection and power. You know that life's problems are not about the food. It's about everything else, and it's time to bring the focus back to healing, love and strengthening the relationship that you have with yourself.

How would your life be different if you consciously sought your spiritual power?

>> Action Steps <<

A) Write in your Self-Love Diet Journal. Put in writing what your spiritual beliefs are. Let yourself write from an intention of letting your hand lead the way, no editing, checking for spelling, etc. Allow all ideas that come be written down. Read it back to yourself out loud. Give yourself permission to have it be a work in progress.

B) Remind yourself daily that your body is allowing your essence to be here on this planet at this time in history.

C) Begin to discover your purpose in life. Realize this is a process, and sometimes asking the question is enough to begin. Give yourself permission to not know the answer and to keep asking the question.

20

Surrender vs. Willpower

Surrender is redefined as a powerful alternative to willpower

Surrender to what is.

Say "yes" to life and see how life suddenly starts working for you rather than against you."

—Eckhart Tolle

How would it be to trust your body to tell you when it's hungry, when it's full, when it wants to move and when it wants to rest? This is the gift of surrender. When you stop trying to control your body, and begin listening to it, you pave the way to a life free from body and food obsessions. What's the difference between living a life focused on willpower versus surrendering to life and all of the unexpected gifts it has to offer?

Willpower

Determination and self-discipline: a combination of determination and self-discipline that enables somebody to do something despite the difficulties involved. (Encarta Dictionary; English, North America)

Willpower is advocated, applauded and encouraged in our culture. When applied to a diet, it is used to disregard your body and mind's desires by strengthening your will. Most people I have worked with use willpower instead of surrender in their lives. Willpower and diets do not work in the long-term. Anne, a client of mine who was in recovery from anorexia, remembered the compliments and praise that she received from family and her parent's friends when she refused to have a slice of her birthday cake.

In the beginning, Anne felt empowered when the adults around her said they couldn't do what she was doing and told her, "I wish I had your willpower." She vividly remembered these statements being connected to her decision to restrict more. Although people always complimented Anne on the strength of her willpower, as she progressed into anorexia, she felt like a failure. No matter how much Anne restricted her eating, anorexia always told her she was eating too much. Anne felt as if she had no willpower, when in fact she was starving herself to death.

On the opposite side of the coin, Barbara, a client of mine who struggled with bulimia told me, "I've never had any willpower. I wish I could be anorexic. All I do is compensate for my binges by purging in some way."

When Barbara first started purging, it was her attempt to control her weight. It has since turned into a nightmare of disempowerment in all areas of her life. Both Barbara and Anne thought having more willpower was the answer.

The Self-Love Diet is not about willpower. The Self-Love Diet incorporates surrender into the healing process. Surrender is about letting go of control and inviting love in to take care of your miraculous body.

Surrender

Declare yourself defeated; intransitive verb to declare to an opponent that he or she has won so that fighting or conflict can cease. (Encarta Dictionary)

Surrender may bring up an image of waving a white flag in defeat. If so, it might be difficult to understand how the concept of admitting defeat can bring about self-love and healing. The trouble may come from confusing surrender with submission. Submission is the experience of being overpowered by someone else. Surrender comes from within; it is a choice. The message of surrender is: "I declare that my opponent has won this battle so I can cease the fighting."

Let's use the game tug-of-war as a metaphor to illustrate the difference between using willpower and using surrender.

Can you imagine pulling with all your might on one end of the rope? Let's agree that this image reflects the part of you that engages in willpower. Visualize that your arms are taut, your feet are dug into the earth and your thighs are contracted as you pull the rope toward yourself. You are using all of your strength to win the goal of weight loss.

Visualize another version of you at the other end of the rope pulling against the first image of yourself. Let's agree that this second image is the part of you that fights against the deprivation of the diet. This part of you is tugging on the rope, arms taut, feet dug into the earth and thighs contracted as you yank the rope back toward yourself. This is the part of you that fights against depriving yourself of foods that you want or rallies against strict rules and regulations about eating. This type of struggle is a familiar story for anyone who finds themselves in a battle with food.

Let's go back to the scene of tug-of-war. What would happen if you stopped fighting back against the determined willpower version of you and released the rope? Can you see that by declaring yourself defeated and letting go of the rope, willpower has fallen down and you are the one left standing?

The concept of surrender depends on you deciding to no longer be in battle with willpower. Once you stop hating yourself for not being able to have willpower and once you stop using your willpower because you know it's leading you to your death, you will be able to make room for love to come in.

This passage from Gloria D. Karpinski's book, Where Two Worlds Touch: Spiritual Rites of Passage, speaks to this idea of releasing your hold on the rope.

Giving Up the Struggle

During surrender we eventually give up the struggle itself. That may be the hardest release of all. We know how to struggle, how to survive by forcing ourselves to cope, and push through odds. What we don't know is how to relax, to trust, to allow the universe to carry us.

What would it be like if you decided to surrender your battle with food and your body and love your body as it is in this moment? My clients have responded with the lament, "Michelle, I'm fat. I need to lose weight, and you are asking me to love my body?"

My answer is "Yes!" When you're on the Self-Love Diet, you love your body to health. Here's an example of what loving your body to health looks like.

Imagine you are hungry. It's breakfast time, and you have a choice: you can eat a donut or you can cook yourself an omelet. Let's compare surrendering to self-love versus using willpower in the following donut versus omelet scenario.

If you are operating on willpower you would likely say, "I'm being good today. I will not have that donut." Willpower is connected to the diet mentality of good food/bad food and good me/bad me, depending on what you eat.

You decide to use your willpower this morning and make yourself an omelet for breakfast. You are proud of yourself for saying "No" to the donut. You were able to deny yourself. You get a sense of power in that moment from dominating the ravenous beast within. You may feel superior to the others in your family who bought the donuts. You enjoy the feeling of control that willpower temporarily provided you when you made the choice to deny yourself the donut. The problem is that over time willpower backfires. The deprivation needed to keep willpower alive invites you to relapse when you continuously deny yourself something you believe you really want.

When you're in diet mode and using your willpower, you may lose the battle and eat the donut. This is a setup for making yourself feel bad because you ate the donut and it was on your bad foods list. Using willpower creates repeated failures because you are constantly battling the bad foods. This creates a pattern of feeling ashamed and discouraged and of mentally beating yourself up throughout the day, or longer, for eating the foods on your bad list.

It's a common notion to think, "Well, I already messed up. So I might as well eat all of the donuts." This irrational idea leads many to overeat to the point of pain and weight gain, when their goal was weight loss. This cycle is similar to the binge/purge cycle of bulimia.

Let's look at how different the morning could be when surrender is used in place of willpower. In the above example, you ate the donut and felt bad about yourself all day. With surrender, you could choose to surrender the battle against the donut and choose to eat the donut without self-hatred, giving yourself permission to enjoy the taste and experience of eating the donut. You would not say, "I blew it by eating the donut, so I might as well eat the whole box of donuts." You remind yourself that you are experimenting with the idea of actually allowing yourself to enjoy and pay attention to the sensations and energy the donut gives you. Eating mindfully, you learn if the donut was a loving decision as you notice your body's response to your choice throughout the day.

Instead of beating yourself up after eating the donut you examine the comfort level in your body. You notice what kind of energy the donut gives you and how long it lasts, as well as how long it is before you are hungry again. By being mindful of your thoughts, you will catch yourself if you begin to fall into the diet mentality of self-condemnation. You remind yourself to be loving and to just notice without judgment if eating the donut is a loving, nurturing choice.

Once you relieve yourself of the diet mentality, you may find that you can actually eat one donut, enjoy it, feel satisfied and not crave the whole dozen. By lingering luxuriously with the smells, textures and tastes, you allowed your mind and body the time to register satiation. When you don't think it's the last donut you're ever going to have in your life, the urgency and zing of the donut is neutralized. This guilt-free eating requires you to legalize all foods. Your decision on what to eat, and being able to freely choose from all foods, gives your body the power to help you decipher what is a loving choice for you in that moment and what is not.

By surrendering to eating the donut with curiosity, instead of self-loathing, you might also discover that you won't choose the donut next time because you really don't like the way it feels in your stomach. It may feel heavy, and perhaps you may even notice a slump in your energy later in the day.

If you have lived with willpower your whole life, it may take some time for you to relinquish the diet mentality and decide to nurture yourself by surrendering to love. If you find yourself continuing to choose foods that ultimately do not make you feel good, begin to ask yourself, "What would love do?"

When you surrender to self-love you learn a lot about yourself. Don't be afraid to seek professional help if you notice you are unable to make loving choices on your own.

Omelet vs. Donut: Continuing the Saga

You may think that the omelet is the self-love choice, but as you learned from the above scenario, all is not what it seems. Let's take a look at the choice of the omelet through the lens of willpower.

You are hungry. It's breakfast time, and you can have a donut or you can cook yourself an omelet. You look at the donut and get nervous and mad at your family for buying them. You think, "Didn't I tell them I'm on a diet?" You tell yourself, "I will not have that donut!"

You use your willpower, and you make yourself an omelet. As you are making the omelet your resentment grows towards your family's "sabotaging behaviors." You eat your omelet with a sense of righteousness. You decide to let your family know how you feel about them buying donuts. You want them to respect your desire to lose weight and not bring food into the house that you cannot have.

I hope you notice that the willpower mentality is still telling you that you can't have that donut. It's also building anger towards your family, and may even be inviting you to feel like a victim.

Looking at the choice of the omelet through the lens of surrender offers the same meal, but a completely different morning. You see your choices and may think, "I've chosen the donut before, and it didn't make me feel very good. It will take longer to cook an omelet than grabbing that donut, but I've got the time, and I'm worth it." When you check in with your body while contemplating your choices, you may become aware of wanting something warm with different tastes and textures and choose the omelet. You may even consider putting your favorite music on while you prepare it.

As you are cutting red tomatoes, yellow onion and adding the spinach you have in your refrigerator, you become mindful of the meditative quality of cutting the vegetables. When you eat your omelet, you savor the tastes. You notice that you feel positive about the choice you made. For the rest of the day you have the knowledge that you are worth the time it takes to cook for yourself. You know this breakfast will stick with you until lunch. You understand that you could have chosen the donut, but you knew the omelet would meet your needs more fully, and you wanted the omelet over the donut.

In the above examples, you chose an omelet in both cases. When you used willpower it led to a sense of deprivation. You also became aware of a sense of entitlement to control the food choices of others in your family. This makes sense if you believe that you really want the donut. When you surrender to your body's cues, you may be surprised to discover what your body really wants. When you surrender to love, you know you could choose either one. The choice is yours. When you choose the most loving thing for you, it is no longer about deprivation. You can release the idea of not being able to eat something to choosing not to eat something. This makes all the difference.

Surrendering Outside of Food

The concept of surrender goes beyond food and body concerns. It is one of the wonderful gifts of the Self-Love Diet. When you release willpower, you are released from its daily struggle.

A story from my own life serves as a good example of surrender. In the beginning of the 1990s, early in my recovery from compulsive overeating, I was invited to be part of a marketing group. Each member had a different career, and we advocated for each others' professions. One member came to my home to sell my husband and I a product he worked with. In the process of our meeting, he told us of an opportunity to invest in an endeavor he was starting. My husband and I agreed to invest ten percent of our retirement fund.

It wasn't long before we found out that 75 percent of our retirement fund had been stolen, our signatures had been forged and this person was not responding to our calls. We felt betrayed, ashamed, embarrassed, outraged and hopeless. We spoke to friends and hired an attorney.

As this was going on, I became aware of a deep need within myself to regain my center. I wanted to feel joy, peace, faith, trust and calm in my life again. I began increasing my time in prayer, meditation, reading spiritual literature, talking with my friends, exercising and going to my support group. Soon I noticed a mini miracle. I was not going to food to comfort myself.

One morning, after speaking to our attorney, I felt unsettled and began to read from an inspirational book. I found a passage that spoke directly to my situation. The gist of the writing was to help me see that my anger and unwillingness to forgive was hurting no one but me. I knew I needed to surrender my anger and resentment.

I began thinking about the person who had taken our money. I realized that he did not have the faith needed to know that he would be provided for. This scarcity mentality was what motivated him to take our money. I began to pray for him. I asked God to give him everything that he needed, most importantly, faith that he and his family would be provided for.

An hour after that prayer, the phone rang, and it was him. He apologized for not responding to my calls, and he promised our money back in ten days with interest. Unbeknownst to him, he would be receiving a letter from our attorney, along with legal proceedings. He followed through with his promise to us, and he returned our investment with interest.

The timing of his call may be seen by some as a coincidence, but I believe my personal work in surrendering was the catalyst in this situation. Through that experience, I learned a valuable lesson about the power of surrender and forgiveness. Surrender continues to sustain me in times when I realize I do not have control of situations in my life that I wish I did. Surrender reminds me of my spiritual connection and also reminds me to have faith and trust that life will find its own way. Life does not always follow the path I think it should, and sometimes that's a good thing.

How would your life be different if you surrendered your will power regarding what, how much or when you should eat, and let love decide?

>> Action Steps <<

A) Choose one day a week, to begin with, as your "Surrender to Love Day." Be mindful of making loving choices for yourself that day.

B) Notice what happens when you choose to enforce your willpower instead surrendering.

C) Write a list of ways you can surrender to self-love. Pay attention to behaviors, beliefs and emotions that foster surrender. Use this list as a reminder that you have alternatives to willpower.

21

Birth of the Love Warrior

Understanding the language of your spirit

Your vision will only become clear when you look into your heart. Who looks outside, dreams. Who looks inside, awakens.

—Carl Jung

When you're focusing on the spiritual aspect of your Self-Love Diet, you need to pay close attention to your ideas, dreams and intuitions. They are the language of your spirit, helping to guide you on your life's path. They are just as important to listen to as your body's signals that tell you when you are hungry, satisfied or full.

The Dream

I had a dream that there was a tiger in the back seat of my Toyota Solara. I knew I needed to get him out of there, but I was concerned that if I let him go, he would hurt the villagers. I thought of putting a leash on him, but even in my dream I knew he was too powerful for a leash to constrain him. While I was in the midst of this dilemma, the blaring beeps of my alarm clock woke me up, and my dream abruptly ended.

The Dream Working on Me

This was one of those dreams that I didn't understand right away. Three months after having that dream it continued to linger in my consciousness as

I went on vacation with two of my cousins. I had been talking to my cousins about getting back into Tai Chi. It had been an important part of my life in my 20s. It helped me to stay grounded and increased my sense of serenity and focus in life. The universe provided me the opportunity to practice Tai Chi again in the form of a class at the resort where we were staying.

I walked into a class of over twenty people dressed in colorful yoga pants, running shorts, tank tops and sweatshirts who were stretching or quietly meditating in preparation for the class to begin. The teacher introduced herself and began to lead us through each step. As we progressed through each movement and moved in unison through the form, I experienced a sense of connection with everyone.

Out of the blue, I heard the teacher say, "Bend down, pick up the tiger, bring it to your heart, raise it to the energy center of your third eye in between your eyebrows and release it."

As I bent down, I felt the pressure in my arms from the weight of the tiger in my dream as I imagined bringing him out of the back seat of my car. Over and over, she led us to repeat this process of lifting and releasing the tiger into the four directions. Each time I bent down, it was as if I was in my dream getting the tiger out from the back seat and releasing him into the world. An incomprehensible, overwhelming energy pulsated within me as I progressed through the remaining movements. Tears streamed down my cheeks. I didn't know why I was crying, but I let my tears flow.

At the end of the class, I approached the teacher and told her of my dream and of my experience in her class. I asked if she knew the significance of the tiger. She responded without hesitation, "The tiger represents creativity. Do you need to release your creativity into the world?"

That questioned burned into my brain. I walked back to the condo, called my life coach and recounted my experience in the Tai Chi class. She suggested I get the tiger from my dream out of the back seat and into the driver's seat of the car. In an instant of clarity, I responded, "No, I need to get the tiger out of the car, get on its back and go for a ride."

She asked me to write, draw or paint it. For the duration of my vacation I worked on this image. I drew myself on the back of a tiger. I found books with photos of tigers and drew my face next to the tiger's with my hands wrapped around his neck. As I continued working with this image it brought more creativity and clarity into my life. This was exactly what I was looking for.

The Dream Takes on Meaning

Later that month I attended a writer's workshop retreat. The weekend began by sharing dinner together. The conversation around the circular dining table was lively, and interestingly intimate for a gathering of strangers. Somehow the conversation flowed into dreams.

After listening to others recount important dreams they had, I shared my tiger dream and pulled out the drawings from my backpack. The woman to my right said, "You've drawn *Durga*!"

"*Durga*? Who is that?" I responded.

"*Durga* is the most powerful Goddess in the Hindu Tradition. *Durga* was created in response to the dark times when a demon was threatening the very existence of the world. She's represented by riding a lion or a tiger."

The Idea of a Love Warrior Is Born

I became more and more interested in this Hindu Goddess. I knew and loved the Blessed Mother of my Catholic upbringing who was a role model of divine motherly love, but a warrior Goddess? This was new to me. How did *Durga* fit in with the Blessed Mother of my childhood teachings?

That night, before I went to bed, I got online to research *Durga*. I discovered that the earth was in peril when *Durga* was created. The male gods each created a part of her body out of their radiance. They did this to counter the demonic influence of a demon named Mahish who was threatening their very existence. *Durga* fought many battles, and in the end she was victorious, killing Mahish and all of his commanders and bringing peace back into the world.

According to Peter Marchand, based on *Tools for Tantra* by Harish Johari, "The name 'Durga' in Sanskrit means 'invincible'. The syllable 'du' is synonymous with the 4 devils of poverty, sufferings, famine and evil habits."

I thought of my clients and their poverty of self-love. Their suffering and famine amidst an abundance of food came to mind. Their addictive, disordered behaviors could be synonymous with the "evil habits" that *Durga* was created to extinguish.

"The '*r*' in the name *Durga*, refers to disease.

The self-hatred experienced through eating disorders parallels the disease of the body and mind that is as destructive as any cancer.

"The '*ga*' in *Durga* is one in the same as the destroyer of sins, injustice, and cruelty."

My clients needed an inner *Durga* to destroy the "sins" of valuing appearance over substance, the injustice of size discrimination and their own inner cruelty that interfered with their ability to remember their inherent value and contribute their gifts to the world.

That night, I realized that *Durga* came to me to help personify the invincible force, self-love, which could combat the demons my clients were battling. I understood that each person I helped get out from under the power of an eating disorder was one extra person capable of pooling their energy towards helping the survival of our planet.

The Battle

I realized that we need a different kind of warrior to fight today's personal and global battles. *Durga* became for me the symbol of the female warrior necessary for healing ourselves and our planet.

We need to be Love Warriors, not warriors of violence and destruction. We need *Durga* for her strength on the battlefields and we need the Blessed Mother Mary to forge weapons of love for the battles to be won. The qualities of love, combined with a fierce passion, are what are needed to put recovery into action. *Durga* tells you that you have to be willing to fight and take action in order to save yourself. Mary tells you that if you continue to perpetuate your own body-hatred, you will drain your life force. She reminds you to love yourself.

If you cannot take action on the fundamentals of feeding yourself, how can you contribute to the healing of our planet? If you are numbing yourself with food and body-hatred, how can you recognize what your unique contribution will be? Before we can change the world, we have to be willing to battle our own body-hatred and the underlining problems that our body-hatred is trying to mask first.

Our planet is in dire need of healing and love, the same healing and love that is needed by each human being who lives on it. By listening to your intuition and paying attention to your ideas and dreams you can have access to a larger realm of healing possibilities for yourself and our planet.

How would your life be different if you became adept at listening to the language of your spirit and gave more credence to your intuition?

>> Action Steps <<

A) Look through magazines and use your intuition to tear out images that call to you. Collect them without having to understand why you chose those particular images.

B) Create a collage of what your life would look like when you love yourself and your body.

C) Keep your Self-Love Diet journal and a pen or pencil by your bedside so you can write out your dreams upon waking.

Body Path

This is a call to arms. A call to be gentle, to be forgiving, to be generous with yourself… When the criticism drops away, what you will see then is just you, without judgment, and that is the first step toward transforming your experience of the world.

—Oprah Winfrey

Body Path of the Self-Love Diet

Ask anyone to define diet and they are likely to say a diet is a plan to lose weight by cutting back on calories and increasing exercise. We have all seen the infamous before and after photos of people who have gone on diets. Our body's appearance has been used as the measure of success.

Although the Self-Love Diet does focus on your body, it does not look for what's wrong and needs to be changed. The Self-Love Diet focuses on what's right with your body and what it needs to be loved to health. The

Self-Love Diet teaches you how to listen to the language of your body and through non-judgmental curiosity, you will learn to listen to what your body needs and how to best care for it.

When you commit to paying attention to how your body communicates, you will find an ease in caring for yourself. Health is the goal, and it comes in a lot of different sizes.

When I ate compulsively in my pre-self-love days, I cared for myself with food. When I was physically hungry, I appropriately gave myself food. Conversely, when I wasn't physically hungry and gave myself food, I was using the one tool fits every situation method for dealing with life. If I was tired, I ate. If I was sad, I ate. If I was nervous, I ate. If I was bored, I ate. I think you get the picture. It's similar to having one tool in your tool belt. If you only have a hammer, and you need to hammer a nail into the wall, it's great. If you only have a hammer, and you need to patch a hole in the wall, it's not so great.

I can still remember the surprise when I listened to my body and realized that I was eating ice cream when I was really thirsty. When I stopped and listened to my body, I became aware of craving cold water. After eating the ice cream, my throat felt coated and I noticed a mucus cough. I felt compelled to drink water to clear my throat. I also noticed my stomach being full and feeling uncomfortable. When I stopped and asked my body what it wanted, I eventually heard, "cold, refreshing water." What a revelation! I enjoy the sensation of swallowing cold water when I'm thirsty so much more than my mismatched ice cream eating days. Another gift my body has given me is the ability to know what I like and what I don't like. Boy did I get a surprise when I first began leading support groups for compulsive overeaters as an intern counselor.

It was early December, and I had not practiced the activity before I offered it that first night in my supervisor's walnut paneled office. I decided to participate along with my five female clients. Three of the women sat on the well-worn green, gold and tan plaid couch in front of me. The other two sat on the grey steel folding chairs to my right. On top of an orange ceramic oblong platter, I placed lemon wedges, chocolate kisses and potato chips each in their own white, paper cupcake holders. The goal was to learn how to eat mindfully. I instructed them to stop and pay attention to how the food looked, how it felt in their hands, the aromas, the textures in their mouths, how it felt to bite into the food and what they noticed when they swallowed the food. I began by asking each participant to use the sense of sight with the first food choice, which was the Hershey kisses.

Darcy, a full-figured, red-haired woman in her late 30s sat in the middle of two other women on the couch. She spoke about the pleasure she took in looking at the candies wrapped in their sparkling silver foil, with an engraved paper slip. "It's like a Chanukah present! I'm aware of feeling anticipation. There's a sensuality of undressing each one as I expose the teardrop, chocolate-colored shape."

Claudette, a petite, blonde-haired Irish woman in her early 30s sat to my right on the folding chair. She noticed the emotion of excitement as her salivary glands were activated when she smelled the scent of the familiar chocolate.

Next, I asked each woman to slowly experience the taste and texture of the chocolate candy in their mouths and the sensations of swallowing it. I placed the chocolate kiss into my mouth and let it slowly melt and soften before I bit into it. I chewed it and as I swallowed, I paid attention to the sensations of it flowing down my throat.

What do you know? I didn't like that awareness. The chocolate had a chalky feeling to it. The chocolate covered the roof of my mouth and stayed in the nooks and crannies of my teeth. The sweetness, when I concentrated on it, was more than I actually liked. I sat there stunned. I had always eaten them by the handfuls, never taking the time to listen to my body's reaction.

Joan, a dark-haired Italian woman in her early 40s who sat to the right of Darcy on the couch told us that, "This experiment confirms my love of chocolate Hershey kisses. What comes as a surprise to me is how satisfied I am with one. I never thought eating one candy would be sufficient. I've enjoyed this one kiss more than the fistfuls I've gobbled in the past!"

Claudette, the woman who sat to my right, had a similarly shocking experience with the potato chips. When she took her time tasting the chip and feeling the texture in her mouth and the sensations of swallowing it, she decided she didn't like it. "It feels like a thin, soggy, tasteless Eucharist."

Your body wants to be loved to health. If you pay attention, it will guide you to well-being. I invite you to regularly offer yourself the experience of paying attention to your body. It has a lot to tell you.

22

Your Miraculous Magnificent Body

Appreciation and Amends, two self-love activities

The Moment of Contact

*Take a deep breath and sing your song, and hear
your music and kiss yourself in the mirror each
time your eyes meet your eyes,*

*And tell yourself how Tantalizing, Marvelous,
Voluptuous, Sumptuous, Divine, and Juicy you
are!*

*You may not believe it, but it's no matter, the act is
the thing; the moment of contact with yourself.*

—Michelle E. Minero

You have a miraculous, magnificent and marvelous body. Your body is
a spectacular, special and stupendous spiritual container.

Have you ever seen the joy on a baby's face when she rolls over for the
first time or when she's able to pull herself up to a standing position? Have
you ever watched a mother or father lift their infant in the air and heard
the delight communicated through their baby's laughter? Witnessing these
transient moments of pure joy a baby experiences in its body gives you clues
to a new appreciation of your own body. If you have not experienced what it
feels like to fully inhabit your body with joy and appreciation, I offer you an

opportunity to think about your body in the following manner.

Your Birth

Your body was majestically and miraculously formed within the body of your mother. You did not instruct your cells to divide and become heart cells, brain cells or the multitude of specific organs necessary for your formation. You did not get directions on how to propel yourself through the birth canal. Nor did you tell your lungs to breathe in air for the first time as you came into this world.

Your body instinctively worked towards your creation and sustenance from the moment of your conception.

Think about the millions of transactions that take place within your cells, bloodstream, bones, organs and your brain. When you stop to take notice, you might be amazed and perhaps mystified by the magnificence of your body.

Think back to Chapter 8, "Is Healing Possible?" and recall all the activity that takes place in your body to heal a cut. Did you have to ask your white blood cells to rush to the cut area and clean out the debris that might cause a threat to your body's well-being? Your body healed your cut and your skin replaced itself while you were going about your life.

Take a moment to thank your body for its tireless effort at keeping you healthy. Thank your heart for continuously beating while you sleep, and thank your lungs for expanding and contracting and helping bring oxygen to all your vital organs through your blood stream.

Also take time to think about what your body allows you to do. Do you enjoy dancing, swimming, walking, painting, sewing or watching the sunset? Whether these activities require simple abilities and movements, like being able to see or use your hands, or more complex movements, like the use of your whole body, they are dependant on your body. Open your awareness to what your body does for you and what your body allows you to do and you'll begin to see just how miraculous your body is.

If you have struggled with an eating disorder, it's likely that you have abused or harmed your body through unhealthy behaviors, as well as cruel criticisms. If you do not have an eating disorder, it's still likely that you have mistreated your body.

Your body deserves an apology. When you ask your body for forgiveness, it's not enough to say, "I'm sorry."

Here are the components to a satisfying apology:

- Take responsibility for your actions.
- Acknowledge how your actions affected your body.
- Try to understand how your body "felt."
- Make amends. Have a plan so you will not hurt your body again.
- Say you're sorry.
- Ask for forgiveness.

After you've finished writing your apology to your body, consider reading it out loud to yourself in a mirror while making eye contact with yourself. This helps your apology feel more tangible.

Here is one person's apology letter:

Dear Body,

I am so sorry for my constant dissatisfaction, belittling, criticizing, and hatred of you. You have done nothing more than constantly cared for me and healed me, and spoken to me to let me know what you've needed.

I have not listened to you. I have not loved you. I have hurt you to the point of having to be hospitalized. You were not able to provide me with my periods, or strong bones. I am sorry. Please forgive me. Please give me a second chance at loving you. Thank you for being the instrument that allows me to make a difference in this world.

This is a good apology. However, your body ought to have more than an apology, it warrants an amends. An amends is a living apology. It is a commitment to change. Amends means you acknowledge you've caused harm, and you promise to stop that behavior. Amends means you have an alternative plan to replace the harmful behaviors of the past, with new loving behaviors.

To regain or create a healthy relationship with your body you must take responsibility for your actions and follow through on your amends.

Here is the amends addition to the previous apology letter:

I intend to take better care of you from this day forward. If I catch myself looking at your reflection and thinking a negative thought, I will stop. I will ask myself, "Who says my shape is not as beautiful as other shapes?" I will remember all that you have done for me and continue to do for me. I will appreciate you and thank you.

Notice how you feel when you read the amends. Adding your amends opens the door for positive change. The focus on what you will do differently guides you as you create a more loving relationship with your body.

The Body Forgiveness Letter template can help you write an apology to your body. You'll find the template in the Appendix. In the Love Warrior Community chapter you'll find another example of a Body Forgiveness Letter, as well directions on where to read more and how to share yours with the Love Warrior Community.

I send you blessings on your journey of self-love and forgiveness.

How would your life be different if you realized your body was miraculous?

>> Action Steps <<

A) Each morning before getting out of bed, focus on your magnificent body. Feel gratitude for what it does for you.

B) Write a Body Forgiveness Letter. Read it out loud to yourself while looking in the mirror.

C) Read your Body Forgiveness Letter to a trusted person who agrees to be your self-love advocate and who will witness and sign your letter.

23

Instrument vs. Ornament?

How do you treat your body?

The surgeons' market is imaginary, since there is nothing wrong with women's faces or bodies that social change won't cure; so the surgeons depend for their income on warping female self-perception and multiplying female self-hatred.

—Naomi Wolf

Have you ever taken the time to sit and view your body as a miraculous instrument? Take a moment now, and notice your breath. Can you feel the air at the back of your throat as you inhale? Can you notice a slight change of temperature as the air flows from your nostrils while you exhale? Do you notice a rhythm in your chest as you breathe in and out?

You breathe every moment of every day and night while doing a wide variety of actions, thinking thousands of thoughts and experiencing a multitude of emotions. You continue to breathe when you are sleeping without needing to tell your lungs to expand or contract. Breathing is one example of the miracle of your body.

What about a woman's ability to give birth? A woman's body does millions of tasks in preparation for a new life. All of this activity is under the threshold of consciousness. Your body has an innate wisdom that is awesome in scope.

Let's look at your heart. Your heart began to beat while you were still in your mother's womb. Your heart continues to contract and pump blood throughout your body without you having to give it a thought. You do not have to authorize your heart valves to open and close. You do not have to measure the amount of blood that goes in and out of your ventricles. Your body's wisdom takes care of this life giving action every moment of every day and night. Your heart is always working for you. If you work as hard at loving yourself as your heart works for you, you will have mastered the Self-Love Diet.

Unlike our body's automatic ability to care for itself, we need to mindfully focus our thoughts and actions towards self-love. This needs to be a daily practice. If you are like me, you may get caught in the *ornament* versus *instrument* outlook, forgetting what an intelligent, proficient instrument your body is.

Ornament

An ornament is an object displayed for its beauty. Beauty is a wonderful part of life. It brings pleasure to you and others. Although bodies are beautiful, they were not solely created for ornamental purposes. When you treat your body like an ornament, you reduce your body to being an object. If you view your body as an ornament, it makes sense that you would want your ornament to be as beautiful as it could be. This way of viewing your body makes sense of plastic surgery, obsession with body sculpting and the diet industry.

Our brains are continually comparing and contrasting our bodies with the ideal that is blown up and plastered onto billboards. We are also bombarded with a multitude of airbrushed images offering only one body type: the thin, young, sculpted body that is currently in style and being sold by the diet, fashion, fitness and beauty industries. Our minds' critical focus as it scans for body imperfections is a detriment to the attainment of inner peace and serenity. Most of my clients have one or two major areas of their body that they either hate or at least are uncomfortable with. Monica is a good example.

Monica is a tall, svelte, dark-skinned, beautiful young woman with long, straight, shiny black hair. When she sat down in my office, the soft green wall behind her was the perfect backdrop to her emerald green eyes. She is a senior in high school and looks like a stunning model you would see in a magazine.

Monica sees herself differently. She hates her stomach and thighs. She thinks her arms are too big. These thoughts plague her every day and interfere with her ability to eat, keep her food and have joy in her life.

Instrument

An instrument is used to accomplish a particular purpose. In this case, your body is your instrument, and its purpose is to house the spirit that will guide you to do your work in this lifetime. If you view your body as an instrument, this way of thinking will lead you towards a loving stewardship of your body.

For instance, if you were out in the sun, you would wear a sun hat, sunglasses and sunscreen to protect your body and eyes from the sun's ultraviolet rays. If you were on a road trip, you would make sure you had money to buy food along the way, or you would bring a cooler with drinks and snacks. If you sprained your ankle, you would not go running the next day because that would not be good stewardship of your body.

Basic, loving care of your body includes getting enough sleep, drinking enough water and eating a variety of foods when you're hungry, and stopping when you are satisfied. Add exercise that you enjoy, loving body talk, expressing your feelings, spiritual expression, healthy relationships and medical attention when needed and you have the basics for loving your body.

Taking Stock

You may not have the same level of discomfort with your body as Monica does, but see if a body part comes to mind when I ask you to think of a part of your body that you do not like or wish were different. If a body part entered your mind, think about it now.

Notice your thoughts as you think about this part of yourself. Observe what your mind is telling you about this part of your body.

If you were thinking in the *ornament model*, you may have noticed critical, negative thoughts about that body part. Here is an example of Monica's thoughts that go along with an ornament perception of the body.

"My thighs are too big. They spread out and take up too much room. I can feel extra weight on them. I don't like the way they feel. I'll usually wear long pants, unless it's really hot. After looking at them, I tell myself I'll have to skip my next meal."

Monica's ornament perception of her body interferes with her ability to enjoy life. If you were thinking in the *instrument model*, you may have noticed appreciation and gratitude for that part of your body. Here are some examples of the instrument point of view. The following examples are Body Love Letter submissions from the Love Warrior Community (lovewarrior-community.com).

A 25-year-old female writes:

"I love the physical activities my body allows me to do: running, biking, playing soccer. I love that as long as I give it what it needs it gives me what I need :)"

A 19-year-old female writes:

"Dear Body,
I know you're really tired. But I appreciate everything you do for me, even when I push too hard. Spring Break is in two weeks, so you can rest up then. Thank you for not breaking down and sticking with me."

A 20-year-old female writes:

"Dear Body of Mine,
There's a verse in a speech-turned-song called "Wear Sunscreen" that reads; "Enjoy your body, use it every way you can. Don't be afraid of it or what other people think of it. It's the greatest instrument you'll ever own." When stripped of all the material aspects in our society, we are all equal in that we are breathing, living, thriving human beings. Our bodies are our most basic and

advanced foundation for our lives. So Body, thank you for being so great. I will still love you when gravity takes its toll on you and the elements wither you away. I'll try to keep you as strong and healthy as possible, because if you are strong and healthy, I will be too. You are the greatest instrument I will ever own.

How would your life be different if you viewed your body as an instrument instead of an ornament?

>> Action Steps <<

A) Whenever you catch yourself thinking in the *ornament mindset*, replace the focus of your body's appearance with an appreciation of what it does for you.

B) Send love and appreciation to a part of your body that you have criticized in the past by creating a daily routine. For example, you can apply cream to your arms and legs daily, or make a routine that fits for you.

C) Write about how you would treat your body if you worked as hard at loving your body as your heart works for you. Take one of your ideas on how you would treat your body lovingly and put it into action.

24

Can I Be Healthy If I'm Fat?

Exposing size bias

The Church says: The body is a sin.
Science says: The body is a machine.
Advertising says: The body is a business.
The body says: I am a fiesta.

—Eduardo Galeano

The answer to this question is yes. Health at Every Size, HAES, is a movement towards acceptance of size diversity, self-acceptance and the debunking of weight related myths. You will find other associations that advocate against size and weight discrimination in the bibliography at the back of the book, as well as a great book by Linda Bacon, PhD, *Health At Every Size: The Surprising Truth About Your Weight.* HAES challenges the wide spread belief that thin equals health and beauty and that fat equals disease and ugly.

Research has shown that fitness levels are much more accurate in assessing health levels than weight and BMI calculations. Deborah Burgard, PhD, a psychologist who is one of the founders of the HAES model, had a chance to show how misleading scales could be when a body composition team came to the dance studio where she took classes.

The technicians weighed her on a conventional scale. She weighed 188 pounds with a BMI of 30, which is in the obese range. Next, they measured her lung capacity and then dunked her into the water tank and brought her back up. Their foreheads wrinkled with confusion. They apologized, "We may have made a mistake. Will you let us dunk you again?" Deborah agreed and was retested. They came up with the same calculations.

Deborah's lean body mass was 144 pounds. Her fat percentage was 22 percent. "Perfect," they declared. Deborah was not thin, but she was an active, fit athlete. In order for her BMI to be in the normal range, less than 25, her body fat percentage would have had to be less than seven percent.

How many times do we inadvertently judge someone by their size? How do the BMI standards effect our perception of ourselves, and others?

HAES, and other organizations, such as the Council on Size and Weight Discrimination and Association for Size Diversity and Health, are working on bringing the issue of fat discrimination to the forefront. They are also helping educate physicians, therapists, dietitians and other mental and medical health professionals to become aware of biases that can and do interfere with providing the best care to all.

Marcy is a case in point. Marcy was a client of mine who was put on a diet in infancy, given laxatives as a toddler and was told to continue dieting in elementary school. By the time Marcy was in junior high school, she was hardly eating at all, and by her freshmen year of high school, she could add bulimia to her smorgasbord of disordered behaviors. Marcy got into treatment while in high school and continued to work on herself throughout adulthood. Marcy became a bright, competent nurse. Marcy helped others, and was especially sensitive to the needs of women with food or body issues.

Marcy told me, "Michelle, I can't seem to lose the 20 pounds my doctor is telling me to lose. I don't know what else I can do. I've battled fat all my life. No matter what I do, I can't seem to lose this weight. What's wrong with me?"

Marcy had been in therapy for a good portion of her life. By the time we met, she was in her 50s and was no longer bulimic or anorexic. She only bought organic foods and planned well-balanced meals for her and her husband. Marcy swam for 30 minutes three times a week, she worked out in a boot camp class twice a week and walked for 20-30 minutes on the other days.

Marcy was conscientious of her health because there was a history of late onset diabetes in her family, on both sides. She went for annual blood tests to assess her blood sugar levels because of her predisposition. She had just returned from her doctor's appointment the week before our session. Her doctor had gotten frustrated with her lack of success in losing the 20 pounds that she wanted Marcy to lose for the last five years. Her doctor indicated to Marcy that she must be eating more than she was reporting, or else she would have lost her weight by now.

"This latest doctor's appointment is an instant replay of the endless appointments my mother took me to as a child for my weight problem," Mary told me.

Marcy signed a release of information form for her primary care physician so I could request the results of her recent physical. Once I received the information, it showed that Marcy's vitals were all in the healthy range. Marcy did not have high blood pressure, nor did she have high cholesterol. Her blood sugar levels were in the healthy range, and she did not smoke or drink alcohol. She slept well, exercised daily and ate well-balanced meals.

While consulting with her doctor, we were in agreement that although Marcy's weight was above the insurance standard's recommendations, she was currently healthy. We were not in agreement that going on a diet would be a good preventive measure for Marcy based on her eating disordered history.

Marcy's doctor was well intentioned but could not see how her own frustration with Marcy's lack of weight loss was not helping. Her size bias interfered with her ability to recognize the healthy woman standing in front of her.

Marcy decided that she needed to change the goal of therapy. Instead of seeking help to lose weight, we explored the goal of maintaining her current weight and continuing her annual physicals due to her hereditary predisposition for diabetes, while working towards the goal of loving the body she had.

The process of recovery using the HAES model is described at its core concisely by Karin Kratina, PhD, MPE, RD as a "return to an eating style most recall from their youngest years - eat when hungry, quit when satisfied most of the time, and go outside and play."

This model of HAES is essential to know and to share with others. After applying these principles in your life, you can share them with your health professionals. HAES is important for all medical and mental health professionals to be familiar with because its concepts are in line with the Hippocratic Oath to do no harm.

In today's fat phobic climate, it is easy for a professional who is not trained in the field of eating disorders to blindly accept a patient's belief that they need to lose weight and go on a diet as part of their treatment plan for self-care. The main task of HAES, and similar organizations, is to debunk the myth that increased weight is an indication of health risks and premature death, as advertised by the current War on Obesity. This correlation is not supported by the literature.

By endorsing dieting behaviors, you and/or your health providers could actually be setting yourself or your loved ones up for yet another failed attempt at weight loss. Repeated failures on traditional diets decrease self-esteem and increase the risk for eating disorders. Dieting, not fat, can put your health more at risk. In contrast, the Self-Love Diet not only focuses on your physical health, but it also encourages you to be mentally, spiritually and emotionally healthy.

How would your life be different if you realized you were healthy and didn't need to lose weight?

>> Action Steps <<

A) Notice if you have judged yourself or others before based on size.

B) Declare freedom from the old fashioned diets, and pronounce your Self-Love Diet lifestyle to whoever will listen.

C) Use your old diet magazines, recipes, etc. as a background to a painting or collage, covering the old beliefs with images of your current dreams and desires.

25

Throw Out the Scale!

Your worth cannot be weighed

In the Middle Ages, they had guillotines, stretch
racks, whips, and chains. Nowadays, we have
a much more effective torture device called the
bathroom scale.

—Stephen Phillips

On October 10, 2009, the sun slipped through my bedroom window blinds as I checked my email before going to work. On my home page, I saw a photo of Tori Spelling. Under her photo was a link to the story titled, "Tori reveals her true weight." It is unthinkable for many to reveal their weight, so I was pleased to read that Tori is doing what she can to destigmatize the numbers on the scale. Although I was pleased to find the article about Tori on the front page, I was struck by the fact that President Obama won the Nobel Peace Prize the day before, on October 9, 2009, and he was nowhere to be found in the headlines. We live in a culture where our President's Noble Peace Prize is old news, upstaged by reporting on a celebrity's weight.

Do you have an ideal weight in mind for yourself? If so, it's important for you to remember that you are more than your body. You were created with a mind, emotions, relationships and a spiritual nature. You are not a number on a scale.

Once you replace control and manipulation of your body with respect by listening to its needs, it will reward you with a size and shape that is innately yours. You will be able to maintain your physique without unnatural, obsessive or compulsive behaviors. You will know when you are hungry and learn how to stop when you are satisfied. Your exercise will be a joy, something you yearn to do.

The Self-Love Diet focuses on you as a whole person. Therefore, having a specific goal weight is not the focus of this diet. Instead, your goal is to learn how to love yourself to health. Although doctors need to assess for a goal weight range for eating disorder treatment for their patients, having a number on the scale you are trying to attain can be confusing, as well as difficult.

Sarah was 5' 7" and weighed 92 pounds when she first came to see me. Her skin was pale and her eyes vivid blue, framed by deep circles and dark brown eyebrows. Her hair was pulled back off her face in a ponytail. Not a single hair was out of place. Her posture was perfectly aligned as she sat straight back on the edge of my brocade couch. She wore a turquoise blue sweatshirt over denim jeans and wore pristine white running shoes with pink shoelaces. Sarah was 18, a senior in high school with anorexia who also suffered from obsessive-compulsive disorder. She was an excellent student, had tested into three AP classes and was involved with gymnastics since the age of three.

After my initial assessment, it was clear that in order for Sarah to see me in my office, she needed to have a medical clearance from her doctor and needed to agree to a treatment team. She agreed to consistently see her physician for weekly vital and weight checks, a registered dietitian to help support her weight goals and me.

Sarah's doctor set her minimum weight goal at 115-125 pounds. Sarah was given this information, but was not told what her current weight was. Instead, the doctor and registered dietitian would let her know if she had a gain or a loss in weight. This is a common protocol, which can help people struggling with anorexia to decrease the anxiety of knowing that the numbers on the scale are rising. People struggling with anorexia can use the number on the scale to drag themselves deeper into their disease.

Sarah had a double whammy of obsessive-compulsive disorder, as well as anorexia. This dual diagnosis made it especially hard for Sarah to accept even the minimum goal weight of 115 pounds. Sarah told me that her obsessive thoughts could not even imagine reaching the number 100.

"I have this phobia about weighing 100 pounds. How does my doctor expect me to get to 115?" she told me.

She reported being constantly barraged by fearful thought such as, "You cannot weigh 100 pounds. If you do, you will you continue to get fatter and fatter until you die." "You cannot eat breakfast. If you do, you will gain weight until you reach 100 pounds, and you will feel disgusting." "If you reach 100 pounds, you will be gross and your boyfriend will leave you."

The goal weight of 115 pounds increased her obsessions, resulting in increased fear, anxiety and distress, which resulted in weight loss. Her doctor adjusted her minimum target weight to 110 pounds. With this new goal, Sarah agreed to take things slowly. She would break it down into small steps. She would work towards getting to 100 pounds and think about the other ten pounds after that. With this plan in place, she started increasing her intake.

After two months, Sarah's dietitian called me and reported that Sarah was getting close to 100 pounds. The obsessive-compulsive disorder continually badgered Sarah by ruminating on the dreaded 100-pound number. Right around this time Sarah began asking her doctor, registered dietitian and me to tell her what her weight was. I carefully took the time to explore the motivation for her request, knowing that the number is always too high for those with anorexia and can instigate more restrictive behavior, as well as mental and emotional self-abuse.

Sarah persisted in telling me and her registered dietitian that it was more anxiety provoking to not know her weight. Her imagination ran away with her, telling her she was over a hundred pounds and no one was telling her. The registered dietitian agreed to let her know when she reached 100 pounds.

The following week Sarah stomped into my office, her blue eyes glistening with tears, ready to spill over. She plopped down onto my couch and exclaimed, "The person who weighed me at the doctor's office left my file open on the counter. I looked at my weight. Michelle, I weigh 101 pounds! I can't trust any of you anymore," she bawled.

She told me that she had been weighed by her registered dietitian the day before who told her that she was still below 100 pounds. She felt betrayed. Anorexia had promised to never allow her to get to 100 pounds.

"I am not going to eat anymore. This is not acceptable. I will not weigh 100 pounds!" she yelled.

We worked with her anger and fear and addressed the obsession with the number 100. I let her know that there could be a four pound difference in one day, depending on the scale used, the clothes worn, the time of day, the time of month and whether or not she has just eaten or just used the bathroom. She was not completely calm by the time she left the office, but she was beginning to feel better. Although she refused to eat her three snacks, she did commit to eating her three meals each day until I saw her again.

Sarah's obsession with her goal weight is common among my clients. I have worked with clients who have gotten on and off the scale consistently, all day and all night. They weigh themselves in the morning, after breakfast and after going to the bathroom. They weigh themselves in the afternoon and before and after lunch. They'll weigh themselves after working out and before going to bed. This compulsion to weigh oneself more than once a day is not reserved for my eating disordered clients or my clients with obsessive-compulsive disorder. It seems to have become an accepted practice for many non-eating disordered people.

What is the obsession with the numbers on the scale? The right number, whatever that is, has become a symbol of self-acceptance, belonging, value and desirability. My clients who don't have eating disorders tell me that when they step on the scale and have lost weight they have increased self-esteem.

This is not possible. A scale cannot gauge your purpose in life or the positive effect you have had in others' lives. The numbers on a scale have no intrinsic ability to add or subtract a sense of esteem. You are the only one that can put a value or a judgment on the worth of yourself or someone else. A scale can only measure quantity, not quality.

In the Self-Love Diet you are encouraged to throw away your scales. When you throw out the scale, it is a symbolic act. It signals your intention to pay attention to your inner self.

Focusing on the traits that you want to promote, such as cultivating patience or increasing time spent nurturing yourself, as well as focusing on characteristics that you want to curtail or change, such as judging yourself harshly or putting undue value on your looks can replace the attention you gave to the numbers on the scale. When you stop focusing on the number on the scale it frees up your time to focus on loving yourself.

The Self-Love Diet provides a vehicle to promote true self-esteem. If the idea of throwing out the scale seems too radical, I invite you to read the story of Helen and how she took back the power from her scale and gave it to herself.

Helen came to see me five years post-bariatric surgery. This surgery left her with minimal capacity for holding and digesting food, forcing her to eat less. She had a history of binge eating, night eating and bulimia. Prior to her surgery, she had reached 348 pounds. This amount of weight on her 5'4" frame had threatened her life. After her surgery, her lowest weight was 125 pounds. Gradually, over the past five years, she had slowly stretched out what was left of her stomach and had gained more and more weight until she had reached 208 pounds at the time of our meeting.

"I want to weigh 125 pounds again." This was Helen's opening statement when she walked into my office and settled onto my plaid love seat.

"My current weight is scaring me and is becoming an issue with my partner." She continued, "He's never known me fat. He met me when I weighed 125 pounds. My current weight is interfering with my ability to dance, hike and camp with him. I workout four to five times a week, but each time I get on the scale it just seems to be going higher and higher, no matter what I do."

When Helen and I investigated what she was doing, we found that she was weighing herself on the scale frequently, each day and night, which increased her anxiety and feelings of loss of control. She quickly realized that weighing herself made her feel helpless, which led her to eat in order to soothe herself. She had created a negative loop.

Action	Thought	Feeling
Stepping on Scale	I'm out of control.	Fear

We discovered that the scale was a measuring stick of her stress in all areas of her life. In her high-pressure career she seldom took time to eat her lunch or take breaks. It was her job to resolve conflicts between the employees in her company.

Helen had learned how to turn off her body's signals for self-care in order to keep up with the relentless demands of her work. Once she got home, she relaxed by drinking wine and eating dinner, followed by continued snacking until she went to bed.

It was clear that Helen needed new skills to deal with the stress at work, and she was motivated to make changes. She began by adding a weekly yoga class to her more strenuous workouts, and I taught Helen how to attune to her body's signals for hunger. We used a one to ten scale, one being starved and ten being painfully stuffed, to help her gauge her hunger. This scale helped Helen to become aware of her body's signals for hunger, satisfaction and fullness, and it helped her to realize when she was physically hungry versus when she needed something other than food.

Helen also became mindful of when she was anxious. She replaced alcohol and food, her past means of relaxation, with breathing exercises, soothing self-talk and consciously asking herself what she needed in the moment. Helen noticed that coming home and exercising helped her to release the tensions of the day more effectively than drinking wine, and it also had the added benefit of helping her sleep more soundly. She was also willing to look at her dependence on alcohol and started making agreements with her partner regarding her drinking.

During one of our sessions, I suggested to Helen that she throw out the scale, but it was a while before she agreed to consider it. Once she was ready, she created a ritual. She took the scale to her favorite spot on her property, dug a hole and buried it. Next to the burial site, she planted a tree. Each time she went out to water the tree she thanked it for the reminder of the new life she was creating for herself.

Helen made many different choices as she used the principles of the Self-Love Diet. During one of our sessions she told me that she had decided to get rid of her clothes with elastic waistbands in lieu of garments with definitive waistlines. "Without my scale, my clothes tell me if my weight is changing or stable," she stated.

After close to two years of working together, Helen began to train for a white water rafting trip with a group of her longtime women friends from college. This trip signified the return of her physical strength and agility. After the excursion, she told me that it was the most physically challenging trip she had experienced and one of the most important things she had done for herself up to that time. "I'm in my body more these days, and it feels great!" she told me.

Helen did lose weight, although she did not attain her initial goal of 125 pounds. She used her increased energy, fitness, stress reductions skills, boundary setting skills and her ability to discern when she was hungry and full as measures of success.

At our last session, Helen and I compared how she thought about herself and how treated herself to her first session. She noticed that she now took her lunch breaks and did not work past her scheduled hours. These behaviors led others to respect her boundaries, which helped her to feel good about herself. Instead of eating or drinking wine to reduce her stress, she continued to attend her yoga classes, had a daily meditation practice, exercised regularly, led active weekends and was able to enjoy dancing with her partner again. She loved and cared for her body in ways that increased her energy, reduced her stress, enhanced her ability to relax and provided restful nights of sleep.

At our last session, Helen told me, "I'm glad I didn't throw out my scale like you encouraged me to. Burying it and planting the tree next to it has meant so much more. As I watch the tree grow, it's like I'm watching myself grow. If I hadn't gotten rid of the scale, I don't think I'd feel the way I do about myself. I really like myself these days. Thank you."

How would your life be different if you didn't measure your worth by a scale?

>> Action Steps <<

A) Notice if you put an inordinate amount of time into thinking about your weight.

B) Measure your worth by the love you give to yourself. Choose self-love actions from the list in the Appendix to begin to find out which behaviors fit for you.

C) Throw out your scale!

26

Mirror Image

What do you see when you look in the mirror?

The human body is the best work of art.

—Jess C. Scott

When you look in the mirror do you see a person of great worth, or do your eyes gravitate toward the imagined flaws in your appearance? Do you accept the image in the mirror with appreciation, or do you hold an ideal image of how you think you should look? Do positive affirming thoughts come to mind when you look in the mirror, or do you begin a litany of criticisms?

Remember the jealous Queen in the story of Snow White? She went to the mirror every day asking, "Mirror, mirror on the wall, who is the fairest of them all?" It can be easy to get caught in the same trap as the Queen if your internal peace and sense of esteem comes mainly, or solely, from your appearance.

Comparing your outsides with the outside appearances of others is like looking at a bunch of wrapped gifts. You have no idea what is inside the boxes. If you pick the most beautifully wrapped gift in your estimation, you are not guaranteed to get the best gift for yourself.

In Sarah Breathnach's book, *Simple Abundance*, she speaks of a group of women who wrote down their challenges on slips of paper and put them into a bowl at the beginning of their weekend retreat. At the end of the retreat, the facilitator guided the group's discussion to the topic of comparisons.

Each woman admitted to comparing herself to the others. Everyone disclosed that they would gladly change places with one or more of the women.

The facilitator then asked each woman to pick a slip of paper from the bowl until she was comfortable living with the challenge that was written on it. At the end of the activity, every woman decided that they would not change places with the other women, even though they had rated them as having better lives prior to reading their challenges.

This resonated with me because the shadow in the act of making comparisons is that we really don't know the whole story of any person until we've lived in their shoes.

I remember being with my cousins at a family party when I was in high school. I was about 17 years old. "Proud Mary" was just released by Ike and Tina Turner. We were talking about how sexy Tina Turner's legs were. We all tried to shake our bodies like her, without success. I know that my cousins and I would have innocently changed places with her if given that magic opportunity. We didn't know what Tina Turner's life was like outside of the glitz and glam and sexy dance moves. If we had known of the violence she endured at the hands of Ike Turner, I know we would not have traded abuse for her thighs and dance moves.

When I sit with my clients who are working to get free from their eating disorders, it pains me when they are unable to see themselves clearly. As I sit with these beautiful women, they describe themselves to me as ugly, hideous, revolting and disgusting. Their self-hatred is tangible in the room. Anyone watching a video of them describing themselves would be looking around the room, trying to understand who they were speaking about. My clients' body image is distorted.

What is distorted body image? There are two aspects to a distorted body image. First is the image you have in your mind of your body and how you feel about it. The second part is the way you imagine others will think and feel about your body.

There is a wide range of effects a negative body image can have. You may have a slight dissatisfaction with your body that pops up during summer when it's bathing suit time. You may have a mental picture of what your body looks like in a bathing suit, but it does not interfere with you buying that new suit, putting it on and going out and having a blast. Or, your negative body image can result in you ruminating about wearing a bathing suit, leading to increased negative thoughts about your body, which can result in depression and isolation. You may make up excuses to friends and family so you won't be in a situation that would require you to wear a bathing suit.

How does a person's self-image get so disturbed?

Malnourished Brain

Clients who restrict their food are prohibiting their brain from getting the nourishment it needs. When this happens, the brain cannot think clearly, has difficulty making decisions and the reward/punishment part of the brain is affected. What would normally be understood as positive now has a negative connotation. What previously would have been negative now has positive associations.

For example, if you find yourself in a relationship with someone who is in recovery from anorexia, you may be thrilled to see a weight gain and color coming back into the face of your loved one. If you tell her, "You are looking healthier." It is likely that she will interpret healthy for fat. If you tell someone, "I'm concerned about you because you've lost more weight." It's probable that your loved one will hear your concern and flip it towards a positive. She may think, "Good, people can tell I'm getting thinner. I'm succeeding." This statement can actually activate more disordered behaviors. This is why I ask family members and support people not to comment on body size or shape.

Life Experiences Lead to Faulty Belief Systems

Debbie suffered years of mental, physical and sexual abuse from her stepbrother until the family dissolved and he and his mother moved away.

Debbie used food to self-soothe as a young girl and developed mistaken beliefs that helped her make sense of her past.

"I must have deserved what happened to me."

"If I hadn't worn that T-shirt he wouldn't have molested me."

"My body was at fault for my abuse"

"My body can't be trusted"

"If I make myself look unattractive, I'll be safe"

This last belief is a common one for many of my clients. It can be the catalyst for either weight loss or weight gain. These mistaken beliefs came from Debbie's past experiences and do not reflect her authentic self today. She is slowly learning who she really is and that her body is not to blame for what happened to her. This process takes time because she has to create new beliefs that reflect her current desires in life. She also has to notice when her old ones are coming back. This is not easy to do.

Ethnic/Family Standards and Beliefs about Beauty

When we look at different ethnic body types we can see the truth of genetic diversity. A family can have a positive or negative influence on their family members' body image. If family members consistently complain about their believed flaws, always battling their bodies and criticizing themselves for being too fat, too tall, too flat-chested, too whatever, this behavior will grow discontent in vulnerable family members. On the other hand, if a family accepts and embraces their body type, skin color, hair texture, etc. it will make it easier for the rest of their family members to do the same. A sense of pride and identification with ancestral characteristics can grow and add to one's positive sense of self.

Culture of Your Friends, What's Acceptable and What's Not

I'd bet most people reading this book can remember when their friends' opinions and standards began replacing the importance of their family's.

We are hardwired to belong. In the caveman days, if you were not a part of a community, your chances of survival were low. Ostracism was a death sentence for many. This helps us understand the need to assimilate into a group mentality.

Young girls and boys want to wear the same name brand jeans and shoes as the friends in their peer group. The academic kids all want to get above average grades. The jocks want athletic prowess. Some groups will gravitate towards disordered behaviors more than others. If you are an athlete and steroids will make you stronger, therefore better at your chosen sport, it is more likely that you will use this illicit drug than a person whose status depends on his GPA. If you are in the popular crowd you may be more likely to go on diets than a girl whose sense of belonging is not as tied to her appearance. If you are a woman living in Hollywood, and if we up the ante and you are in the entertainment business, it's more likely that you would go on a diet to lose weight or consider elective surgery to "enhance" your appearance more than a housewife in Middle America.

Media Influence

By now we all have heard about the common practice of airbrushing photos of bodies to create the ideal image marketers want to sell. Concerned individuals have been teaching media literacy classes to the upcoming generations. We are just beginning to feel the positive impact of the media classes taught in schools and colleges.

Kate Winslet helped us all when she let it be known that she did not give a magazine the right to change her image. They made her look much thinner than she really was, and she complained. Jamie Lee Curtis and Oprah Winfrey provided us with the ultimate before and after pictures so we could see for ourselves that the images we have of our stars is just that, images airbrushed and Photoshopped, even after a team of makeup artists, hairstylist, clothes stylists, along with the photographer who uses the most flattering profile and lighting imaginable have done their full day's work.

It's hard to know what real looks like if it's not presented to us in movies, magazines and television. The Self-Love Diet reminds you to regularly offer yourself large servings of positive self-talk when you look in the mirror.

How would your life be different if you felt love when you looked at yourself in the mirror?

>> Action Steps <<

A) In your Self-Love Journal, write about the Queen in *Snow White*. Do you see any part of yourself in her? If so, describe this part of yourself so you can get to know it and can recognize it when it shows up.

B) Do you see how your ethnicity, family or peers contribute to your self-love, body dissatisfaction or body-hatred?

C) Go to www.lovewarriorcommunity.com and hover over Create/Explore. A drop down menu will appear. Hover over Positive Images. Click on Non-Airbrushed Real People Portrait Gallery. Notice how you feel about yourself when you look at this gallery of non-airbrushed people rather than when you look at fashion magazines. Go a step further and add a photo of yourself in your everyday look, and ask your friends and family to do the same.

27

How Can I Change My Negative Body Image?

A "bag of tools" is provided to bring love to your body image

> *Body acceptance allows for the fact that there is a diversity of bodies in the world, and that there's no wrong way to have one."*
>
> —Golda Poretsky

This is a big question, and there have been whole books and programs created to specifically address this phenomenon. In this chapter I will share some of the strategies I have used with my clients that have helped them change their negative body image into a loving body image. By regularly putting the following Self-Love Diet tools to use, moment-by-moment and day-by-day, you will strengthen your ability to change your body image into a more loving and accepting one.

If you notice that you are spending an inordinate amount of time in body-hatred, and it is impacting important areas of your life, please do seek out professional assistance while you are working on your Self-Love Diet.

Pay Attention

Notice when you are criticizing your body. You may have been criticizing your body for so long that you don't even notice yourself doing it any more. It can be similar to our heartbeat. Our hearts beat without us thinking about it. You probably don't think too much about your heartbeat until it becomes more noticeable by exercise, fear or bad health.

Start paying attention to what your mind is saying about your body. Does your mind have a consistent monologue about specific body parts that it replays over and over? Does your mind tell you that you must change your body in order to be happy? Does your mind tell you that others are spending as much time as you in assessing and criticizing your body?

Assess Your Body-Talk by Writing in Your Journal

Write out the negative body thoughts you noticed when you were paying attention to what your mind was saying about your body. If you live with others, make sure your journal is in a safe and sacred place, just for your eyes, which will allow you to write freely.

Writing out your negative body thoughts will help you to notice them whenever they're running through your mind. The next time you catch yourself thinking negatively about your body, pay attention to how your negative body thoughts make you feel and write down your observations in your journal.

Notice how your body feels when your mind is criticizing it. Notice what emotions you are feeling when your mind starts mentally abusing your body. Notice what circumstances or people trigger your negative body talk. Notice the fears you have of others bashing your body. Throughout the day, pay attention to all the times your mind criticizes your body. Estimate how much time you spend on thinking negatively about your body each day. Notice how that time spent on negative body talk each day affects you.

Confront Your Negative Thoughts

Using the information you received from paying attention to your thoughts, begin the process of confronting each body-hatred thought you wrote down. Maybe you noticed that a lot of body-hatred talk revolves around a specific body part, like your thighs. Confront your thoughts by questioning them.

"Is it true that I am nothing more than a pair of huge thighs?"

As you question your negative thoughts, find examples that disprove them. Do you have an identity outside of your thighs? What about your thoughts, emotions, relationships and life experiences? Create a statement to disprove each negative thought.

"I am a complete human being with thoughts, emotions, relationships and life experiences."

Strengthen Your Inner Observer

Your inner observer is that part of you that pays attention to your thoughts and can observe yourself thinking. Strengthen your inner observer by mindfully distinguishing yourself from your thoughts. There is a difference between thinking, "I look horrible" and "My mind is telling me that I look horrible." This seemingly small shift allows you the power to notice what your mind is doing.

Once you notice your mind's thoughts as an observer, it allows you to see your thoughts as being separate from your identity, which makes it easier for you to let go of them. By thinking, "I look horrible" you are making a statement about your appearance and are perpetuating a negative belief about yourself. When you view your thoughts from the perspective of an inner observer, you remove the power that your thoughts hold over you. When your thoughts become objective observations, instead of statements, they lose their connection to your identity and their ability to perpetuate your negative body talk.

Letting negative thoughts go can be difficult. Here are two practices to add to your Self-Love Diet that can help you with letting go of your negative thoughts.

In Chapter 6, "How Do You Begin to Love Yourself?" you learned how to use visualization to initiate healing, relax your body, calm your mind and soothe your spirit. You can also use visualization as a practice to strengthen your inner observer and to help you notice, and then let go of your negative thoughts. Many of my clients have found the image of a stream useful for this visualization practice.

Imagine sitting by a stream, looking straight ahead at the gentle current. Keep your focus in front of you so you can only see the imagined stream that is within your peripheral vision. To practice letting go of thoughts of body-hatred, imagine putting one of your thoughts on a leaf that is floating down the stream. Watch it float by you and out of sight. Repeat this visualization with each of the thoughts you wrote down from paying attention to your body talk. You can use this Self-Love Diet tool anytime you notice yourself thinking negatively.

Another Self-Love Diet tool you can use to practice strengthening your inner observer is watching clouds pass by while lying down outside. When watching the clouds, you repeat the pattern of noticing a cloud and then watching it vanish as it passes through the sky, which mirrors the process of noticing your thoughts and then letting them go. The goal is to have your reaction to your thoughts be as neutral as your reaction to watching the clouds move across the sky.

Focus on Your Body as an Instrument vs. an Ornament

Reminding yourself about what your body does for you is another Self-Love Diet tool that can help you in transforming your body image. Bring in appreciation for the miraculous body you have. Remember to thank it. Think about all it does for you until you can feel the appreciation. Throughout the day, remember the things you take for granted, like breathing, walking, talking and seeing. Keep in mind the things your body allows you to do. Tell yourself, "My hands allow me to make the jewelry that I love to create which provides me with an income."

"My legs allow me to ride my bike to work each day, which keeps me and the earth healthier."

By paying attention to what your body does for you, and allows you to do, you can begin to view your body with more appreciation.

Refocus Your Attention on What You Do Like about Your Body's Appearance

Our brains are wired to look for what is wrong in order to survive. As humans, we even train ourselves to look for what's wrong. Do you remember the children's magazine Highlights? I remember one of my favorite activities in the magazine was to find all of the mistakes in the picture. I would circle the sunglasses that were missing a lens or the woman's purse that was missing the shoulder strap. When it comes to body image, this survival skill of looking for what's wrong is causing more pain than help.

Practice bringing your attention to the aspects of your appearance that you like. When you look in the mirror, focus on what you like about your appearance and say it out loud or write it down in your journal.

"I like the shape of my eyebrows."

"I like how my hair is thick and shiny."

"My toes are cute."

"I like the shape of my legs."

Notice how you feel when you focus your attention on what you like about your appearance. When appreciating the thickness and shininess of your hair, notice the thoughts that pop up. When appreciating the shape of your legs, notice your emotions. How does it make you feel to positively focus on your appearance?

Write out a list of the body parts that you think are attractive so you can remind yourself about what you do like about your body when you get caught in the body loathing mindset. If focusing on what you like about your appearance isn't helping you get out of the body loathing mindset, call upon the other Self-Love Diet tools until you begin to feel a shift in your mindset. Focus on what your body does for you and allows you to do. Remember that once you notice your thoughts, you can confront them, question them and disprove them. Practice your inner observer. Allow yourself to notice your negative thoughts, and then let them go. The more you put these Self-Love Diet tools to use, the more natural regularly offering yourself love becomes.

How would your life be different if you saw and thought about your body positively?

>> Action Steps <<

A) Commit to loving your body by paying attention to how much time you spend acting negatively towards and thinking negatively about your body.

B) Start journaling your negative body thoughts so you are able to notice them when they are happening, and then either confront them or let them go.

C) Practice confronting your thoughts. Choose three negative thoughts that you wrote down in your journal. Beside each thought, write down a statement that disproves it.

28

Mirror Neurons/Mirror Work

Utilize your body's inherent capabilities for learning new behaviors

We feel what we see, we experience others as self.

—Diane Ackerman

Mirror neurons are the newest craze in neuroscience. This discovery has been labeled by neuroscientist V.S. Ramachandran as the "fifth revolution"— "the 'neuroscience revolution,' the first four being Copernican, Darwinian, Freudian, and the discovery of DNA and the genetic code."

The reason I am excited about this discovery is because of the possible implications that mirror neurons can be used to show us how to love ourselves.

Mirror neurons were discovered by Giaccomo Rizzolatti in Italy in 1995. Rizzolatti was studying the motor neurons in the brains of Macaque monkeys. He discovered the specific neurons that fired when the monkeys reached for peanuts. He named them motor neurons. What he was not anticipating was the discovery that these motor neurons fired when the monkey watched a scientist reach for a peanut.

The implications are manyfold. This insight into the brain helps us understand how we as humans learn. We learn by *mirroring* the people around us. When we watch others make physical movements mirror neurons are activated in our brains as if we're making the same movements. This process shows us that we learn through imitation. The brain sees someone else doing something and it's as if we're doing it. This has been coined as the Mirror Neuron System or MNS.

These mirror neurons are also connected to our emotions. This accounts for our ability to have empathy. It's why we get excited when watching a sports game or cry at a sad movie, even though our loved one has not died.

As humans, our survival has depended on our ability to belong to a greater community. Therefore, these mirror neurons help us discern the intentions of others so we know if they are trustworthy and safe.

What happens if we don't have people around us who are connected and attuned to us with loving intentions? Can receiving and being aware of receiving loving behaviors and intentions later in life activate our mirror neurons to help us love ourselves? Can we learn to love ourselves through the use of mirror neurons interspecies? Can we learn to love ourselves through the mirroring of the love shown to us by our pets? If we can discern emotions and intentions due to our mirror neurons, could we use this MNS to develop self-love and increase our body satisfaction by looking into our own eyes? Does our brain know the difference between watching someone else's loving gaze and our own in the reflection of a mirror?

This last question is at the crux of the mirror work I propose we use as a self-love practice. Even if our mirror neurons are not firing when we look into our eyes and tell ourselves that we love ourselves, something is happening.

The eyes have been called gateways to the soul. If you have had the experience of taking the time to look into the eyes of an infant, you will understand the profound experience this can be. When I looked into the eyes of my first grandchild while she silently looked into my eyes, I felt a soul-to-soul connection.

If you were lucky you had an alert, present, loving mother who held you close to her heart, offered you her breast or bottle and looked deeply into your eyes with love overflowing. Your mirror neurons were able to let you know that this person's intentions were to love you, and from that you learned that you were lovable. This bonding is at the heart of attachment theory, which elucidates your ability to love yourself and to create healthy attachments and relationships throughout your life.

Even if you were lucky enough to have this loving bond at the start of your life, over the years, life interferes with your sense of self as a lovable, whole person deserving of all good things. You soon may have come to believe that you are not good enough, that your body is not right and that all is not well.

Mirror Work, Connecting with Your Soul

When I am working with people who have negative body image, it can be difficult to get them to look in the mirror. I have a full-length mirror in my office, as well as a mirror that is positioned to reflect my clients from the chest up. I quickly realized the smaller the mirror the better to start off with. I use mirrors approximately three inches in diameter for the mirror work I am about to describe, which is about the size of the mirrors used in compacts for face foundation.

Step One

Look into your eyes in the mirror, not *at* your eyes or face. This is not the activity you may be accustomed to if you have a daily routine of wearing makeup. You will not be looking *at* your skin, or your eyes or eyebrows.

Step Two

Continue to look into your eyes until you feel yourself *sink down* and connect with your authentic self, or soul. When I first began this practice of looking into my eyes and settling my gaze, I felt a *sinking into* myself.

I've had numerous clients tell me that they have a decidedly different *feel* when they look into their eyes compared to when they look at their eyes. Your goal is to connect with your authentic self or your spirit. Stay with this part of you for as long as you can.

Step Three

Tell yourself that you are lovable and that your worth transcends the size or shape of your body or body parts. This is the time to be your own loving mother who looks into your eyes and tells you how loved you are. Smile at yourself, sending love deep into your soul. Be gracious, grateful, accepting and positive toward yourself.

Step Four

Take another moment to silently look into your eyes with love, committing the experience to memory as you start your day. By using your gaze to look *into* your eyes, I believe you are activating your mirror neurons to bring back the experience of yourself as a lovable human being.

There is much research yet to be done. In the meantime, do your own research and see what you find out.

How would your life be different if you started each day by looking into your eyes with love?

>> Action Steps <<

A) Start each day by looking into your eyes with love.

B) Notice what happens when you do the above activity. How does the loving presence and messages you give yourself in the morning affect your day?

C) Write about your experience and share it on the Self-Love Warrior group blog at www.selflovewarrior.com.

Mind and Emotion Paths

I think... if it is true that there are as many minds as there are heads, then there are as many kinds of love as there are hearts.

—Leo Tolstoy

Mind and Emotion Paths of the Self-Love Diet

The Mind and Emotion Paths are presented together because these two paths are interconnected. When you think thoughts they lead to emotions. When you feel emotions they lead to thoughts. Actors use this neurological and physiological process to their advantage.

When an actor is preparing for a scene that requires a certain emotion, let's say sadness, the actor remembers something that was personally sad to her. Once the actor recalls this event, and lingers on it, bringing all the details into focus, the emotions kick in and elicit the response required for the scene. Her body also reacts to this memory, bringing physical sensations of sadness.

Perhaps her face becomes slack, a frown appears across her forehead and tears begin to swell in her eyes. This interconnection between the mind, emotions and the body is why subtle shifts in muscular movements are visible on the big screen, lending authenticity to an actor's performance.

If the very next scene requires the same actor to feel silly and to giggle, she will use the same process. In the Self-Love Diet, you can be the actor in your own life story, and you can begin to have the same power to elicit the emotions you want to cultivate in your life.

This ability to utilize the connection between your thoughts and your emotions is the beauty of the Self-Love Diet. This mindfulness allows you to linger and luxuriate in the sensations, cognitions and emotions that bring love, joy and contentment into your body, mind and relationships. It can also keep you ruminating about all the pain and suffering in your life. Knowing this helps you to be mindful of those thoughts, emotions and sensations that can lead you away from loving yourself.

One common self-defeating thought pattern is a negative loop. If you repeatedly hear from others that you are no good, it is quite common to begin to tell yourself the same message, over and over again. These repetitive thoughts actually create neuropathways in your brain. It's like working with clay. If you are creating a face of a person and want to create a deep frown line, you will start by tracing a line in the clay where you want it. You can deepen the line by repeatedly stroking with more and more pressure until you have made a deep frown in the clay. What started out as a scratch in the clay can become a deep channel with repeated swipes of the carving tool.

In this carving metaphor, you can see how your effort created a deep channel in the clay. You have the same power to create new neuropathways in your brain. Instead of a clay tool, your thoughts become the instrument for creating the pathways in your mind. You control the depth of the pathway by the repetition of your thoughts.

By thinking loving thoughts repeatedly, and adding your visual, auditory, olfactory, sensate and energetic senses, you can help develop the belief that you are valuable, worthy and lovable. I will provide you with more information on how to do this in this section of the book. Your thoughts can lead you to self-loathing or to self-love. You are in charge.

Another way of working with your thoughts is to just notice them. If you have ever sat quietly and paid attention to your thoughts you may understand the term monkey mind. This term describes the way your thoughts jump around, like a monkey swinging from one tree to another. The simple act of noticing, without judgment, allows the observer in you to detach from the emotions of those thoughts. If you notice the thought, "I'm fat," instead of reacting negatively to the thought, you would be able to think, "There's that fat thought again. Isn't that interesting?"

By strengthening your inner observer you will be able to watch your thoughts come and go, like waves that ebb and flow. Through this practice you can separate your emotional reactions from your thoughts, and you can just notice them without buying into them, as well as offer yourself loving thoughts in place of them.

29

Treasure Chest of Emotions

Deciphering the messages of your emotions

*But some emotions don't make a lot of noise. It's
hard to hear pride. Caring is real faint - like a
heartbeat. And pure love - why, some days it's so
quiet, you don't even know it's there.*

—Ernest Hemingway

When I was in Kindergarten, my mother would drop me off at my grandmother's house on the way to work and pick me up at the end of the day. Each night on our way home to Daly City we stopped at Ocean Beach in San Francisco. We sat side by side in the car watching the colors of the sunset turn the sapphire sky crimson, gold and amethyst before continuing on home.

As we sat in the car, I watched the same man walking along the beach holding something in his hand. It looked like a thick steel cane, except it had a handle at the top, and on the bottom, a small, flat, round, steel plate set parallel to the sand. As we watched the sun gift its cascade of colors into the ocean, this man would walk along the beach swinging this tool back and forth like a blind man using a seeing-eye cane.

"Mom, what is that man doing?" I asked.

"He's using a metal detector to look for treasure."

I was excited to think that treasure could be found on our beach. I was ready to go with my mother and begin looking for our own treasure.

"Can we find our own treasure chest?" I asked.

"No, honey. There are no treasure chests in the sand. This man is looking for coins, watches or jewelry that people have left or lost at the beach."

"Can he keep whatever he finds?"

"Absolutely," my mother responded.

It was a marvel to me that treasures could be so easily had. All he had to do was look for it, and they were his. It was hard to contain my excitement. I bounced up and down in the car, hoping to get permission to get out and find my own beach treasures.

"How does he know when he has found treasure?" I asked.

"When the man swings the metal detector back and forth, it beeps very quickly if it finds something made of metal. Then he knows to dig at that spot, and he'll find his treasure."

"Why doesn't everybody come looking for the beach treasures?"

"Well, Michelle. That man has to go through tons of sand before he finds a treasure. Most people think it's too much work. They think it will take too much time, and they don't believe they will find anything worthwhile. Most people are just too busy."

I didn't understand her at first, and then I realized that my mother and I were most people. We never bought the metal detector. We never joined that man in seeking treasures, and I don't remember asking my mother about it again.

The quest for self-love is similar to the process that man went through looking for the beach treasures. It takes time to become familiar with and name your emotions. You may feel like you're shifting endlessly through grains of sand to uncover your emotional treasures. When you do find an emotion it may beep at you to get your attention. Once you recognize it, you can listen to what it has to tell you. The messages your emotions impart are the treasures. It's up to you to allow them to guide you in your life, rather than deny, avoid or distract yourself from them. Once you recognize a feeling, it's your job to dig for the treasure. Here are some tools you can use to excavate your treasures.

Tool #1: Use Your Mind

When you are aware of an emotion, ask yourself: What is this feeling? The acronym HALT can also be used to help discern emotions.

+ H = Are you hurt? If you are hungry, is it physical or emotional?
+ A = Are you angry? Are you anxious?
+ L = Are you lonely?
+ T = Are you tired?

See the appendix for a list of more emotions. If you still are unable to recognize your emotions, try asking the following questions.

+ Have I felt this before?
+ What is this emotion trying to tell me?
+ When is the first time I remember feeling this?
+ How does this feeling connect to what's going on in my life now?

Here's an example of how I used my mind to discover my emotions. I woke up to a sunny summer morning feeling off. I noticed I was having a good day; the sun sparkled on the water as I stretched in my backyard spa, but the usual lift that comes from a relaxing morning just wasn't there. That was my metal detector telling me there was a treasure waiting for me.

I crossed over to my meditation bench. Red roses cascaded over my head and shoulders along the weathered wooden arch. I began to remember bits and pieces of a dream. My mother, father and uncle, who have all died, were in it.

When I asked myself, "How does this feeling connect to what's going on in my life now?" I realized the anniversary of my mother's death was the following day. The gift of digging for this treasure made me conscious that I was still grieving and needed to be more nurturing to myself. By sharing this information with my family, they were able to be more supportive of me that day.

Tool #2: Use Your Body

When you are aware of an emotion ask yourself:

- Where do I feel this emotion in my body?
- Is it in more than one place?
- What does it feel like?
- How big is it?
- Does this emotion have a color?
- Does it have a sound?

If you still don't have the answers try the following:

- When is the first time I can remember feeling this sensation in my body?
- How does this feeling connect to what's going on in my life now?

Trish is a 58-year-old, robust, brunette. She is a successful business-woman. Trish is intelligent and aware. She can catch thoughts when she's being critical and change them, but she still has difficulty being with her feelings.

She marched into my office and chose to sit in the sunlight on the tan, green and red plaid love seat. "I've been crying for no reason at all. I don't know if it's menopause, depression or just sleep deprivation. My partner and I produced a great company, we do good work in the world and my employees are all wonderful."

Trish continued to give me lots of reasons why she thought she should be happy and grateful. She said that she counts her blessings every day and writes them out each night.

"Are you willing to write them out now?" I asked her.

"I just told you, Michelle. I do this every night, but I'll do it again if you want."

In three minutes, Trish had filled the entire page with bullet after bullet of things in her life that she was grateful for. I started with the first bullet.

"Trish, you've written, 'I love my partner, and she loves me.' Will you put your hand on your heart, breathe quietly and let yourself feel the truth of this statement?"

Trish put her hand over her heart and sat there quietly a few moments before her dark brown eyes began to glisten. Soon tears spilt down her cheeks.

"What are you feeling?" I asked her.

"I'm not sure. It's not sadness."

"Sit with it a little longer. Let me know where you feel this emotion."

"I feel it in my heart."

"Do you feel it anywhere else?" I asked.

"I feel it in my chest."

"How big is this feeling?"

"I feel it from my waist all the way up to my throat."

"Does this feeling have a color?"

"It's pink. Michelle, this is love! My whole chest has expanded to let it in."

When Trish allowed herself to sit with and feel the emotion in her body, it gave her the gift of the sensation of her passion, not just the idea of it. This incident brought clarity to Trish. She wanted more time with her partner. It was time for Trish to make some changes at work. She shortened her workweek, delegated work that others could do and had more time for her relationship.

Tool #3: Just Notice

Once you are aware of a thought or an emotion, use the tool *just notice* to observe it. Pay attention to the sensations in your body that accompany the thought or emotion. If you begin to judge yourself as good or bad, stop. Neutralize your experience by thinking, "Isn't it interesting that I seem to judge things as good or bad?"

In a support group I ran for many years, the women had an inside joke. Each time someone would share an uncomfortable emotion or experience that they were judging as bad, horrible or intolerable, one of the other women would say, "Isn't that interesting?" It was their way of using the *just notice* tool.

When Lynne was experiencing the travails of her husband being out of work and in her hair, she found herself over eating fudge brownies. "I feel ashamed for slipping back into my old ways of coping," she said.

"Isn't that interesting?" all of the women said in unison and laughter filled the room. Lynne's shame changed to camaraderie as the group helped her neutralize what she called the brownie incident.

Tool #4: Allow Yourself to Feel

There is no such thing as a good or a bad emotion. Some emotions are more comfortable than others, but emotions are just sensations in your body that give you information to help you deal with any given situation. Once you understand the difference between feeling your uncomfortable emotions and reacting impulsively to them, you will have freedom to experience your emotions safely.

Anger is an emotion that is usually judged as dangerous, scary or bad. Remember that the emotion of anger itself is not bad. You may be fearful of this emotion because of how you or others in your life have acted it out. Anger has a lot of energy, and this energy can be a catalyst for positive change in your life if you learn how to work with it.

Anger is generally easy to identify. If you are angry, your body may beep at you like the metal detector by increasing the rate of your heart and your breath. Perhaps you'll feel a rush of blood to your head, or your face may flush. Your emotions send you a treasure chest full of sensations and signals so you will understand what they are trying to tell you.

Once you know that you are feeling angry, you can tweak the old adage of counting to ten by taking ten full diaphragmatic breaths. This slows your heart rate and helps to calm and soothe you before you respond. Once you are soothed you will be able to use the power of your anger to act responsibly.

By using different modalities you will be able to decide how to express your anger in a way that doesn't hurt you, others or destroy property. By being alert to your body's emotional sensations, you are more apt to become familiar with them. This can help stop impulsive, hurtful or irresponsible statements or actions towards yourself or others. By becoming aware of your emotions, you can manage and express them responsibly.

Tool #5: Writing

Writing works to clarify emotions. First, you have to stop and pay attention to the feeling so you can write about it. Once you have clarity, you can explore your sensations and emotions in more depth through the process of writing.

Stream of consciousness writing is one technique that allows you to write freely as your thoughts come to you. This method is a process of writing without regard to spelling, grammar or punctuation. By getting uncomfortable feelings out of your body and onto the paper you can discover the gifts your emotions have for you.

When I was a marriage and family therapist intern, I used to get home at 10:30 pm or 11:00 pm. Everyone was asleep by the time I stepped into the kitchen to pour myself a bowl or two of cereal before I went to bed.

One night as I poured cereal into my bowl for the second time, I realized I wasn't really hungry. I decided to write about it. As I let my hand write down whatever came to mind, it was as if a wise inner self was communicating with me. I reread what I had written and examined the words on the paper. *I'm not physically hungry. I'm tired. I just want to go to bed and be held.* The words jumped out at me. I was using cereal to soothe and comfort myself. What I needed was sleep. What I wanted was to have my husband hold me.

Tool # 6: Talk to Someone

Talking to someone who is trustworthy and a good listener allows you to process your emotions verbally.

I watched a sitcom where a teen seeks out her mother and asks for her advice. The mother is pleased to have her daughter confide in her. She sits down, and her daughter launches into a diatribe about how angry she is with her best friend. The mother tries to get a word in edgewise, but her daughter leaves no space for her to speak. As the daughter continues to rant about her girlfriend, she begins discussing her friend's strengths as well. Soon the daughter has come to a balanced perspective, has decided to talk to her friend and is confident that it will all work out. The daughter hugs her mother, who has been silent the whole time, and thanks her for, "being such a help!"

Talking to someone you trust can be a valuable tool for gaining clarity with your emotions. If there is someone in your life who is a good listener, talking to that person may help you find the treasure in a confusing or overwhelming emotion.

You can easily review these tools in the appendix "Deciphering Your Emotions" to help you get the treasures waiting for you in your emotions. If you are uncomfortable feeling your emotions, remember that feelings have gotten a bad rap. They are not good or bad; your emotions are just information waiting to be deciphered. Some of the following beliefs may be getting in your way of receiving the treasure chest of gifts that your emotions can offer you.

"If I let myself cry, I will never stop."

"I can't let myself feel that. If I do, I will die."

"My emotions are too overwhelming."

"Crying is a sign of weakness."

"My emotions are too much for people."

"Feelings are supposed to be kept to yourself."

"I'm annoying if I tell people how I feel."

"No one likes a whiner."

"If people really knew how I felt, they would abandon me."

Take some time and notice what beliefs you may have about your feelings that may not be serving you.

_____

_____

_____

Many people think this process of digging for their emotions will take too long or is too big of a task. Some of my clients have told me that they don't think they can do it. They say they are too busy with life to stop and go to the beach looking for their treasures. Sadder yet, some of my clients don't believe they have a treasure within to find, so they never begin the search.

Some of the people I work with are brought in by their parents or partners. The beginning of their journey can seem to fall into their lap. For others, the motivation comes from the desire to make changes in their life, or the path towards finding their own treasures begins by wanting a loved one to get help.

Once you commit to healing yourself, even if you are ambivalent, an inner-motivation or a consciousness that there is more to life emerges. This is when your inner metal detector can provide the awareness that emotions can be tools to find your inner treasures.

The gift of searching for the meaning of your emotions is similar to the treasures found by that man at the beach. He found lots of bits and pieces, most of it commonplace, but every once in a while he have found something so valuable that he continued his daily search.

If you take the time each day to look to your emotions and try to discover their meanings, you will store up a mountain of invaluable treasures. You will learn about yourself, what motivates you and how you can better love yourself. You may decide that you are worthwhile enough to continue the daily search.

Lori is a good example of someone who was not motivated to search for her emotions. In fact, she was so afraid of her feelings that she did just about anything she could to not feel them.

Lori was 21 when I first met her. She was tall, had short platinum blonde hair, blue eyes, freckles and a contagious smile. Lori was a swimmer. She had broad shoulders, lanky legs and a muscular, athletic body. I could not tell from the outside that Lori had a long history of physical, sexual and mental abuse.

Lori had been working with a therapist in Southern California before coming to Northern California. I asked Lori why she was seeking therapy. She told me that the counselors at her college referred her to me. I asked her what current symptoms she was engaging in that she wanted to change.

"I cut myself three to four times a week, I purge one to three times a day, I stay under a certain amount of calories and I swim and or run daily."

Lori had a common fear that her feelings would take her over. She believed her emotions were out of control, and she confided that she sometimes felt crazy.

"I don't want to die. I just want to stop feeling," she told me.

Lori suffered from post-traumatic stress disorder, anorexia and recurrent major depression resulting from over a decade of nearly daily abuse, torture and death threats.

After five years of our working together, Lori no longer cuts herself in an attempt to punish herself for imagined wrong doings or to translate her inner emotional pain in an outward fashion. She has recently been able to go back to swimming at a recreational level without overdoing it. Lori is beginning to work from an intuitive eating model, although when under stress she will go back to the food plan her registered dietitian helped her create. She replaces running with moderate hikes. She was able to gain weight, and her weight remains stable within a healthy range. Although from time to time she has suicidal thoughts, she does not act on them.

Our work together has not been miraculous. It has been a strenuous, focused, persistent commitment on Lori's part to stay the course of learning that she is lovable, worthy and deserving of good things. Her lesson is to know in her cells that the things that happened to her were not her fault. Her challenge is to trust one other human being with her vulnerability.

I sit with Lori while she hesitantly describes the flashbacks and memories of her childhood. She is no longer alone with the emotions and sensations that flood her body. Lori has learned how to manage her emotions. When she begins to sense that they are overwhelming, she has learned to contain them until our sessions. She has developed a safe place within herself where she can go to find peace. She knows how to ground herself and how to deal with her emotions that she once described as over the top.

Lori still has work to do. Loving herself when she carries a past in which she was treated so horrifically can still be challenging. Learning to ride the wave of her emotions and experiencing the truth that the uncomfortable ones will pass has created her mantra: "Emotions come and go whether I act on them or not." Reliving with me, in the moment, the emotions and body sensations from her past trauma has been her gateway to feeling love, laughter, safety, happiness, trust and joy.

If there is trauma in your background, I encourage you to get professional help to learn how to manage your emotions. Your pain can become the pathway to healing.

How would your life be different if you thought of your emotions as treasures?

>> Action Steps <<

A) Practice spending time with your emotions. Just notice them.

B) Practice one or more of the six tools mentioned above and spend time deciphering the message in your emotions.

C) Write in your Self-Love Diet journal and describe the sensations in your body and their corresponding emotions.

30

Facing Fear

False expectations appearing real

Fear is the cheapest room in the house. I would like to see you living in better conditions.

—Hafiz

Sometimes your emotions don't feel like treasures. Fear is one of those emotions. It can activate your flight, fight or freeze response and be life saving, but it can also overwhelm you with intense sensations when you are not really in danger.

When you are living from a place of fear, love does not have much room to grow. The limbic system, located on the top of your brainstem and buried under your cortex, is involved in the activation of your fear response. You are programmed for survival. Your brain is on the lookout for things that will endanger your life so it can protect you. This ability to spot danger was especially important to early humans. When our ancestors hunted for food, many times they ended up becoming the food. It was imperative for survival that our ancestors' fight, flight or freeze response was intact.

Today, when you imagine a fearful situation, your brain can still release adrenalin in an attempt to keep you alive. The problem for many is that they are no longer in life and death situations, but their brains are still releasing adrenalin as if their life depended on it. Panic attacks are a good example of this survival mode backfiring.

Putting the Self-Love Diet into place requires you to listen to and let yourself feel your emotions so you can understand the messages behind them. When fear is the emotion you are experiencing, it can be very uncomfortable to sit with it. Here's what you can do when fear is the emotion you are learning from.

#1: Learn Your Body's Fear Response

How does your body tell you that you're afraid? Do you notice your heart rate increase? Perhaps you get sweaty hands or begin to breathe more shallowly? Notice your body's sensations so you will be clear what your body is telling you.

#2: Assess the Situation

If you are in danger, do the next right thing to move you towards safety. Run, fight, scream, hide, etc. If you are feeling intense fear but are not in danger, then you have fallen for false fear. Experiencing fear before giving a talk in front of an audience is an example of feeling fear when you're not in danger. You can use the acronym F.E.A.R. to help you decipher if what you're afraid of can cause you harm or if your emotions are sending you a false message.

F = false

E = expectations

A = appearing

R = real

If your fear is sending you false messages, realizing that your fears are really false expectations appearing real can help you to let go of them. Here are some tools to use when you are not in danger and need to self-soothe.

#3: Develop Your Loving Observer

This loving part of yourself can notice the sensations in your body without falling into fear. This observer self can let you know that you are not in danger and can guide you to love yourself by using the following self-love tools.

#4: Soothe Yourself with Deep, Diaphragmatic Breathing

This is my favorite because it's free, always attainable and once you've got the practice down, you've got it for life. Practice diaphragmatic breathing until it becomes second nature to you. You can tell if you are breathing from your diaphragm when your stomach protrudes as you fill it with air before bringing the air up into your lungs.

Practice this technique before you need to use it. Lie down and put a book on your stomach. Breathe in such a way as to lift the book up and down as you inhale and exhale. Once you have the sensation of breathing in this way you can graduate to using two books.

Put one book on your belly and the other book on our chest. As you begin your deep breath the book will rise off of your stomach before the second book rises off your chest. It's like a wave. The air will first rise in your belly and then in your chest. You will feel your chest open up and your shoulders rise as you bring in this deep, full breath.

When you breathe in this manner, your heart rate will slow down, your muscles will relax, your brain will stop releasing the adrenalin and soon you will feel calm. Once you've mastered diaphragmatic breathing laying down you'll be able to do it sitting and anytime you need it.

#5: Just Notice the Sensations of Fear

Here is another example of how just noticing can help. When Anne had daily panic attacks she started getting afraid to leave her house. I asked her to keep a journal and to notice her sensations as well as their sequence, intensity and duration. This required astute attention from Anne. She told me it helped her to get out of her body and into her head. Soon she was familiar with the beginning sensations that signaled a panic attack and she was able to start her diaphragmatic breathing before it got out of control. When she wasn't able to prevent her panic attacks, she knew that they would end soon once her hands got sweaty. "Just noticing the sequence of my symptoms helps me," Anne told me. Just noticing allowed her to prevent and manage her panic attacks.

#6: Imagine Being in a Safe Place Until Your Body's Reaction Matches the Picture in Your Mind

Even if you had an idyllic childhood, the very process of living life brings with it experiences that can interfere with the feeling of safety and calm. It's important to have a safe place that you can see, hear, smell, taste and feel in your mind's eye. Here are some examples.

"I see a clear turquoise lake. The sun is out and the sky is clear."

"I can hear the birds overhead and the lapping of the water against the boats on the dock."

"I smell the fresh air and the pine trees along the left side of the shore."

"I taste the lingering flavor of the iced lemonade that I always had at the lake."

"I can feel the cool breeze move my hair at the same time that I feel the warmth of the sun on my shoulders."

When you are choosing your safe place imagine a place where you have always been safe and only good things have happened. If nothing comes to mind, create your own safe place in your mind. Remember that this place is just for you, and no one else can come into your safe place unless you invite them.

Once you have all of your senses activated, tell yourself, "I am safe."

There's a difference between knowing you're safe and feeling safe. It's important to bring your awareness to your body. Notice how it tells you that you are safe. Pay attention and see what you are able to discern. I will walk you through this safe place practice in more depth in chapter 45, Safe Place Visualization Script. Once you have established your safe place, the next step is to commit to a daily practice of visiting it. Within about a month's time you will have a lifelong means of soothing yourself. If the 6 Self-Love Diet tools above are not sufficient you may need support from a psychotherapist or medication from a psychiatrist.

By regularly offering yourself time to slow down and gain clarity when you are feeling sensations of fear, you will decrease the time spent in over-whelming emotions that are based on False Expectations Appearing Real.

How would your life be different if your fear no longer over powered you, but rather signaled you to self-soothe?

>> Action Steps <<

A) Notice your body's signals when it is responding to fear.

B) Decide if you are in danger, or if your body is reacting to false expectations appearing real.

C) Practice self-soothing tools such as the observer, diaphragmatic breathing, just noticing and the safe place visualization.

31

Thoughts, Feeling, Actions Loop

Be in charge of your thoughts, feelings, and actions

When you make a choice, you change the future.

—Deepak Chopra

The following diagram of the Thought, Feeling, and Action Loop is the basis of Cognitive Behavioral Therapy, or CBT, an evidence based treatment modality for recovery from eating disorders, depression, mood disorders, substance abuse, as well as other diagnosis.

Here is a visual that will help you see that you can create your emotional life based on what you think or do. Using the metaphor of being the star of your own movie, imagine that you are preparing for a scene. This scene requires that you express anger. Unfortunately you have just had a great day, and are feeling very happy. How do you create the emotion of anger for this scene in the movie?

Start by thinking of a time when you were really angry. Focus on that experience until you can see yourself in that time and place. Bring all your senses to mind. Continue to remember what happened, until you can actually feel the anger in your body.

Now pay attention to the emotion of anger. When you are feeling this anger, what are you led to do? Using the metaphor of preparing for the scene in the movie, you will have a number of different options to express your anger. Perhaps you will clench your jaw, swear, or hit something. The action you take doubles back on the feeling of the emotion, increasing your experience of that emotion, and the thought contributes to continuing the loop so you can sustain this emotion for the scene in your movie.

In this example, anger is elicited by the memory of a lie. Since this is what was required for the scene in your film, WALA! You've created the exact emotion you needed to bring realism to the scene.

Unfortunately many of us use this powerful method of emotional control without even knowing, or understanding it. Here is a common Thought, Feeling, Action "loop" many people get stuck in when dieting in the old diet mentality paradigm.

If you look at this loop, you can see how the thought created the feeling that lead to the action that confirmed the thought. The person with this thought pattern is off and running and may be quite capable of eating the whole cake.

Let's take the same situation and use the TFA loop with self-love as the focus.

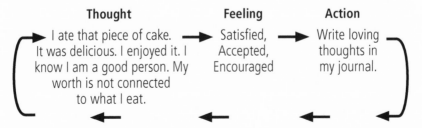

With the above examples, the behavior of eating a piece of cake is the same. Look at the difference of the feelings based on the thoughts about eating that piece of cake. This is how the Self-Love Diet gives you back control of your emotional life.

You can also choose what emotion you want to feel, and just like the actor, choose a behavior, or a thought to elicit that feeling. Let's say you want to feel happy. Start with the emotion you want to create, and use actions and thoughts to bring that emotion to you. Here's an example:

In this life you are the star of your own movie. You are in charge of your thoughts, emotions and actions. You can create your own "feel good" movie by recognizing the power you have to create and change your emotional life depending on what you think or do. Make your life's screen play a love story, not a horror film.

Word of Caution

Emotions are gifts that give us information about our life. Just like you need to listen to your body; you need to pay attention to your feelings. Don't rush into getting rid of your difficult emotions before you have the information they are giving you. If you have a genetic pre-disposition for a mood disorder that can put you at risk, please use the suggestions in this book as adjunctive help to therapy if you find yourself contemplating self-harm or thoughts of harming others. That being said, the above activity is a powerful antidote to chronic ruminations, worries, and negative thought patterns that are no longer serving you.

How would your life be different if you were able to manage your feelings based on what you do, or what you think?

>> Action Steps <<

A) Pay attention to your emotions. Use your journal to decipher what they are telling you.

B) Begin by committing one day at a time to observing your thoughts and the resulting emotions and behaviors.

C) Keep a journal of the impact of your actions on your feelings.

32

Learning to Love
through a Daily Practice

Gaining clarity on how you feel when you love yourself and others

You can only feel love by expressing it.

—Amma

Do you remember any of your teachers asking, "Okay students, who can tell me the definition of love?" My guess is you were never taught the definition of love in school.

If you were to define love, what would you say? Take a moment and think about your response. Was a quick and ready answer available to you? If so, I wonder if you asked someone else if they would have the same answer?

Love is not as black and white as math. If someone asked you what 2 x 2 was, you and most others would be able to answer almost instantly with the number 4. When asked about the definition of love, you may encounter more difficulty.

My daughter Kristina's answer was, "Love means loving someone just the way they are."

My son Albert's answer was, "Wow!" followed by silence. "Let me think", followed by more silence. "I guess, commitment. Yeah, commitment would do it."

My husband Al's response was, "How would you define love? What do you mean?"

I told him I was writing about it for my book and wanted his definition. He responded with, "I don't know. There's a lot of stuff. I mean, I'd have to think about it. It's too early."

I have to admit, it was 5:30 am, and he was just coming out of the bathroom after taking his shower, but I do think if I had asked him what 2 x 2 was, he would have been able to answer it, even that early in the morning.

After thinking for a while, he said, "Love means never taking your partner for granted."

I believe love is a noun and a verb. As a noun, I believe love is healing energy. You can feel it when it's directed your way, even if you can't touch it. Love becomes a verb when you take action.

Below are two examples of how you can cultivate love. When driving across a toll bridge, pay for the driver behind you. Imagine how you would feel if you were driving across the bridge, stopped to pay the toll and the toll collector told you that the person ahead of you had already paid for you. How would that make you feel? If you pay for the person behind you, imagine how they will feel when they find out what you did for them. Spreading small random acts of kindness can create a sense of love.

Another example of cultivating and spreading love is to let someone go before you in line at the grocery store. Remember that love as a noun is healing energy. Practicing these small acts of kindness spreads positive, healing energy to others, and in return, to yourself.

Practicing love in your relationships, you can begin by thinking about something that you are grateful for in your loved one, and then take a moment to tell them.

Before moving on, stop for a moment, and remember an experience where you felt love. Perhaps you felt love when you met your niece, son or granddaughter for the first time. Maybe you can remember the first time you said, "I love you," to your best friend. Perhaps you feel love when the little kid that you babysit, teach or mentor lights up and greets you with a running hug every time they see you, or maybe you felt love when a stranger shared a genuine smile with you.

Continue to think about this loving memory until you can feel it in your body.

Where do you feel it? Many people feel it near their hearts. It may be different for you.

How does it feel? I've heard the words, "warm, fluid and tingling." Notice what you feel.

Become familiar with how love expresses itself in your body. Practice focusing on what love feels like by using those memories that elicit your love response. Focusing on bringing love to your mind and body not only lifts your spirits, but it actually is physiologically healing.

Love needs to be practiced. Just as you had to practice your time tables in school in order to be able to tell me automatically that 2 x 2 equals 4, love needs to be practiced until it becomes an automatic response.

For most people, the definition of love has been diminished to an emotion, a surge of adrenalin that makes your heart beat when you see that special someone. Yet movie theatre love is only one dimension. Love, the way I see it, is an active, spiritual command. It's a healing energy and a positive mindset that you can cultivate. It's an energy that you can bring into all of your actions. You can choose to live your life with love. Unfortunately, many of my clients come in to see me because they're living their lives from a place of self-hatred. Over and over again, they share hateful, hurtful and critical thoughts about themselves.

We have all spoken harshly to ourselves at some point in our lives. When you do this, you are dismissing love from your life. When you catch yourself focusing on your negative traits to the detriment of your well-being, practice the following exercise to teach yourself how to treat yourself with kindness.

+ Think about the last time you remember being critical with yourself. Perhaps you called yourself stupid or criticized your body, calling your body or yourself a derogatory name.

+ Hold on to this memory. Allow yourself to feel the negative emotions it brings. Notice where you feel it in your body. Put the feeling aside for now.

+ Next, think of a person that you love. This person is your encourager, someone who wants the best for you, someone who brings you joy.

* Now imagine that the two of you are visiting in-person. Imagine yourself saying what you said to yourself to your loved one.

* Experience in your mind's eye the reaction of your loved one if you were to talk to them the way you spoke to yourself.

* Notice how you feel when you imagine this scene.

If you would never talk to the people that you love in this manner, why would you speak to yourself in such a way?

Remember the reference I made earlier to the character Giovanni in Elizabeth Gilbert's book, *Eat, Pray, Love*? He told Liz to be very polite with herself while she was learning something new. This is advice well taken. As you progress through this book, the concept of self-love still may be new to you. This may be your first time hearing about a lot of these practices and concepts. At first, practicing self-love does not come easy. If you find yourself struggling with practicing self-love as you continue to read this book, and as you continue to practice the Self-Love Diet once you've finished the book, remember the basic etiquette. Being polite to yourself is a good start.

How would your life be different if you offered yourself regular opportunities to feel the emotion of love?

>> Action Steps <<

A) Commit to your Self-Love Diet by creating a daily practice of self-love actions. Refer to the appendix to find self-love practices you can choose from, or create your own.

B) Before you go to bed each night, recall your thoughts and actions throughout the day that were focused on loving yourself, and congratulate yourself for choosing to love yourself in those moments.

C) Write a list of your positive attributes that you believe are true. Continue to add to the list as you gain more and more evidence of your positive qualities.

33

Are You an Inny or Outty?

Self-Love looks inward; diets look outward for answers to health

> *Don't let the noise of other's opinions drown out*
> *your own inner voice. And most important, have*
> *the courage to follow your heart and intuition.*
> *They somehow already know what you truly want*
> *to become. Everything else is secondary.*
>
> —Steve Jobs

Are you an Inny or an Outty? I'm not asking about your belly button right now. I'm addressing the quality of life that comes from looking within and trusting yourself versus looking to others for the answers to your life. By changing from an outty to an inny life perspective, you have the authority to dramatically change your life for the better.

The diet mentality is an outty life view. When you look outside of yourself for answers you are forfeiting the wisdom that's inside of you.

The Self-Love Diet perspective is an inny viewpoint. When you look inside of yourself for answers you discover the personal power that lives within you.

Personal power is the ability to say what you mean, mean what you say and do what you say you will. This is living congruently. In order to develop the skills to live congruently you need to learn more about yourself. What do you believe? What are your opinions? What do you want to do? In order to love yourself you need to find out who the self is. Looking inward is a good start to discovering your uniqueness.

Personal power shows up as self-confidence that comes from knowing and loving yourself. This self-confidence allows you to share who you are with others, even if you think they may disagree, be disappointed or get angry that you hold a different opinion or choose a different path.

Focusing inward for your answers brings with it the ability to listen to and learn from your intuition. This ability enables you to live an authentic life, a life that is uniquely yours.

Jane is a good example of a woman who was infused with the diet mentality. Here is her journey of how she changed from an outty to an inny perspective, which allowed her to love herself more fully.

Jane called me on the phone and told me, "I hear you work with eating issues. I've lived my whole life on and off of diets, and now I'm fatter than ever. My doctor told me yesterday that if I don't do something about my weight I'm going to end up like my mother and wind up needing knee replacements. I don't want that. I'm on medication to lower my cholesterol because my knees don't let me exercise to get it down naturally. My left knee gives me the most trouble. I start to exercise, and I keep it up for a while, and then I hurt myself. I'm at the starting point all over again. Can you help me?"

Jane came into my office the following day. "Whew! I had to stop at the middle of your flight of stairs before I got to the top," she told me as I met her in my waiting room.

Jane's salt and pepper hair was cut in a pageboy style. Her startling blue eyes matched the blue of her jogging jacket. Her black pants stretched across her ample hips, and I could see that she was walking with a limp.

When I asked Jane what her therapeutic goals were, she responded, "I want to finally lose this weight, keep it off and feel better about myself."

Jane was viewing her problems from an outty perspective. Below are some of the outwardly focused diet mentality beliefs and behaviors she brought with her to therapy. You'll notice that as Jane progressed in therapy, her beliefs and behaviors changed to an inny, self-love approach, which ultimately did allow her to feel better, not only physically, but also emotionally.

Jane had a history of putting her faith into the latest diet "expert" whose book would tell her how to eat properly for her body.

Outty

By looking toward the latest "expert" Jane would look outside of herself for the answers. She had lost faith that she had any expertise when it came to knowing how and what to eat in order to maintain a healthy weight range.

Inny

To help Jane change to an inny perspective I had her recall when her children were infants. She remembered they intuitively knew when they were hungry and when they were satisfied. She was open to relearning her body's hunger and satiation signals. Jane also began to explore the message her body and mind were giving her when she had food cravings but realized she was not physically hungry.

Jane would ignore her physical hunger cues if it wasn't time to eat according to her new diet.

Outty

Jane was disregarding her body's signals. Her history of being an outty did not prepare her to look within to assess when it was time to eat. Jane looked toward the experts outside of herself for the answers. When Jane felt hungry, but followed her outty rules, she disregarded the treasure chest of information that lived inside of her. The answers she sought were within her all the time, similar to Dorothy in the Wizard of Oz.

Inny

When Jane developed an inny focus, she began to trust that her body knew what, when and how to eat. She learned to track her level of hunger on a one equals starving to ten equals stuffed scale. In time, she began to trust her body to tell her when she was hungry and when she was satisfied.

Jane would eat things she didn't like because they were on her diet plan.

Outty

Jane didn't question the fact that she didn't like cabbage. If her diet said this is what she should be eating, she obeyed the rules.

Inny

With Jane's new inny focus, she began to ask her body what it wanted and was given the answers. She allowed herself to slow down and enjoy her food. She found that her eating experiences were much more enjoyable from this inny way of choosing what, when and how to eat.

Jane looked for the next new diet that would propose the "right" way of eating, or the newest product that would jump start her towards her goal after she regained her weight back from her latest diet attempt.

Outty

Instead of looking within, Jane kept an outty focus by believing that the answer was waiting for her if she could just find the right diet. This approach kept Jane blaming herself for failing.

Inny

When Jane began thinking from an inny perspective, her focus expanded beyond eating. She began journaling, drawing, meditating and writing. These activities helped her focus inward for her answers. She later joined a support group where she felt safe to verbally explore what she wanted in her life beyond losing weight.

Jane counted calories, carbohydrates and fat content when deciding what foods to buy.

Outty

Jane told me that she had two kinds of shopping experiences. If she wasn't hungry, she was in her numbers crunching mindset. She would focus on the calories, the percentage of fat and the nutrients of her foods.

"It felt as if I were eating numbers," she told me. "In fact, I'd enjoy eating a food because I would compare it to a higher cal food that I didn't choose at the store. While I was at home eating, I wasn't thinking about eating. I wasn't tasting the food. My mind was still absorbed in the calories and the smart choice that I had made with the food with fewer calories."

Jane's second type of shopping experience happened when she was hungry.

"I'd impulsively buy foods because I saw them, not because I had any food plan or menu in mind," she told me. "I leaned toward convenient, starchy foods, or sweet deserts, like cookies, cracker jacks, pies or puddings."

Inny

Jane transformed her food shopping experience when she used her inny perspective versus her old numbers crunching method of buying foods. She became aware of the beautiful colors of the vegetables and the texture of the grains. She enjoyed the aromas of the fruits. Once she was inner-focused, her trust in herself grew as she chose foods that were attractive, flavorful and satisfying.

Jane got triggered by foods that were off her list when she saw or smelled them, even when she wasn't hungry.

Outty

Jane's outty way of living made her vulnerable to her external surroundings. She instantly desired food that she saw on T.V. commercials, even if she had just finished a complete and satisfying meal. If Jane was out shopping after a full lunch and walked by a bakery, the sight and smell of the bakery goods grabbed her attention. She was unable to enjoy the artistic displays and aromas without compulsively eating them.

Inny

Jane's new inny approach to life allowed her to check-in with herself when she noticed she was craving a food. She was learning to assess if she was physically hungry or if this craving was some different need within her. She was making progress on eating when hungry and redirecting her desire to eat when her appetite was not related to physical hunger.

Jane felt responsible to eat something if someone offered it to her, even if she wasn't hungry, or even if it wasn't on her diet, so she wouldn't offend the person.

Outty

Jane had a complicated relationship with her mother-in-law. They loved each other and had created an eating relationship. They were eating buddies. Her mother-in-law baked goodies when she came to visit. Jane was pressured to eat the baked goods, even when she was full or didn't want to. She was eating to please her mother-in-law. Jane believed that if she said no to the food, she would be saying no to her mother-in-law who she loved dearly.

Inny

When Jane stopped using food as a substance, and only ate when physically hungry, her relationship with her mother-in-law became strained. Jane struggled to focus on what she wanted, instead of what others wanted or needed from her. Jane made a major life shift when she began telling her mother-in-law "No thanks" when she was not hungry. "I love my mother-in-law. I don't have to eat to prove it," she told me.

Jane would walk-jog for a specific amount of time, tracking her heart rate, although it was not enjoyable to her.

Outty

Jane knew that she needed to exercise more, and so she would punish herself by walk-jogging after eating more than she thought she should have.

"This is my pay back for overindulging," she told me.

This diet mentality approach to exercise kept Jane from enjoying exercising and created a punishing attitude toward her body.

Inny

At this point in Jane's self-love work, her outty focus of what she "should do" became her guiding light. Whenever she recognized that she was shoulding, she knew it was an invitation to check-in with her intuition, which she was beginning to trust. Jane explored the question, what do I enjoy doing? She soon discovered that she loved dancing. She began line dancing, swing, and even tango lessons.

Jane had faith that a new diet would be the right one that would fix her problem.

Outty

Jane's outty viewpoint kept her continually on the lookout for the next messiah that would save her from her life of indentured servitude to her past diet guru. She believed that the problem was her inability to stay strong.

"If I could just lose this weight and keep it off everything would be fine," she told me.

Inny

As Jane continued to work with me, she began to realize that her problem wasn't really about weight. What she discovered was that she needed to learn new ways to recognize, feel and express her emotions. She learned new ways to self-soothe when she was anxious, and as she continued to choose more loving behaviors, she began to think more lovingly towards herself and towards the important people in her life.

Jane was irritable and felt deprived of the foods she wanted.

Outty

When Jane was hungry but knew that it wasn't time to eat, or when she had eaten foods that she didn't find satisfying, she would get angry, irritable and be difficult to get along with. She had given her power to the diet and often felt angry and deprived of the comfort her favorite foods gave her.

Inny

As Jane learned how and why she was craving certain foods, she was able to decide what choices made her feel good and what choices didn't. Soon she was not depriving herself any longer. She was now in charge of deciding what and when she would eat. She noticed that sometimes she chose to eat even though she wasn't physically hungry. She told me, "When I consciously choose to eat something, even if I'm not hungry, I don't' punish myself, and I find that by giving myself permission, I eat less than if I'm rebelling against my diet.

Jane tried her best not to eat past 8 pm at night.

Outty

Nighttime seemed to be the most difficult time for Jane. She reported, "I can be good all day, eat a healthy dinner, then I blow my diet each night."

Inny

Jane learned about HALT, trigger emotions.

H = Hungry? Hurt?

A = Angry? Anxious?

L = Lonely?

T = Tired?

Jane soon realized that she was eating because she was tired. Just like babies get fidgety and irritable when they're tired, Jane found that she was wound up after dinner. She was using food to soothe herself. As Jane learned how and why she was craving certain foods, she was able to decide what choices made her feel good and what choices didn't. Soon she was exchanging late night eating for going to bed. "When I'm tired, sleep makes more sense than food."

As Jane learned to focus inward for her answers, she became her own expert. As you continue practicing the Self-Love Diet, notice when you begin to change from an outty to an inny perspective.

How would your life be different if you trusted your inner wisdom?

>> Action Steps <<

A) Spend time each day or night focusing inward for your answers.

B) Notice when you're looking outside of yourself for answers, and ask yourself what would love do?

C) When you have a decision to make, ask yourself what you're feeling, why you're feeling it and what you want.

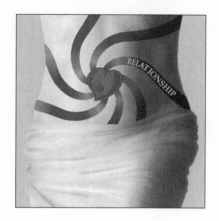

Relationship Path

When we seek to discover the best in others, we
somehow bring out the best in ourselves.

—William Arthur Ward

The Relationship Path of the Self-Love Diet

The most important relationship begins with you. The way you think and feel about yourself affects the way you act with others.

Carol came to see me for her weight problem. We were soon able to uncover that Carol used food to mask her feelings of not being good enough. Carol had created a pattern in her family of being the go to girl. Whenever her widowed father, older sister or younger brother needed help, they would go to Carol because she would always say yes.

This didn't seem to be problematic until Carol got married and started her own family. Soon she found herself stretched too thin, trying to balance her time between her husband, her two young boys and her family of origin.

Carol and I worked together on setting boundaries, and she was eventually able to realize that she didn't need to be helpful to be loved.

"Focusing on me, being more myself and being more grounded helps me connect more with my family," Carol told me. "What I offer my family is now more true and rich. I'm finally doing things for the right reasons. I used to say yes when I really wanted to say no. Now when I say yes, I mean it, and my joy has increased when I'm helping them out. I'm not feeling used or resentful because I say no when I mean no. Now, when I help my family I'm more in the present. I have a feeling of love and connection with them because when I'm with them, I really want to be there."

Setting boundaries is one way to love yourself, and ultimately, it strengthens your relationships with others. Having healthy, loving relationships is an inside job. In the Relationships Path of the Self-Love Diet, you will learn, and soon experience, how self-love is the means in which your relationships are improved.

34

Gratitude

This emotion is an essential building block for a healthy relationship

Gratitude unlocks the fullness of life. It turns what we have into enough, and more. It turns denial into acceptance, chaos to order, confusion to clarity. It can turn a meal into a feast, a house into a home, a stranger into a friend.

—Melody Beattie

Sometimes the simplest suggestions are the most powerful. If I were to choose only one activity that would have the most impact on the largest number of people, I would choose to have everyone start each morning by focusing on what they are grateful for. I'm not asking you to make a cursory list. Instead, I invite you to consider staying in bed each morning while you think about what you are grateful for until you can feel the sensations of gratitude throughout your body.

The emotion of gratitude is healing, and thoughts of gratitude set your mind in the right direction for each day. If you wake up each morning lethargic and not wanting to get out of bed, there's a good chance your thoughts are to blame.

Imagine putting water in the gas tank of your car, instead of gas. How would your car run? By having a practice of counting your blessings before you get out of bed each day, you are fueling your mind and emotions with quality gas to get you through your day.

While thinking about what you're grateful for at the start of the day, it can help you to appreciate the everyday occurrences that you take for granted. You may realize that you're grateful for sight, to see beautiful sunsets, for hearing, to listen to your favorite music or for your legs, to get you where you want to go. When you start your day grateful for the gifts your body gives you, you are appreciating your body for what it does and how it makes you feel, rather than putting its value on how it looks.

When you use this same strategy towards the important people in your life, magic can ensue.

Gratitude is an essential building block for a healthy relationship. When you practice gratitude you will enhance your relationships, whether the relationship is with yourself or another. Maggie and David are a good example of how focusing on what they were grateful for in one another strengthened their relationship.

Maggie and David came to see me because they were having trouble in their marriage. They both had high-power jobs before they had children. They decided to wait to have kids until they saved enough money so that Maggie could stay home with them. David had recently become the Vice President of the company he had been working for and was providing financially for himself, Maggie and their three young children. Although Maggie and David had agreed that she would stay home with the children, Maggie was seeing the toll this position was having on David.

Maggie wanted to get a job and contribute financially for the family so David could step down or change careers. David was not open to Maggie working outside of their home. They stated that they loved each other deeply, but they found themselves arguing and feeling resentful and angry towards each other. They came to an impasse on this issue.

I asked David and Maggie to put the issue aside for the moment and to describe each other's contributions to the family in positive terms. As we continued exploring their roles and contributions, it became clear that this session was the first time they had expressed their gratitude towards each other. "We don't do what we do for compliments," David stated.

With a little prompting, both were willing to look into each other's eyes and tell one another what they appreciated about each other. Maggie expressed her gratitude to David for showing his love by working so hard to provide for them financially. She also shared her loneliness and told him that she missed him. I watched as David's face softened, shoulders relaxed and eyes glistened.

I am always touched and impressed by the power that gratitude and emotional honesty have in relationships. David was able to repeat what Maggie said to him, thereby expanding and strengthening his experience of the moment and confirming that he had heard her correctly.

Next, David expressed his gratitude to Maggie. Looking into her eyes and touching her knee, he told her that he was grateful for the 24-7 care and love she provided for their children. He spoke about his appreciation of her decision to nurse them all, and acknowledged that he could sleep through their youngest one's cries in the middle of the night. He thanked her for getting up with their baby, even when he knew that she was just as exhausted as he was.

I noticed Maggie's reaction when David acknowledged that she was just as exhausted as he was. Her next breath was deeper as she inhaled fully, and she nodded her head up and down. She kept contact with David's eyes. Next, she laid her hand on top of David's hand, and the two of them sat silently as they continued looking into each other's eyes.

There is an energetic field that is tangible when I'm working with my clients. In the silence between Maggie and David, I could feel the gratitude and love between them.

David and Maggie were right on target with what they shared with each other. Not all of my clients are able to do this activity on the first time with such attunement.

I offer this as a practice for you. If you are not as smooth as Maggie and David were, it's okay. It's a skill that grows with practice. Below is another practice to help you become aware of the shift in your emotions when you bring your attention to gratitude.

Think of an important person in your life who you are not totally happy with in this moment. Focus on what you don't like about their behaviors. Now bring your attention to how you feel. What do you notice? Where do you notice it in your body?

Thinking of the same person, focus on the qualities that you are grateful for. Remember the attributes that attracted you to this person. Allow yourself time to feel how their positive traits make you feel. What emotions are you aware of? Where are you aware of these feelings in your body?

Write your experience in your Self-Love Diet Journal. Notice the shift in your emotions when you bring your attention to gratitude. Remember that your emotions affect the way that you interact with others, which affects your relationships either positively or negatively.

If you are not a journal writer, take a few moments now to expand on this experience by reviewing the previous questions and by noticing the difference in your emotions and in your body when you switched from what you didn't like to what you were grateful for. Take notice and sit with this awareness a while before you continue to read on.

Being grateful for your partner, friend, family member or coworker will not automatically fix the problem, but it will allow you to have a wider perspective and will facilitate more positive conversations. When you take people out of the black and white, good and bad categories, you are able to clearly see their strengths and weaknesses. When you work with the whole person, rather than focusing on their faults, you invite their better selves to join your better self.

By regularly offering yourself love through the practice of gratitude, you are creating your best self.

How would your life be different if you brought gratitude into all of your relationships?

>> Action Steps <<

A) Start each morning with thoughts of gratitude for your body and yourself until you can feel the positive sensations of this emotion.

B) End the day with thoughts about the people, occurrences and circumstances that you're grateful for. Stay with this activity until you can feel the benefit in your body, mind and spirit.

C) Write in your Self-Love Diet journal to focus on the positive qualities of someone you are having a difficult relationship with. The difficult relationship doesn't have to be with someone else. You can work on your relationship with yourself.

35

Curiosity

The power of asking vs. assuming in relationships

The first and simplest emotion which we discover
in the human mind, is curiosity.

—Edmund Burke

When you are curious it infers that you don't know the answer and are interested in finding it out. Curiosity keeps you on the edge of your seat and fully present in your life.

According to *Self Magazine*, "People who describe themselves as intentionally curious report greater life satisfaction and a deeper sense of meaning. They're also apt to push themselves to learn and meet their goals."

Curiosity may have killed the cat, but it puts life back into important relationships, including the one with yourself. If you have been in a relationship for many years, you can begin to assume that you know the other person inside and out. That assumption is not always true. Even in your relationship with yourself you may assume certain truths about yourself that are incorrect.

Candy is a good example of someone who assumed she knew herself better than I would as her therapist. On the outside, we would all assume that she was right. She came in for her first session and I had sat with her for only an hour. How could I know her better than she knew herself?

I have a belief that everyone is inherently lovable and deserving of good things. I know everyone does not share my belief.

Candy did not. She assumed that she was worthless, and although she agreed that her husband and son saw her differently, she believed they were wrong. She suffered from depression all her life, and when she came to see me she had struggled with bulimia for over 20 years.

I began to get curious and asked her about the important relationships in her life. Candy told me about her father who provided for the family financially, but was seldom home. When he did come home, she never knew what to expect. He was often drunk and dangerous. He was violent with her mother, and as she and her brother got older he began beating them as well. Her mother did not protect them. "It felt like my mother, brother and I were siblings," she told me.

The assumption that she was worthless began to make sense as we talked about how she survived those years. As a young girl, it would be unlikely to believe that she was lovable and worthy of loving treatment when she all too often experienced the opposite. In order to survive her chaotic and uncertain childhood, it certainly made more sense to believe that she was deserving of maltreatment. If that was so, life made sense. If she was to blame for making her father so angry, then she could fix it. If she kept her bed made just right, he wouldn't scream at her and tell her how sloppy she was. If she brought home straight A's, he couldn't beat her for getting a B–. Candy began to recognize how important it was for her to believe that *she* was not OK in order to give her a sense of power that she could change things by controlling her actions.

She was beginning to understand why she held herself to such high standards and felt as if she had to be perfect. As a child, these behaviors were coping mechanisms that helped her to survive. Even with this awareness, Candy's beliefs about herself would take a long while to change. In the mean time, when she noticed herself thinking longstanding beliefs about herself, she began to ask, "Is that true?" Curiosity helped her to live in the moment rather than reenacting old stories from the past.

When I work with couples, I teach them about the importance of curiosity right away. It is vital to add this skill to your repertoire of relationship abilities.

Todd Kashdan, PhD, author of *Curious?*, states, "As soon as we think we're an expert in something we usually stop paying attention and switch into autopilot ... Rather than starting with a rote, 'What's going on at the office?' Find out what weird or funny or interesting thing happened that day ... You'll both end up being more engrossed in the discussion, and the result is a stronger relationship."

The majority of couples I have worked with in my private practice have fallen into behavioral patterns, or roles, that lead to assumptions about one another. The companion to curiosity is a conscious commitment to replace assumptions with agreements. If you think you know what your partner's response will be, you won't even ask. Many lovely surprises can be missed if you don't ask because you believe you already know the answer.

Joseph and Malinda had a library of stories about one another by the time they came to see me. Malinda felt alone in the relationship and complained that Joseph did not know how to express his feelings. She had instances dating back 20 years to prove her point. Joseph complained that Malinda constantly criticized him, and he felt that no matter how hard he tried he would never be able to please her. He was discouraged, angry and felt hopeless. Each time Malinda initiated conversations or conflict, Joseph retreated further and further away.

They assumed the worst of each other, and in doing so, actually invited the worse from one another. They had long ago lost their curiosity about each other, assuming they would never change. Even when Malinda was encouraging and complimentary, and even when Joseph was heartfelt and supportive in session, it was hard for both of them to see the progress they were making. Their litany of stories about one another got in their way of seeing each other clearly, even when there was evidence to support the changes they were making.

Soon after we began our work together they agreed to be curious and to work on asking each other questions rather than making assumptions. In our next session, Malinda bypassed her assumptions about Joseph not liking sentimental movies and asked if he would like to go with her to watch the movie *The Notebook* the upcoming weekend. Joseph's response was, "That's a chick flick." Next he suggested, "Why don't you invite Carol?"

"See? I do know him," Malinda smiled smugly, although I sensed sadness around her eyes.

I became curious about Joseph's sentiments regarding chick flicks. As we continued to explore his response to Malinda's request, Joseph recalled watching the movie *Bambi* as a seven-year-old boy. He told us that he remembered crawling into his mother's lap and crying when Bambi's mother died. His brows furrowed and his shoulders tensed as he recounted his father ridiculing him mercilessly by calling him a crybaby and a girly girl and by garnering his older brothers into laughing at him. As Joseph recounted this memory, he was surprised and confused by the tears in his eyes and the lump in his throat. As I guided him to experience his sensations and learn where they lived in his body, he was better able to glean the information they were providing him. After taking a deep breath, he was able to connect the dots of this memory to his current day judgments on chick flicks.

"I've always known emotions were not comfortable for me, but I thought it was a gender thing. I never put two and two together."

After that experience in my office, Malinda and Joseph made a commitment to ask questions of each other and then make agreements rather than assumptions. With the marriage of their daughter coming up, they agreed to be curious about each other's thoughts and opinions regarding all the decisions they would be making.

As Malinda and Joseph continued to work on improving their relationship, Malinda confessed, "We've been together long enough for me to know what Joseph's responses will generally be, but I can still be surprised when I'm curious and ask instead of assume."

How would your life be different if you consciously brought curiosity into your relationships?

>> Action Steps <<

A) Start by being curious about how you think about yourself. Challenge the ways you see yourself.

B) Be mindful of making assumptions. Even if you think you know the answer, ask an important person in your life what their opinion is.

C) Use your Self-Love Diet journal to recount those times that curiosity helped you experience life in a fresh and vital way.

36

An Invitation to Look Within

Seeing what you don't like in others
is an invitation to change yourself

We don't see things as they are;
we see them as we are.

—Anais Nin

Have you ever looked at an important person in your life and criticized or blamed them? When you do this, it can be an invitation to turn your focus onto you. Mary and Tom are a great example of using blame as a signal to look inside and learn important things about yourself and others.

Mary called to make an appointment for her and her husband Tom. She stated on the phone that their youngest child was ready to graduate from high school. Mary had recently gotten a promotion as an information systems manager, which required extensive trainings and much more responsibility. Just when they needed the comfort and closeness that a healthy sexual relationship needs, they found themselves fighting and distant. They both were worried because soon they would have an empty nest, and they were experiencing difficulty with sex for the first time in their relationship.

They came into my office the next day. Tom was a tall burly man with a ruddy complexion. He was a lineman and had recently gone back to work after a work-related injury. He stated that Mary was not interested in sex anymore even though she talked about it all the time. He said that she was blaming him for not wanting it, but it was her who didn't want to have sex anymore.

Mary was a short woman, less than 5 feet tall, and petite. She was upset with Tom because he had not initiated sex for over a month. She thought he must be interested in someone else. Why else would he not want sex with her anymore?

After I brought their blaming communication style to their attention they agreed to put the blaming aside while in my office, and they began to speak honestly and listen openly as I asked them more questions.

Mary had failed to see that although she initiated sex once, she too was not initiating sex like she used to. As I continued to be curious she was able to say that it took her longer to climax now that she was in menopause, and this caused her some frustration with herself and Tom. She also noticed that she did not speak to Tom about wanting to be sexual until she was hurt, angry and blaming him for the situation.

When Mary brought her attention to herself, she realized that although she wanted to receive Tom's touch and sexual attention, she was overworked and the thought of having to reciprocate made her feel tired and angry. The traveling that came with her promotion was draining and not as exciting as she had anticipated. I helped Mary to take the focus off of Tom and helped her refocus her attention on her feelings and beliefs. Soon she became aware of a number of beliefs she had not been conscious of.

Mary's Beliefs

#1 Tom should initiate sex more than me because he always has. He's a man, and men have a higher sex drive.

#2 If Tom doesn't initiate sex, then it means he doesn't like having sex with me anymore.

#3 We should take turns initiating sex. After I initiate, it's Tom's turn.

#4 It's selfish to want to receive sexually without giving back.

#5 It makes you a better person if you please the other person rather than receive sexual pleasure.

#6 If we don't have the same passion as the movie stars we see in the movies, then that means there's something wrong with our relationship.

#7 Tom should make me come each time we have sex. If I don't orgasm, he has failed.

#8 If Tom is not initiating sex with me, perhaps he's having sex with someone else.

If Mary had stayed focused on blaming Tom and had not looked inside herself, she would never have discovered her beliefs. Now that she was aware of what her thoughts were on the subject, she could understand her behaviors and emotions more clearly. She had greater compassion for herself and Tom.

She looked at the bigger picture and realized that she needed comfort and support from Tom while she was going through this career transition. She discovered that they both had used their sex life to reduce stress and increase comfort. She learned about the changes her body was going through with menopause and learned ways to work with the changes. When Mary took the time to delve within herself, she felt more attuned to Tom because she was not the victim. She could clarify her questions and assumptions, and she could see her part in their struggle with their sexual relationship.

Next, I helped Tom take the focus off of Mary and helped him to look at his feelings and beliefs. Soon he became aware of a number of thoughts he had not been conscious of.

Tom's Beliefs

#1 Sex should be fun and easy.

#2 It's my job to make Mary orgasm. It's taking her much longer to come, and sometimes she doesn't achieve an orgasm at all. I am failing.

#3 If Mary loves me, she'd be excited enough by me to come.

#4 I work hard all day and now sex feels like it's work too.

#5 I've started watching porn to try to bring back the spark in our sex life. Mary does not want to watch it; she is not trying to make things better.

By looking inward, Tom learned that he had been feeling confused, resentful and guilty about Mary's changing sexual responses. He also realized that he felt neglected when she was home. Now that he was aware of what his beliefs were, he understood his behaviors and emotions more clearly. He had greater compassion for himself and Mary.

He saw the bigger picture and realized that he needed comfort and support from Mary while they traversed menopause and her new career together. He discovered that their past easy sex life had contributed to confidence in himself. He needed to be curious about how he could still feel sexually competent even if Mary didn't orgasm as easily as she used to.

After Tom took the time to investigate his beliefs, he felt more attuned to Mary. He stopped feeling as if he had to know what to do. He worked with Mary to be curious and figure out together what worked.

Tom and Mary worked well together once they adopted the tool of curiosity. They could see the impact these beliefs and emotions had in their sexual relationship. Once they stopped blaming each other and themselves, they were able to talk constructively and figured out how to work together towards their common goal of more sexual intimacy.

If you are thinking about a relationship that you are in and you can't think of your piece of the problem, notice when you are pointing your finger at your partner and imagine that there are three fingers pointing back at you. When you catch yourself blaming someone, this is a practice you can use in any circumstance to help you put the focus on yourself to better understand your feelings and beliefs that are surrounding the blame.

(Pointing finger by Adam Crowe)

1 The first finger tells you to ask yourself, "What am I feeling?"

2 The second finger informs you to ask yourself, "Why am I feeling this emotion?"

3 The third finger reminds you to ask yourself, "What do I want?"

When you realize that you are blaming someone, it becomes an opportunity to look within and become more attuned with your emotions and thoughts. You are able to get to know yourself better, and if you find yourself in a relationship where someone is doing something you don't like, you will have the clarity to share with them what it is you are feeling, why you are feeling it and what you want. They will no longer be put in the position to be mind readers because you will have done your work and spoken your truth. Bringing your focus to the three fingers pointing back at you when you are focusing on someone else allows you to communicate your emotions, motivations, needs, wants and preferences in an honest, respectful and assertive manner.

Suzanne and Pat are an example of a couple that I worked with where one of them couldn't see their part of the problem. Suzanne did not believe she had a part of the problem. Her husband Pat had the eating disorder, so why did she need to look within herself?

This is a common dynamic that shows up when I'm working with a family or a couple where one person has an eating disorder and the other partner, or family members, do not. The non-eating disordered person is always affected by the eating disorder, therefore always has a part. Usually, the non-eating disordered person tries a number of strategies that do not help the situation, and can actually make it worse.

Suzanne loved Pat but was at her wits end. She was frustrated and tired of Pat's failed attempts at weight loss. She had been cooking for Pat and serving him portions she considered adequate because she was concerned about his health. This set up an unhealthy dynamic between the two of them. Pat would sneak extra food when Suzanne wasn't looking, or he would make excuses to go to the store so he could buy himself food he was craving that he knew Suzanne would not allow him to eat. When Pat ordered his meals at restaurants Suzanne would answer for him, "No, he doesn't want the bread. He'll take the fruit." Pat would get angry and they would end up fighting. Although Suzanne was correct in seeing that Pat was having a problem with eating, she couldn't see her contribution to the problems they were having with their relationship.

Once Suzanne was able to see her piece, and how it was setting up a power struggle between them, she said to me, "Well, that's great. What am I supposed to do? Just sit at the restaurant and watch Pat order a double bacon cheeseburger?

The answer to that question was "Yes."

Pat had to learn how to make his own food choices without the dynamic of choosing something because Suzanne wouldn't want him to. He had to learn how foods made him feel and how much energy they gave him, or took from him. He had to learn when he was hungry and when he was satisfied. As long as Suzanne was trying to help him by making those choices for him, he would never learn those lessons for himself.

"So what do I do when Pat eats too much, or chooses foods that aren't healthy?"

"Use the three fingers pointing at you exercise," I responded.

Here is what Suzanne shared in session with Pat.

- First Finger: "I feel angry, scared and frustrated."

- Second Finger: "I feel these emotions because I love you, and I want you to be healthy so we can live a long life together and enjoy our upcoming retirement together. I'm afraid you're killing yourself to spite me."

- Third Finger: "I want you to make healthy choices for yourself so you will be around for me."

When Suzanne did her work of gaining clarity of her feelings and sharing her emotions and thoughts with Pat rather than trying to control his behaviors, it changed the dynamic between them from one of power and control to one of respect and emotional honesty.

By doing your part by going within, you gain clarity about your emotions, the reasons behind them and what you want. Once you have calmed down enough to do this work, you are in a better position to have a constructive conversation where the goal is to be emotionally honest. Even if the circumstance doesn't change on the outside, you will have gone within and spoken your truth.

By going within and gaining clarity about your emotions, needs and wants, you can then stop blaming your partner and communicate to them how you're feeling and what it is you need and want, which fosters emotional honesty and healthy relationships.

How would your life be different if you stopped blaming others and looked inward with curiosity and compassion?

>> Action Steps <<

A) Pay attention to when you are blaming others.

B) Write out a time when you blamed someone. Be curious and find your part in the situation. Compassionately look for patterns in your behaviors and beliefs that don't serve you.

C) If you don't believe you have a piece in a problem, use the Three Fingers Pointing at Me exercise to gain clarity on how you feel, why you feel it and what you want, then share your insights with your partner.

37

Will the Real You Please Stand Up?

Speaking your truth builds lasting relationships

*It takes courage to grow up and turn out
to be who you really are.*

—E.E. Cummings

Growing up in the 60s, I enjoyed watching a television show called *To Tell the Truth*. Each show featured a person with an unusual occupation or life story, along with two other people who tried to trick celebrity panelists into believing that the story was theirs. Three contestants would state that they were the real Mr. Smith, or whatever the person's name was. The two imposters could lie, but the real Mr. Smith had to tell the truth. The basic premise of the show was to see if the four celebrity panelists could guess which one of the three people sitting behind the desk was the real Mr. Smith.

If you've ever been in a relationship where you have found it difficult to discover who the person is that you were dating, then you'll know the difficulty of creating a lasting, healthy relationship if your partner is not showing up authentically.

Have you ever said yes to an activity that you really didn't want to do because you were trying to be pleasing? If this becomes a habit, it can become a problem in a relationship. Maybe you've been on the other end and have experienced the eventual exasperation of the response, "It doesn't matter to me. Whatever you want is good." You may begin to feel like you're losing touch with your partner and that you're no longer recognizing who they are.

Telling the truth is not always easy. Fear of rejection is a human experience that harks back to evolution when our survival depended on our ability to belong to a group.

Old misguided beliefs such as, "I'm not good enough the way I am" or, "I better pretend because if he/she really knew me, I'd be rejected" get in the way of your ability to live authentically, and ultimately get in the way of your ability to be emotionally intimate. The amazing truth is that when we tell people our secrets, we are surprised to find out that they actually bring us closer together.

I have experienced this myself with my Circle Sisters, a group of women who I have been meeting with once a month since 2007. We start off our circle with drumming, silence, writing or meditation. Then we each light a candle and speak our intentions for the evening, or in life. We use a talking stick to take turns sharing our responses to the prompts that guide our sharing. Other times we speak spontaneously from our hearts. Over the years, we've noticed a willingness to delve deeper and share things that we may or may not have realized we were withholding.

One night, I got caught in the trap of comparisons. During our silent meditation time, I looked around the circle and made contact with the startling blue eyes of one of my Circle Sisters who bicycles in races. I smiled, averted my eyes and began to think, *She trains for bicycle races by riding 10 miles, and the eventual race can be up to 100 miles. She has a lean body. I don't see any extra fat anywhere.* I then brought my attention to my midsection and noticed my stomach pouching as I sat on the soft sofa in the muted light of the floor lamp.

The next woman who caught my attention is adept at yoga. She is so flexible that her legs are able to stretch outward in a straight line from her hips. She's also an avid hiker. Again, my eyes went to her slight frame. For the second time that evening, I compared my body's appearance and abilities, and came up short.

I was now on a roll. My eyes scanned for more evidence of my inadequacy, and I landed on another fit woman in the group who is a physical therapist. She's trained to be of service to those with injuries. As I was observing her well-defined muscular arms, I began to notice what I was doing. I took a breath to ground myself and to just notice and then let go of my critical thoughts, but my eyes began to stray to the three other women who are professional artists.

One woman had a successful career in the world of design. She is also a talented music teacher, has published a spiritual based book and is trained in Reiki. The other two are living a consistent dream of mine as professional artists. Their work has been in galleries, and they have a flair and ease with their artwork that felt better than my abilities. The last woman my eyes landed on just finished her dissertation and now has her PhD.

That night, our prompt was honesty. We hit the Tibetan bowl to signal the transition from silence to sharing. My Circle Sisters began taking turns speaking about their lives, their struggles and their intentions. When the talking stick was laid down next to our white ceramic bowl of four Indian women holding our flickering candles, I felt my heart pounding in my ears. I told myself it wasn't necessary to share these thoughts and feelings because I knew what was true: our bodies' shapes do not reflect our value. However, since honesty was our prompt for the evening, I decided to share my self-critical thoughts in comparing myself to them.

As I shared my mental act of comparing myself to them, it was astounding to feel my connections grow stronger and more intimate. The talking stick was picked up by woman after woman as each Circle Sister shared similar feelings and thoughts.

We discovered that we were not alone in thinking that others were better than us in some way. This simple act of truth telling helped us all to connect with each other in a way that went beyond the outer comparisons. By sharing our vulnerability, we became stronger and surer of ourselves, and of each other.

How would your life be different if you consistently spoke your truth?

>> Action Steps <<

A) Think of a relationship where you relinquish your desires to someone else. What do you notice when you don't speak your truth?

B) Write about a time when you said one thing, but meant or believed something else. How did that make you feel?

C) Decide to tell the truth next time someone asks your opinion. Let them know how you feel or think about the situation. Remember it's okay to agree to disagree. Notice what happens.

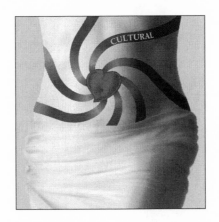

Cultural Path

*You are the most powerful cultural force
in the world.*

—William J. Clinton

The Cultural Path of the Self-Love Diet

You are the culture. Every action you take is reflective of the myriad of choices available to you. You are bombarded with choices. Pay attention. Our culture teaches you to be unsatisfied with yourself. There is big money in products and services that will make you "culturally acceptable".

Love yourself enough to fight back. Use self-love as your weapon.

When you read magazines, notice how you feel about yourself before you read them. Then check in with yourself after you read them. Research has reported self-esteem declines after viewing the airbrushed images in magazines.

When listening to music, pay attention. What are the messages you may be singing along to? Do they help you to feel good about yourself?

Notice the physicality of our movie actors. Do you see your body type typically portrayed? What types of stories are being told on the screen? Pay attention to how you feel after watching a movie. Was your money well spent?

Our capitalist country and our culture operate on how we spend our money. Spend it well. Pay attention to what cultural messages you are supporting with your money.

Although will live in a culture that tells us we need to look a certain way, dress a certain way and act a certain way to be accepted so that we will buy into the latest trends and buy the latest products, there is a growing counter culture. The good news is that progress is being made internationally in the area of self-love and body love. Kate Winslet confronted the practice of airbrushing when her body was changed without her permission on the cover of a national magazine. Emme, a plus size super model, is an advocate for body acceptance. Celebrities are sharing their personal stories of recovery from eating disorders, resulting in fewer stigmas towards eating disorders. People in the eating disorder field organized a boycott against Ralph Lauren's clothing line that featured an airbrushed image of an already ultra thin model, creating an image to anorexic standards.

As you focus on increasing loving thoughts and actions towards yourself, notice how your perception of our culture begins to shift. You may see things in a different light when you look through the lens of self-love. Together we can make our culture reflect our highest ideals, one person at a time.

38

Wars and Diets

What do they have in common?

*To go against the dominant thinking of your
friends, of most of the people you see every day, is
perhaps the most difficult act of heroism you can
perform.*

—Theodore H. White

In 1996, C. Everett Koop, the prevailing Surgeon General, declared
"War on Obesity." A CNN Health article announced, "Koops organization,
Shape Up America, introduced new medical guidelines … urging doctors
to treat obesity as a dangerous and chronic disease to be treated with diet,
exercise, drugs and even surgery.'"

What do wars and diets have in common?

Just as diets, drugs and even surgery are not the answer to long-term maintenance of weight loss, wars have not been the answer to long-term maintenance
of peace. Although wars have been started to end the violence of people who
are being victimized, every war creates new victims and new enemies. The war
business, like the diet industry, actually creates the necessity for their services.

Diets create an environment for gaining back more weight, developing
disordered eating, or encouraging eating disorders. The common phenomenon
of yo-yo dieting creates new victims continuing the demand for the products
sold by the diet industry.

Beyond the established eating disordered categories, there are 25 million other people who struggle with compulsive overeating, or binge eating syndrome. Many more "normal" eaters fight their bodies to try and create the culturally acceptable size or shape that cannot be attained through natural, healthy means.

We have been brainwashed into believing our bodies should look like the ones we see in the media. This body-dissatisfaction has led to body-hatred and self loathing for many.

You may never have sought help or treatment, but rather have thought that *you* are the problem. If so, you have mistakenly blamed yourself for a lack of will power to commit to a diet and exercise regime. It may not have occurred to you that the problem lies with the diets and weight loss programs that are offering you a body that does not fit your genetic engineering.

Hence, you may be gripped by a yearning for a body that was never meant to be yours.

This trancelike state of body obsession can numb you to your personal challenges as well as to the atrocities of our world. In fact this is the "gift" of body obsession or eating disorders: if you continue to focus inward on losing weight your energy is diverted to this never ending enterprise. This ongoing focus helps to keep you distracted from the uncomfortable realities of your life.

In the 1997 movie, "Wag the Dog," the theme of distraction and the power of the media are cleverly portrayed by Robert De Niro and Dustin Hoffman. De Niro plays a Washington "spin doctor" who distracts the citizens from a presidential sex scandal by hiring a Hollywood producer played by Hoffman to construct a fake war with Albania. This scenario works like magic, the uncomfortable reality of the president's sex scandal is eclipsed by focusing outwardly on the media produced war.

The collaboration of the billion-dollar weight-loss industry, Hollywood, Fashion, and Media create a fertile environment for eating disorders and self-loathing.

Does it seem simplistic to blame the weight loss industry, Hollywood, Fashion, and the Media for the creation of body-hatred?

If we take the human tendency for blame and utilize it for heath, pointing the finger in this direction actually can empower us, because WE are these industries.

If we purchase diet pills or sign up for a "too good to believe" weight loss program, we are sustaining the status quo. Even when we go along with fashions' latest trend which brings body dissatisfaction, or buy magazines full of images of airbrushed bodies, we are saying, "I support your business of selling your products that make me feel bad about myself."

Instead of a war on obesity, let's become Love Warriors.

Commit now to spending your money in ways that support self-love and body acceptance. Imagine the ability we could have as a nation if we allocated 1% of the money spent on war towards research, prevention, education, and treatment of eating disorders.

Since WE sustain these industries, we now have the power to change them.

When you stop warring with your body, and start focusing on loving your body, you will connect with the power you have to change the way our culture currently sells products through body-hatred.

How would your life be different if you stopped the war with your body and started loving it?

>> Action Steps <<

A) Remember the similarities of Wars and Diets.

B) Write, blog, post, or twitter your thoughts.

C) Become a conscious buyer. Ban certain products from you home if they are supporting body dissatisfaction or hatred.

39

Body-Toxic Culture

Why is it so hard to heal from an eating disorder?

It's hard to be healthy in a sick society.

—Ivan Illich

The reason it's such a struggle to recover from an eating disorder is because there are so many different components. Remember back to chapter 16, "How Do You "Catch" an Eating Disorder?" There are a variety of factors that contribute to someone developing an eating disorder. The genetic, emotional, psychological, physical, behavioral and spiritual aspects of a person need to be addressed within the forum of relationships that are influenced by our body-toxic culture. Plop all of this in the middle of our planet, which is struggling for its own survival, and you can see the dilemma many find themselves in.

Our culture affects us all. You may not have an eating disorder, but you may be aware that you need to change your thinking about yourself and your body. Changing how you think and feel about yourself and your body is hard enough without being continuously bombarded by unrealistic images of our culture's idealized body.

Television, magazines, radio and the internet give you a daily dose of the latest weight loss program, exercise equipment, diet pills and diet food products. This 61 billion dollar U.S. diet industry relies on you to be dissatisfied with yourself (prweb.com). For you to be a return customer; it's best if you experience continual body hatred.

This quest for body perfection is the backdrop our culture provides for those in recovery from an eating disorder, along with everyone else.

Mary, a friend of mine who has never had an eating disorder, told me about her experience at her gym. "When I walked in the gym, I found new posters all over the walls with images of young women in gym shorts and gym bras sporting six packs. They all had firm thighs and buttocks, all promising the "ideal" body if I continued working out. I felt so inadequate in comparison. All I wanted to do was hide my body under a sweatshirt and sweat pants. I know I will never look like them no matter how much I work out. The images are all of 20- and 30-year-old women who obviously spend a lot of time at the gym."

This Western culture of body perfection is spreading across the world. There are many people on this planet who share the faulty belief, "Once I lose weight, everything will be great. I'll get … the love of my life, that new job, I'll be happy." We speak different languages, experience different cultures, we have different spiritual and political beliefs, and we choose different lifestyles. Nevertheless, I believe our similarities include having difficulty assimilating the current state of our world, as well as the shared challenge of learning how to love ourselves.

Although Mary's drive toward health was not compromised by comparing herself to the gym media campaign posters, she definitely was affected emotionally. Following is a global example of how devastating comparing ourselves to media images can be.

In 1995, Anne Becker, a Harvard researcher, arrived in the Pacific Island of Fiji. She surveyed the girls of that island, finding three percent who reported trying the practice of vomiting in order to control their weight. That was the year television was widely introduced to Fiji. Three years later, Anne returned and found a fivefold increase of this behavior among the teenage girls. "They look to television characters as role models. While it's an everyday concept to Americans, reshaping the body is a new concept to Fijians," she said. One girl in the study said that the teenagers on television are "slim and very tall" and that, "we want our bodies to become like that … so we try to lose a lot of weight." Though Becker cautioned that the study does not establish a definitive link between television and eating disorders, she said that the increases were dramatic in a culture that traditionally has focused on the importance of eating well and looking robust.

When I'm working with someone with an eating disorder, there are always other issues in their lives that need to be addressed other than food and body.

When people are in relationships that are unhealthy and not supportive, it is an extra challenge to recover from an eating disorder and/or a negative self-image, and the thoughts and behaviors that go with it.

Chelsey recounted the numerous attempts her father made to get her to lose weight when she was in elementary school. He cut a photo of a little girl her age out of a magazine and put it on the refrigerator. He said, "Don't you want to look like that? I'll give you a dollar for every pound you lose." The message she received was, "You're not okay the way you are. You need to be different in order for me to love you." When family members do not work on their own issues with body and weight, it can make the journey of healing harder for their loved ones.

Our current global state of affairs is unlike any other time in history. We are hearing the message that our world's survival is in danger. Your television can bring world trauma right into your home with the flick of a remote control. You hear of murder, rape, kidnappings, fires, floods, tsunamis and a sundry of violence. This daily diet of chaos and trauma can create a subtle and sometimes unconscious overload.

If you are battling an eating disorder, it can be difficult to create a more positive mindset when you experience anxiety, depression and the negative thoughts that accompany your eating disorder. When you add the assimilation of daily news and the current state of our world, you can see how your environment does not facilitate recovery.

If you do not have an eating disorder, it can still be hard to create a positive mindset and a loving, healthy lifestyle for yourself when you encounter the stressors that come with living life. That's why it's so important to regularly offer yourself love.

This is an inside job. Although it is not easy, there are pathways waiting for you to begin or to continue your return to optimal health. Therapy, support groups, reading books and committing to loving yourself no matter what, are all pathways to health and happiness.

How would your life be different if your environment was conducive to recovery?

>> Action Steps <<

A) Think and/or write about your road blocks to a healthier you.

B) Which thoughts, emotions and relationships help or hinder your personal growth?

C) Commit to creating a supportive environment. Perhaps you will:

Boycott magazines that glorify the overly thin body.

Stop diet talk when you're with your friends and family.

Spend more time with people who focus on their life passions instead of their bodies.

World Path

Never doubt that a small group of thoughtful committed citizens can change the world; indeed, it's the only thing that ever has.

—Margaret Mead

The World Path of the Self-Love Diet

How can we approach the change needed in the world through our personal self-love work? On the eve of January 20, 2009 during the Inauguration of our 44th President, Barack Obama asked a similar question. He spoke to the previously unimaginable idea of a black man becoming President. At the Youth Ball, he spoke about young people showing incredible energy, persistence, hard work and commitment. Parents told him how their children inspired them to vote for him by witnessing their children knocking on doors and traveling by bus to canvas neighborhood after neighborhood with a passion and focus that has been unparalleled in recent times. President

Obama asked that we all continue our work, and stated that our focus must be maintained if we are to see the changes in the world that we want.

Accomplishing our goals as a nation to create an efficient and affordable health care system, address our economic crisis or heal relationships with other countries seems to be a herculean task. My dream of eliminating eating disorders and transmuting body-hatred and self-loathing to self-love and body acceptance may also be viewed by some as impossible.

I sit with adolescents and young adults who are working hard to confront their beliefs about their appearance and their ability to eat or abstain from bingeing and purging, exercising or overeating. The same dedication, persistence, focus and hard work that President Obama stated were necessary for our nations' recovery are necessary ingredients for personal recovery.

It will take focus, passion, persistence and awareness, not only from our youth, but also from our nation, and our world communities, to attain the goal of self-love on a global level.

I believe that when we go out into the world with positive attitudes and beliefs about ourselves, and our bodies, our love can be contagious.

The adolescents and young adults I work with are being transformed slowly but surely, one at a time, into Love Warriors. Have you come in contact with one? You'll know if you have because their attitudes, statements and actions are congruent with each other and positive. Their hearts' desire is to love themselves and others through working toward health and healing of our world.

Your attitudes, thoughts, statements and actions will positively influence those of the lives you touch. Your self-love can become contagious. This is how change begins. Just like the young political canvassers who knocked on one door at a time, when you change one thought at a time, one action at a time, you will be a part of the global change that begins by loving yourself.

40

Self-Love's Impact on the World

Personal choices foster global change

Every great dream begins with a dreamer. Always remember, you have within you the strength, the patience, and the passion to reach for the stars to change the world.

—Harriet Tubman

How can a personal issue become a social one? How do our personal choices affect the global community? In the March 2008 Volume 9, Number 3 edition of Oprah magazine, I read about young designers who are creating eco-conscious fashion. Before reading the article, I had clumped all fashion designers into a category of people who were part of the problem when it came to body dissatisfaction and eating disorders. After reading the article, I got excited because even in the fashion industry I was learning that there are designers who are conscious of the impact of their work on our world. It gave me hope to think that their eco-consciousness could be expanded to include body diversity in their designs if they became aware of the benefits of the Self-Love Diet.

Stella McCartney's eco collection is inspired from her personal values as a committed environmentalist. She was the first-ever Green Designer of the Year named by the Accessories Council. Her animal advocacy comes from the influence of her parents Paul McCartney and the late Linda McCartney, both avid animal activists. Stella uses no fur or leather in her fashion collections. Stella's decision comes from her conviction that the leather industry is not only an agent of animal cruelty, but that it is also bad for our environment.

Noted in *Global Magazine*, "Tanning, the process of turning skin into leather, requires massive amounts of energy and dangerous chemicals, including formaldehyde and coal-tar derivatives, which can end up in nearby soil and water supplies. These toxic chemicals pose a deadly threat to those who work at the tanneries as well as the humans and animals who live nearby."

Stella challenges her customers to pledge to never wear animal skins again. She reminds us of how the leather industry harms our environment and that our leather bag, shoes or belt were once a living being.

John Patrick is the designer of Organic, which he founded in 2004. John Patrick is part of the movement towards using organic materials in clothing. He developed a line of clothing using plant-based, non-toxic dyes. He created colorful, eco-clothes, expanding the color choices for his customers. Like Stella, he shows us how personal values can be directly connected to positive change in our world by his refusal to use toxic dyes and by raising awareness about the environment through his business.

Rogan Gregory, cofounder of Rogan, Loomstate and Edun, grew up with parents who modeled the importance of stewardship of the world. Like Stella and John, Rogan integrated his values into his work. He uses organic fabrics for his clothing line, Loomstate, and through Edun, he is helping build manufacturing companies in Africa to employ workers, to help establish Africa as a contender in global trade and to help combat poverty in Africa. Rogan is another example of how one person can make a global impact.

If the next fashion designer grows up in a family of Love Warriors what might the impact be on this designer's choices of sizes and style? What if Love Warriors begot Self-Love Fashion Warriors whose passion fueled size diversity and body acceptance?

I invite you into my imagination. In a future *Oprah* magazine, I imagine an article about you or someone you've impacted who is leading the fashion industry towards body acceptance.

Self-Love Fashion Warriors

Leading Fashion Designer (Put your name here) states, "In the past, designers used people as hangers for their clothes. They would design the clothes, and then people would change their bodies to accentuate the artwork of the designer. As we know today, the fashion industry's past focus on unrealistically small sizes was detrimental to its models and played a part in the development of eating disorders and widespread body dissatisfaction. Today, we embrace the body in its natural state. I create fashions to inspire self-love, freedom of movement and celebration of the body. The organic element of diversity in shape and size is the muse of creating my designs. I allow the natural variety of bodies to inspire me."

Progress is being made slowly but surely in the fashion industry for women of larger stature. All Walks Beyond the Catwalk is a London-based organization founded by Caryn Franklin, Debra Bourne and Erin O'Connor. These women are motivated to expand the concept of beauty and to encourage positive body image. The models involved in this organization represent different ethnicities, sizes and ages. Some of the designers who have joined forces with the founders of All Walks Beyond the Catwalk include Stella McCartney, Vivienne Westwood and Mark Fast. Alexandra Groover, another designer involved with this organization, stated on the All Walks Beyond the Catwalk website, "I have always believed that some of the most unique, beautiful, interesting, photogenic, catwalk-worthy models do not fit the current and very limiting modeling industry standard."

This slow and steady shift towards body acceptance in one of the most traditionally damaging industries for self-image is encouraging. On a personal level, as you continue your daily practice of self-love, there will be a slow and steady shift within you until you will wake up one day and find that you are a living model of body acceptance and self-love.

How will your personal self-love focus begin to influence those around you? How can it affect change on a global level?

The women and men I work with in my private practice become

advocates for healing in their own spheres of influence. They are part of a growing army of Love Warriors affecting personal and global change through their everyday healing, loving practices. They choose love as their weapon against their eating disorders and body-hatred. They spread the message of the Self-Love Diet.

Caitlyn is a good example of this growing army of Love Warriors. Initially, she struggled with her recovery from anorexia and body-hatred. By the time Caitlyn left for college she had made wonderful progress. She had become an outspoken advocate for body acceptance and was a positive role model for a peer-counseling group in her high school. The part of herself we coined her Love Warrior continued to flourish during her first year of college when her college roommate, Amy, started each morning with condemning statements about her body as she got dressed. Caitlyn used her roommate's diatribes as an opportunity to share her personal struggles and to share how important it was to her to focus on what her body did for her, rather than how it looked. They made a pact that they would catch each other if they criticized their bodies, and would replace negative statements with appreciations. Caitlyn gave credit to this simple agreement for helping her stay on track with her recovery during the beginning of her freshmen year. The bonus was that Amy benefitted from Caitlyn's personal work as well.

People who have begun the work of replacing self-hatred with self-love are at the center of change, not only for themselves, but also for our world. Can you imagine a world where love replaces hatred? As we heal our bodies, minds and spirits, we can't help but effect healing in the world we live in.

The Peace Alliance, a 501(c)3 non-profit organization founded by Marianne Williamson, is working on a national and international level to replace war with peace, which is similar to Caitlyn's personal work of trying her best to replace self-hatred with love.

The Peace Alliance was launched in the spring of 2004. One vision they champion is to establish a U.S. Department of Peace at the cabinet level of our government to counterbalance the Department of War, now called the Department of Defense. Their teams of leaders are activists focusing on bringing peace into the world through policy and legislation.

The Peace Alliance responds to a hate- and fear-based society by educating and encouraging peace. Caitlyn responded to her roommate's body-hatred through educating her about the inner peace that comes from focusing on self-love. These two examples, although one is personal and the other global, parallel how healing can spread.

If you want to join the ranks of the Love Warrior Community, begin by choosing love instead of hate, compassion instead of criticism, forgiveness instead of judgment, acceptance instead of shame and action instead of complacency. Choose to be mindful of the way you think and speak about yourself, your body and the choices you make. By choosing to offer yourself and others love, and living by your convictions, you can impact the world for the better.

How would the world be different if we all practiced self-love?

>> Action Steps <<

A) What are you passionate about? Let yourself dream.

B) Write how the practice of loving yourself can help you fulfill your passions.

C) Decide how your Self-Love work can be spread to a wider audience, involving the healing of our planet.

Part Five

*What lies before us and what lies behind us are
small matters compared to what lies within us.*

*And when we bring what is within out into the
world, miracles happen.*

—Henry David Thoreau

Taking Action on the Self-Love Diet

As you read this sentence you have already taken action towards self-love by learning about the Self-Love Diet and what the concepts in this book can offer you. But reading about the Self-Love Diet, and then closing the book and forgetting about it is not going to bring you closer to your goal of self-love and healing. Accept the invitation to take action in 7 paths of your life and see what happens.

Now that you have redefined diet to mean a diet of regularly offering yourself love, you can begin taking action by:

- Being conscious of what you think. Choose to love yourself enough to stop abusive, hateful thoughts and to replace them with loving, encouraging and compassionate beliefs.

- When you are at a choice point in caring for yourself, ask yourself what would love do?

- Choose to offer others the same love you want to receive.

- Remember that you are more than your body. You are a spiritual being. Take action by recognizing that your intrinsic value comes from within.

- Share what you've learned with others. Create your own Love Warrior culture in your home, workplace and within your circle of friends and family.

- By healing yourself, know that you are impacting the world in a positive way. Choose to take positive action to make an impact in the world beyond yourself and local community.

In the following chapters, you will read about how others have taken action in their sphere of influence. Let yourself be inspired to make grand gestures, or personal ones, that may never make the front-page news. Remember, each moment you choose a loving thought or action, love is growing. In this section, I will explain how morphogenetic resonance and the concept of the tipping point will spread the message of the Self-Love Diet. Take action as a Love Warrior in your special way. It will be exactly the right way.

41

A Call to Action

Love as a verb

Vision without action is merely a dream. Action without vision just passes the time. Vision with action can change the world.

—Joel A. Barker

Whether Darryl Roberts knows it or not, he is a Love Warrior. Darryl Roberts, director of the eye opening, educational, and inspirational documentary about our obsession with beauty, titled *America the Beautiful*, has this to say about his movie and the fashion industry;

> *Considering that we're challenging an industry that has been assaulting our self-esteem for a long time, this isn't just a movie opening, it's a movement. It's how each and every one of us can say ENOUGH! The reason I believe a movie about our unhealthy obsession with beauty is important is because it really effects young girls. The average girl, 8 to 18 years of age, doesn't like her body, doesn't feel she's attractive and is contemplating dieting or even worse, plastic surgery. This is very unhealthy because as we all know, a healthy self-esteem is the engine that makes you assertive, confident and ready to take on the world. Unfortunately, this has been taken away from a lot of us, so that some beauty companies can sell more products and the CEOs of these companies can drive Bentleys.*

My daughter and I went to the opening of *America the Beautiful* in Marin County, California, in 2009. After the showing of the documentary Darryl told a story that illustrates the power one person can have to change a culture.

He recounts the evening he was in New York and there were only 4 people in the theatre. The host of the evening was very apologetic, and asked Darryl if he wanted to cancel the show. He told us, "I said to her, if even one person comes to watch my movie, I will play it for that one." As he continued, we found out that one of the four audience members, an adolescent girl, came up to him after the movie, and said, "My mom would love to see this movie". It turns out the girl's mother was Meredith Louise Vieira who was a host on the TV talk show, *The View*.

Darryl's audience of four turned into over a million viewers. While he was being interviewed by Meredith the topic came around to MTV's pilot TV show that was in the making. It was a pilot reality show which featured people with eating disorders. The eating disorder community was trying it's best to communicate with MTV to ensure that people with eating disorders would not be used as entertainment. Darryl had unsuccessfully talked with the MTV people asking them to drop the show. NEDA, National Eating Disorders Association, had also been in contact with the MTV staff, and had not been able to get them to "be responsible programmers" by changing, or cancelling the show. Darryl used his time on *The View* to ask the audience, and the people watching to call, write, or email MTV and let their concerns be known. Darryl left the studio that day and later found out that MTV had over 10,000 emails, letters, and phone calls asking for the cancellation of the show.

Each individual person did one small action, which resulted in MTV cancelling the show. Thank you Darryl, and thank you to everyone who emailed, called, or wrote to MTV.

We do have power to change our culture, because *we* are the culture. What we buy, watch, and participate in reflects our values. *Put your money where your love is.*

Don't buy magazines that foster body-hatred, don't watch TV shows that encourage fat discrimination. Use your power. The power of self-love is more powerful than ignorance and self-hatred. Start with yourself, and let the love flow from there.

What actions will you take? Each time you catch yourself criticizing your body, stop and apologize to your body. Tell someone it hurts your feelings to hear them talk so negatively about themselves, you, or others, when you do this, you are channeling your Love Warrior.

The following are more examples of what Love Warriors have done.

Kevin J. Thompson and Leslie J. Heinberg's article, The Media's Influence on Body Image Disturbance and Eating Disorders: We've Reviled Them, Now Can We Rehabilitate Them?, identified "a relationship between magazine reading frequency and women's desire to look like a model.'" This article has inspired me to do my best to minimize the amount of airbrushed bodies my clients will see by carefully choosing the magazines I have in my waiting room.

Remember Caitlyn who I introduced to you earlier in this book? She is the young woman who left for college and made a pact with her roommate that they would catch each other's negative criticisms, and replace them with positive attributes that they liked about themselves. Although Caitlyn reports that she sometimes struggles to believe she's beautiful on the outside, she understands that by accepting and loving the way she is now, she is practicing the perfect antidote to body-hatred, and as she does her own self-love work, she has impacted her roommate.

Caitlyn is one person, who has made an inner change that has positively affected her, and one other person. We now have the potential of two young women who are learning to love themselves. If these two women have children, they are more apt to pass along love and acceptance of their children's bodies. They can be the force that stops body-hatred from continuing to the next generations. We can see how, in time one person has the potential for healing beyond their own thoughts and actions.

How would your life be different if you became a Love Warrior and took action to increase self/body love?

>> Action Plan <<

A) The next time you're at the super market looking at magazines, resist buying one that glamorizes the "ideal" thin female body. Go to www.lovewarriorcommunity.com and hover over Create/Explore. A drop down menu will appear. Hover over Positive Images. Click on Non-Air-brushed Real People Portrait Gallery and look through the images. Send a photo of yourself to be included! To do so, go to www.lovewarrior-community.com and hover over Submit. A drop down menu will appear. Click on Submit Positive Images.

B) Go to www.edrs.net and click on the Resources page. Once on the Resources page, scroll down and click on Organizations and Associations. Pick an organization and take action by making a donation. You will be supporting body/self-love.

C) Pick an organization and take action by volunteering in your community, or nationally via online involvement.

42

Love Warriors Are Regular People

You don't have to be a super hero

A warrior's life is not about imagined perfection or victory; it is about love. Love is a warrior's sword; wherever it cuts, it gives life, not death.

—Dan Millman

What does a Love Warrior look like?

It is difficult to pick a Love Warrior out in a crowd. A Love Warrior can be a man or a woman, an adult, adolescent, or child. Appearance will not help you single out who is a love warrior and who is not, but you'll know when you are with one.

What does a Love Warrior feel like?

When a Love Warrior looks into your eyes, you feel accepted and loved. When a Love Warrior listens to you, you feel heard. You'll feel a Love Warrior's self-confidence and passion. You will feel inspired, motivated and experience a desire to join in and make a contribution. When you are with a Love Warrior, you will feel connected.

You will realize that a Love Warrior is not some magical, bigger than life hero. A Love Warrior inspires you to come into contact with the Love Warrior that resides in you. Love Warriors can teach you to love yourself just by watching how they treat themselves.

What does a Love Warrior Sound Like?

A Love Warrior may sound strong and opinionated. You may hear passionate conversations regarding aspects of our culture. A Love Warrior may also sound soothing, calming, and nurturing. You may hear soothing words that help you remember your value, and direct you to see the worth in yourself and others that may have gone unnoticed.

How Does a Love Warrior Smell?

A Love Warrior may smell of perspiration from the effort it takes to confront the culture of our idealized physique which is plastered on billboards, airbrushed into our magazines, imbedded into the lyrics of our music, and written into the dialogue of our movies. A Love Warrior may also smell clean and fresh as if just stepping out of a shower after washing off all the falsehoods that have glommed onto her regarding the culturally sanctioned shape and size she is supposed to seek and attain in order to be desirable.

The First "Official" Love Warriors

Eating Disorders Recovery Support, EDRS, sprung out of my desire to create a website that offered a list of referrals of therapists, doctors, registered dietitians, and related professionals who could be of assistance in the treatment of eating disorders in Sonoma County.

It was my husband's business sense that actually led to the creation of EDRS. When he saw the referral list on the computer, he asked why I was promoting other professionals on my website. I let him know that I had a full practice, and wanted to let the community know who else could provide help. It occurred to me that if people were getting free publicity they may be willing to give free services. I asked the professionals I had on my site if they would be willing to do one pro-bono service for the community each year in exchange for their contact information, as well as any group listings they may be offering to be posted on the site. The response was overwhelming. We offered our first community conference during Eating Disorders Awareness Week, EDAW in 2007. Professionals as well as community members gave of their energy, experience and expertise.

Love Warrior 2007

One Sonoma State University student who stood out was named Lindsey Wert. Lindsey wrote and performed a one woman play as part of her course work, and scheduled it for EDAW. The moving performance was about Lindsey's journey of healing from chronic sexual abuse, self-harm, and anorexia.

Her personification of the negative mind portrayed by "Ed" (eating disorder) was complete with sun glasses, and a smooth talking message of hope through being skinny. Each time she donned the sun glasses, we heard the voice of her eating disorder. She portrayed her innocent little girl with equal sincerity. The audience felt the joy that this part of her brought into her life, as well as the grief of her innocence lost. When Lindsey became her wise healer the yearning for health and healing was transmitted through her voice as she sang of her desire to love herself, and asked the audience to stop their body hatred, and join in, committing themselves to self-love. It was a magical performance.

At the end of the show Lindsey invited the viewers to come to the stage, light a candle and speak. One audience member was moved to commit to go back to residential treatment to recover from anorexia. Other people in the hall spoke of feeling more self-love and acceptance, and others resolved to go to therapy and seek help for themselves. There was laughter and tears.

All who attended the play were moved by the power of the message. Lindsey became the first EDRS Love Warrior. Thank You Lindsey for your passion, honesty and courage in telling your story.

Love Warrior 2008

The second Love Warrior distinction went to a senior in high school named Lauren Sowell. In honor of Eating Disorders Awareness Week she produced a dinner/raffle fundraiser in collaboration with her school and her community. Lauren received help from a 4 star chef who worked in a rehabilitation program that treated people with eating disorders. She got donations for dinners, art work, massages, jewelry, and assorted gifts. The money she earned was donated to a deserving young woman named Lindsey. Yes, Lauren gifted Lindsey, our first Love Warrior, with the profit from the fundraiser to help Lindsey finance her continued recovery work. Thanks Lauren. You are a Love Warrior!

Love Warrior 2009

Audrey was our third Love Warrior recipient. Audrey courageously and lovingly told her story of recovery from anorexia and bipolar disorder at the Eating Disorder Awareness Week (EDAW) Conference in 2009.

Audrey's life story was a valuable contribution to our audience. She was able to personalize the complexity of recovery, and the extra challenges that occur for those with a dual diagnosis. She spoke from the heart, and touched many people with her story of hope, and successes. Her personal choice to continue with ongoing therapy in order to stay balanced and healthy helped others view therapy as a supportive process versus something you do if you are sick. She ended her presentation by reading a poem she wrote which helped the audience understand what recovery is.

She received a standing ovation. We thank you Audrey for your honesty and courage.

Your story will help others to trust that they can heal.

Here is Audrey's poem:

Recovery Is...

Looking in the mirror and liking what you see
Knowing that life is not about weight, numbers,
   or the size that you wear
About taking risks
Knowing that life is about love, friendship,
   happiness and peace
Asking for and accepting help
Living life, enjoying every moment
   and doing what you love
Having faith
Trusting your body and its wisdom
Believing that life is unfolding just like it is
   supposed to be and that everything happens
   for a reason
Remembering to slow down and breathe
Celebrating your successes
Treasuring your existence and valuing yourself
Continuing forward in the fight against your
   eating disorder when you have grown tired
   and want to give up
Never forgetting to have fun
Holding on to those you love and telling them
   how much you care
Enjoying wonderful, pleasurable things
Remembering that life is a gift not to be taken

for granted
Learning who you are
Respecting the amazing body you were given
Using your voice
Believing in yourself
Feeling your feelings
Following your dreams
Speaking your truth
A sometimes difficult, often wonderful,
  life altering journey
For me this is recovery

Thank you Audrey for sharing your story of recovery.

Love Warrior 2010

Our Love Warrior for 2010 was a woman whose life was touched by eating disorders within her circle of relatives. She took these challenging life occurrences and used them to educate herself, to help those she loved, and to answer the invitation to do her own personal growth work. Her further response was to be an advocate for families, and friends of people suffering from eating disorders. She also collaborated with other eating disorder organizations to become a support for therapists and other professionals to find the resources they needed to help their clients. Heartfelt gratitude goes to our fourth Love Warrior for her dedication and compassion.

Love Warrior 2012

When a group of Eating Disorder specialists from EDRS, (Eating Disorders Recovery Support Inc.) Beyond Hunger and The Body Positive gathered to prepare for the 2012 conference, they nominated and unanimously agreed upon the 2012 Love Warrior.

This woman moved to California in 1985, it was her vision to develop an organization that replicated the clinic she had left in Manhattan which had a direct-service clinic, a training program, a prevention division, a research component, a group department, an intake department, and a community outreach effort. In addition she wanted to create an opportunity for eating disorder therapists and other professionals to know one another, network with one another, and have access to learning opportunities and collaborative opportunities with one another. Out of these goals she created the Association of Professionals Treating Eating Disorders, a non-profit organization in San Francisco, serving the Bay Area for over 25 years. Her life's passion has been to promote recovery from eating disorders.

Thank you to Deborah Brenner-Liss, PhD, for your passion and activism in the eating disorder field. You are our Love Warrior for 2012!

How would our world be different if we each became a Love Warrior?

>> Action Plan <<

A) Look for aspects of the Love Warrior in yourself.

B) If you've advocated for others, how could you be your own Love Warrior?

C) Decide to be a Love Warrior, and be open for opportunities.

43

The 100th Monkey Phenomenon

How information is passed along

There are exceptional people out there who are capable of starting epidemics. All you have to do is find them.

—Malcolm Gladwell

The *100th Monkey Effect* originated from Lawrence Blair and Lyall Watson. A group of monkeys on an island were being studied. The scientists who were observing the monkeys dropped off sweet potatoes, which were not indigenous to that island.

One monkey began a new behavior by washing the potato in the river before eating it. This behavior over the course of six years became common knowledge for the majority of the monkeys on the island. This part of the story is not earth shattering news. The part that is much more interesting is that over on a neighboring island there were monkeys who had no contact with the potato washing monkeys. When the scientists dropped off sweet potatoes to these monkeys, they all had knowledge of how to wash the sweet potatoes without any modeling.

This phenomenon has garnered the attention of many. One theory that has been hypothesized is that a certain magical number is required for a new behavior to be passed along, in this case the 100th monkey.

Malcolm Gladwell's book, *The Tipping Point*, speaks to the observable fact of how social change can move very quickly, similar to an epidemic when a disease reaches a critical mass. "It's the moment on the graph when the line starts to shoot straight upwards."

Eating Disorders have been described as epidemics. I believe there are many people who do not have eating disorders, but still are under the influence of a diet mentality epidemic. The diet mentality is not a healthy paradigm, even if it seems normal.

The following are definitions of the word *epidemic* from dictionary.com:

– A disease affecting many persons at the same time, and spreading from person to person in a locality where the disease is not permanently prevalent.

This definition does not fit for the spread of eating disorders and the diet mentality in the United States because both are prevalent.

– Extremely prevalent; widespread.

This definition fits better because the incidence of eating disorders is extremely prevalent and the diet mentality is widespread.

– Noun: A temporary prevalence of a disease.

I like this definition because if we use it with the focus of eating disorders and the diet mentality, we can think of these occurrences as temporary.

–A rapid spread or increase in the occurrence of something: an epidemic of riots.

When you look at this last definition, let's substitute "*the Self-Love Diet*" for the word *something* and for the word *riots*. It would read like this:

–A rapid spread or increase in the occurrence of the Self-Love Diet: an epidemic of the Self-Love Diet.

How can we create an epidemic of self-love? If we want a rapid spread or increase in the occurrence of loving thoughts, emotions, relationships and actions, how can we facilitate this?

Can the story of the 100th monkey give us some food for thought?

How was the sweet potato washing behavior information passed along? The monkeys on the neighboring island did not have any contact with one another, and yet this new behavior was transmitted somehow across the islands.

Rupert Sheldrake from the UK suggests that patterns of behavior are influenced by morphogenetic resonance. Sheldrake suggests that we do not hold our memories in our individual minds, but rather they exist in fields of memory which we can tap into, similar to tuning into a radio station. He suggests that the more people who have learned a certain skill, the easier it will be for future people to learn the skill.

How can we use these ideas to foster the growth, or the "epidemic" of self-love?

If we get a large enough number of people engaging in the Self-Love Diet here in the United States, will it be easier for these skills to be learned and practiced daily by others around the world?

Keeping these ideas in mind has lead to the Love Warrior Community site where we have faith that simple, consistent, little self-love behaviors will grow in prevalence until we have a full-blown self-love epidemic.

How would your life be different if the concept and practice of self-love was widespread?

>> Action Plan <<

A) Begin a daily practice of self-love. Choose behaviors from Self-Love Practices in the appendix.

B) Share your ideas and practices of self-love with others.

C) Write on the Love Warrior Community blog and share your progress online (www.selflovewarrior.com).

44

Love Warrior Community

Continuing your Self-Love practice

In every community, there is work to be done. In
every nation, there are wounds to heal. In every
heart, there is the power to do it.

—Marianne Williamson

I have read many great self-help books. While I'm reading them, I'm
inspired and motivated. I tell other people about the new ideas or practices
I've started. This continues to happen until the book moves away from the
side of my bed to be replaced by the *new book*.

I don't want you to forget the loving messages and practices that you
have started incorporating into your mind, body and spirit.

I want you to continue to enhance your relationship with yourself, your
body and others in your life.

So how can you change that old behavior of being excited about a book
and then forgetting all about it? One way is to join a group that continues to
meet and share their experiences, ideas and encouragement.

You may want to use this book in a reading group you already belong
to, or you may decide to start a book study group using the concepts and
suggested practices in the Self-Love Diet. There is a benefit to meeting face-
to-face with like-minded people. I'm sure you've heard about the "buddy
system." The buddy system is the act of teaming up with at least one other

person in order to support each other in achieving your objectives.

But what if you decide you don't have the time or the inclination to start a book study group?

Another way to continue your Self-Love Diet is to join the online Love Warrior Community. By connecting with people online, you don't have to be in the same city or time zones. You can make time to work on your Self-Love Diet through the online tools provided for you, when it works for you.

Reading body positive content is inspiring, so is sharing it, commenting on it and talking about it. This is the basis for the tools you will find on the Love Warrior Community: body positive writing, images, music, art and videos.

The Love Warrior Community uses creativity as the conduit for healing. So often we are surrounded by negative media telling us we have flaws that need to be fixed with the newest makeup product, wonder bra or diet. The Love Warrior Community provides a counter-culture of self-empowering, body positive media and tools to help you foster your own self-love practice and to help you create the culture that you want to live in.

Being a Love Warrior is not necessarily going to be easy. It may well be the most important thing you do. It takes the heart of a warrior to love yourself when you are feeling down. It takes the courage of a warrior to look into aspects of yourself that you may want to turn away from. It takes solidarity with other warriors to speak up against the current culture of self-hatred and body loathing, especially when you believe it to be true or hear it from your loved ones.

The Love Warrior Community fills the need for an online presence that represents a new culture, one that we actively create together. You can change your culture because you are the culture.

What you buy, what you read, what you consume, what you say, what you write—your actions and thoughts contribute to your culture.

Can you imagine a place where you could look at images of real un-airbrushed people? How powerful would it be to read about people who are on the Self-Love Diet, instead of finding articles about the newest weight loss trend? What if there was a website where you could read body love letters and body forgiveness letters? Now there is. The Love Warrior Community is a welcoming and supportive space for you to use the Self-Love Diet tools you want to incorporate into your life. It's also a place for discussion, to talk with others who are also developing their self-love practice. The Love Warrior Community is a jumping off point for you to take action. By starting with yourself, you can change our culture into a more self-loving one, and ultimately heal our world for the coming generations. Use these resources for healing, exploration and continuing the Self-Love Diet.

Here's how it works. When you go to www.lovewarriorcommunity.com, you will see "Create/Explore" as one of the options in the menu. When you hover your mouse over it, a drop down menu will appear with these categories: Writing, Positive Images, Art, Music and Video. Each of these introductory pages works as a guide on how to use writing, positive images, art, music and video as tools for your self-love practice. Each introductory page also works as a directory of all previously published works. Each published piece will be viewable individually as a post, and some of the work, like the images, can also be viewed collectively as a gallery. If you click on a link within one of the directories of published videos, writing and other media, you will be directed to an individual post. At the end of each blog post, there will be a prompt inviting you to share how the content relates to your own self-love journey. To submit your creative works, hover over "Submit" and click on the category you want to submit to. If you want to submit writing, hover over "Submit," then hover over "Submit Writing" and you will see the different writing categories pop up in a new menu. From there, you can select the writing category you want to submit to.

Writing

Writing is a window into your soul. It has a magic that bypasses grammatical rules and punctuation. Writing is one way to discover the many aspects of yourself. Embrace all of yourself, those parts you love easily, and those parts you don't. To find out if writing is a healing and Self-Love Diet tool that works well for you, take a look at the Writing section of the Love Warrior Community at www.lovewarriorcommunity.com/writing. We explore writing through self-love journaling, poetry, short fiction, quotes, body love letters and body forgiveness letters. Take the time to explore which one best speaks to you, and begin exploring others' writing.

Reading others' writing can be empowering in itself. Let the words of others' soak in, and if you feel inspired, leave a comment on how their writing impacted you. If you don't feel comfortable commenting on the site, write your response in your personal Self-Love Diet journal.

Self-Love Warrior Group Blog

Contributing to the Self-Love Warrior group blog is one way to continue your Self-Love Diet. By regularly offering yourself a space and time to write about your personal journey, you are solidifying your Self-Love practice for yourself through self-reflection. By sharing your writing on the blog, you get an added benefit of connecting with others, and knowing that others will read your writing helps you see yourself from another perspective.

You can contribute to the group blog anonymously, or you can include a bio and photo of yourself with each blog post. If you have a blog or website that is aligned with the Self-Love Diet, then you can include a link in your bio.

You will find a monthly prompt on the Self-Love Warrior group blog (selflovewarrior.com). Each prompt is only a suggestion. Give yourself permission to write what is healing for you, whether or not it fits the prompt for the month. Use the blog in whichever way helps you on your journey to self-love. If it would be helpful to see different prompts, you can scroll down on the Self-Love Monthly Writing Prompts page and find a list of the current and all previous prompts from each month. In order to keep our blog centered on the concepts of the Self-Love Diet we have created posting guidelines.

Posting Guidelines

You can use self-love journaling as a tool to enhance your self-love practice. You can use it to reflect on large portions of your life or to reflect on a specific moment in time.

How have you overcome struggles or obstacles relating to your Self-Love Diet?

What successes have you experienced?

What revelations have occurred for you while actively working on bringing more self-love into your life?

Here are seven aspects of the Self-Love Diet that you can use as a guide to help you get the most out of your self-love writing practice.

Seven Paths of the Self-Love Diet

Body

How can you love your body?

Give examples of challenging times with a positive "turn around" through appreciation, gratitude or by focusing on what your body does for you vs. what it looks like.

For example: I rub body love lotion on my belly, and I tell my belly that I love it because it's the one area of my body that I used to criticize daily. I noticed that my love for my belly grew as my critical thoughts dissipated.

Emotions

How can you love yourself when you experience difficult emotions?

Show examples of self-love through the ability to self-soothe without using eating disordered or addictive processes. Give examples of how your thoughts or behaviors had a positive effect on your emotions.

For example: I noticed I was going to the pantry looking for cereal to eat. I stopped and went through my check list of emotions HALT: Was I hungry or hurt? Was I anxious or angry? Was I lonely? Was I tired? I noticed I wasn't hungry. I was tired. Going to bed was a more loving choice than eating the cereal.

Thoughts

How can your thoughts reflect self-love?

Give examples of moments where you became aware of your thought process. Have you ever caught yourself thinking negatively, stopped yourself and then changed those thoughts to positive ones? Have you ever noticed your negative thoughts, then confronted and disproved them? Give examples of the effect this had on your ability to experience self-love.

For example: I noticed I was focusing on what wasn't going right one day. I began to feel frustrated. I caught my thoughts and consciously began to count my blessing. I felt so much better!

Spirit

How can your spiritual self increase your ability to love yourself more?

Write about how focusing on your spiritual nature vs. your physical body allowed you to be more loving to yourself and others.

For example: I have a practice of looking into my Self-Love Mirror. Rather than looking at my eyes, I look into my eyes, into my soul, and tell myself that my value does not depend on how I look, or what I do, but rather on who I am, a valuable, lovable human being. This also helps me to be more accepting and loving of others.

Relationships

How can your relationships help your Self-Love Diet?

Give an example of how your relationship with yourself is improving, or notice how you are improving your relationships with others, which empowers you to love yourself more.

For example: I notice less self deprecating thoughts flit by. When they do, I let them go without hanging on to them. If someone compliments me, I receive it and enjoy it. This is an example of my relationship with myself improving. I am letting in praise and letting go of self-deprecating thoughts, which strengthens my Self-Love Diet.

Setting boundaries in my relationships and saying "no" when I'm asked to do something for someone else that would take away important time from me are both examples of taking care of myself, and improving my relationship with others by stating my truth. When I say "yes" when I mean yes, and say "no" when I mean no, people in my life trust that when I do help them, I am doing so freely and without resentment. I am putting my needs and self-care first when I establish boundaries in my relationships. By doing so, it strengthens my relationship with myself, which strengthens my relationship with others.

I can also say "yes" when it would take important time away from me, but the others request is a priority. For example; I may be working on a project and get a call that someone needs to go to the emergency room and needs a ride, or a good friend may call and tell me that her mother died. In those cases it helps me to love myself by knowing that I am a person who can be counted on to help others in need even when it is not convenient. By practicing the Self-Love Diet you will get clear on when to set boundaries, and when to help others.

Culture

How can I practice my Self-Love Diet in our weight-obsessed culture?

Tell a story of how you were able to love yourself in spite of our unsupportive culture, or tell us how you created a self-loving culture.

For example: I've carefully chosen the magazines in the waiting room of my office. I don't allow *People*, *Cosmopolitan* or other magazines that focus on the "ideal thin body" with images of airbrushed bodies. I've created a haven from these images for people who wait in my office.

World

How can loving yourself translate to loving the world?

Give an example of how loving yourself has expanded your ability to be of service to others.

For example: A by-product of my personal Self-Love Diet is this book. By focusing on loving myself, I've been able to share my knowledge and experience to help others. Since I no longer wake up each day focusing on what I am going to eat, not eat or what I weigh, I now have the energy to focus on helping others in the world.

How can loving the world translate to loving yourself?

Give an example of how focusing on helping others helped you to love yourself more.

For example: Perhaps you've contributed to supporting a child in a less fortunate country. By helping others and realizing that there are so many people who don't have the basic essentials of food, shelter, clothing and clean water, it can help you to catch obsessive thoughts about your body and food. By helping others, it also helps you to love yourself more by touching into the compassionate part within you that reminds you to love yourself.

Here is an example of a self-love journal entry from the Love Warrior Community's group blog, Self-Love Warrior.

Earth Day 2012

Posted on April 24, 2012 by Michelle E. Minero

I've been recuperating this past week from the "knock you out, drain you out" flu.

I woke up on Sunday feeling better than I had in six days. My stomach felt neutral, I was able to eat a solid breakfast and the sun was shining! I had energy to spare, so I decided to go outside and wash my car.

This led to me placing the garden hose with running water next to our liquid amber tree trunks while I soaped up the car. After drying the car, I kept the water flowing as I stood and gave each tree a deliberate soaking all around their trunks and three to four feet beyond their trunks in a circle. I felt a sense of well-being as I communed with each tree and appreciated the sun shining on my body that had been cooped up in bed most of the week.

This led me to take a look at all of our plants and trees around our house. I started at the side of our house, and I worked my way around the house and up to our front door, watering every living thing in the early morning warmth of the sun.

The earthy smell of wet dirt greeted me along with the sweet fragrances of the roses and the delicious aroma of the tangerine bush.

It was a sensual delight to spend close to two hours in the sunshine in front of my house caring for my car, all of my trees and plants. I have not been in contact with the feel of dirt on my feet or the tickling sensation of ants doing their best to crawl up my legs for a long time. The feel of the cool water running over my feet and legs, washing the ants off of me was refreshing. I had forgotten how gratifying it is to smell the earthy fecund aroma of wet shredded bark, mixed with decomposing leaves and fragrant fresh budding roses and camellias.

It wasn't until I came inside that I realized it was Earth Day! Was it a coincidence that I chose this day to reconnect with the earth around my home? I don't think so. The Earth Day Network estimates that more than a billion people now participate in Earth Day actives each year. I believe in collective resonance. I think at some level I connected with the energy of all the other people focusing on our earth in their own unique way.

My dream is to see a billion Love Warriors participating in Self-Love Day before I die. Wouldn't it be great for someone to wake up one morning and behave in more loving ways than usual and then realize it was Self-Love Day?

Better yet, wouldn't it be awesome to have a billion people waking up each morning treating themselves and others with love every day of their lives?

You and I can start. We can start right now with this day. Let's see what happens!

Blessings,

Michelle

What can you do right now to treat yourself with love?

_____

_____

_____

Self-love journaling is one tool that you can use from the Love Warrior Community to add to your Self-Love Diet. To read others' self-love journaling on the Self-Love Warrior group blog, visit www.selflovewarrior.com. To submit your own self-love posts, visit www.lovewarriorcommunity.com/contribute-to-group-blog.

Poetry

Poetry uses words like painting uses colors. When you read or write poetry, you can suspend the laws of gravity and reality. Trees can be metaphors for people, and ideas, feelings and experiences can be experienced in new and surprising ways. Pay attention to how you feel when you read a poem out loud. Notice the cadence, rhythm and energy of the words. How does a poem make you feel? How are you impacted by reading a poem? Poems can reveal aspects of yourself or the world that lied dormant until called upon through the creative process of reading or creating your own poem. Here is an example of one poem on the Love Warrior Poetry Directory. See what emotions it evokes from you.

We Have Come To Be Danced

We have come to be danced
Not the pretty dance
Not the pretty, pretty, pick me, pick me dance
But the claw our way back into the belly
Of the sacred, sensual animal dance
The unhinged, unplugged, cat is out of its box dance
The holding the precious moment in the palms
Of our hands and feet dance.

We have come to be danced
Not the jiffy booby, shake your booty for him dance

The Only Diet That Works

But the wring the sadness from our skin dance
The blow the chip off our shoulder dance.
The slap the apology from our posture dance

We have come to be danced
Not the monkey see, monkey do dance
One two dance like you
One two three, dance like me dance
but the grave robber, tomb stalker
Tearing scabs and scars open dance
The rub the rhythm raw against our soul dance.

We have come to be danced
Not the nice, invisible, self-conscious shuffle
But the matted hair flying, voodoo mama
Shaman shakin' ancient bones dance
The strip us from our casings, return our wings
Sharpen our claws and tongues dance
The shed dead cells and slip into
The luminous skin of love dance.

We have come to be danced
Not the hold our breath and wallow in the shallow
    end of the floor dance
But the meeting of the trinity, the body breath
    and beat dance
The shout hallelujah from the top of our thighs dance
The mother may I?
Yes you may take 10 giant leaps dance
The olly olly oxen free free free dance
The everyone can come to our heaven dance.

We have come to be danced
Where the kingdoms collide
In the cathedral of flesh
To burn back into the light
To unravel, to play, to fly, to pray

To root in skin sanctuary
We have come to be danced
We have come.

—Jewel Mathieson (www.jewelm.net)
from the book, *This Dance: A Poultice of Poems*

What emotions are you aware of after reading this poem?

_____

_____

_____

Poetry is one tool that you can use from the Love Warrior Community to add to your Self-Love Diet. To read other poems on the Love Warrior Community and to find inspiration on creating your own self-love inspired poetry, visit www.lovewarriorcommunity.com, hover over Create/Explore on the LWC menu, then hover over Writing and click on Poetry. To submit your own poetry or your favorite poems by others, visit www.lovewarrior-community.com, hover over Submit, then hover over Submit Writing and click on Submit Poetry.

To learn more about the healing power of poems, or how to write your own, go to: www.poeticmedicine.com/

Body Love Letters

Have you ever written a love letter to your body? If you haven't, your body will thank you for doing it. If you find yourself resistant to the idea, I invite you to move forward anyway. Reading, writing and sharing body love letters can be a life changing experience.

Body love letters are an avenue to begin an emotionally honest and vulnerable relationship with your body. Your body love letter offers you a powerful, intimate, honest and genuine experience with your body. Most people don't write letters to their bodies, and yet when I've written my own, or witnessed my clients writing and reading their body love letters, there's a deepening that happens. When you write about your personal relationship with your body, or read what others have written about their bodies, it helps you to stop minimizing the abuse you've given your body through criticisms, judgments or physical harm. It is also a powerful way to begin focusing on what you are grateful for and what you appreciate about your body. It is the door to a new, consciously loving relationship with your body.

Sharing body love letters helps bring us together because it lets us know that we are not alone. We share similar struggles, desires, needs and wants. We all yearn to have a loving relationship with our bodies.

Reading or writing body love letters helps you to see how amazing your body is. By writing and then establishing a daily practice of reading your body love letter you can bring balance to a lifetime of body criticism or hatred.

Here is one example from the Love Warrior Community website.

Dear Body,

I love you. I might not have said that many years ago. I despised my tiny frame, my brown skin; my big lips … the list could go on. When I was younger, you were my worst enemy, but things have changed. Getting older, I realize how much I love you. The features that I had despised are things that I come to love and the things that people love about me. My tiny frame is valued, my brown skin glows and my lips are luscious. More importantly, I'm learning to love my body from the inside out. I'm not only feeding my body with vitamins, healthy food and water, but I'm feeding my soul with laughs and love from friends and family and my brain with knowledge and wisdom. If I wanted to know what unconditional love is, all I have to do is look in the mirror. Thank you for being there for me and just know I'll be there for you.

Sincerely,

Nada Abdulhaqq

What thoughts or feelings did you notice as you read this body love letter?

_____

_____

_____

Body Love Letter Template

Dear Body,

When I think of you as an instrument instead of an ornament, these are the things I appreciate that you do for me:

_____

_____

These are the things I love about your appearance:

_____

_____

I commit to love and honor you by

_____

_____

Signed: _____

Witnessed by: _____

You can keep your body love letter private, or you can have a trusted person witness it. Sharing your body love letter with someone else, when you are ready, can strengthen your resolve to love yourself and help keep your gratitude toward your body more mindful.

Body love letters are one tool that you can use from the Love Warrior Community to add to your Self-Love Diet. To read others' body love letters on the Love Warrior Community website, visit www.lovewarriorcommunity.com, hover over Create/Explore on the LWC menu, then hover over Writing and click on Body Love Letters. To submit your own body love letter or to download the body love letter template, visit www.lovewarriorcommunity.com, hover over Submit, then hover over Submit Writing and click on Submit a Body Love Letter.

Body Forgiveness Letters

Body forgiveness is important in the Self-Love Diet practice. Writing a body forgiveness letter is a powerful process because you're acknowledging the hurt you have caused your body and are asking for your body's forgiveness.

By writing a body forgiveness letter, you're making peace with your body, admitting your self-criticisms and unhealthy care and are committing to actively treat your body, and yourself, healthier and with love.

Here is an example of a body forgiveness letter that was submitted to the Love Warrior Community:

Dear Body,

There's not really a good place to begin to apologize for all the shit that I put you (me) through. I'm sorry for many, many things, indulging in snacks a bit too much, the constant pushing you to keep going (even when you're exhausted), and my own mentality as well. I need to take responsibility for all of these things, and realize that you are not just a shell in which I live, but you are wholly a part of my psychological being as well. I commit to take time to stop and consider YOU for a few minutes every day. I trust that will be good for both of us. You are AWESOME and amazing; I know that you have been able to perform some amazing feats in the past, and you won't let me down in the future. In return, I will take better care of you!

Meghan

What do you want to ask your body forgiveness for?

_____

_____

_____

Body Forgiveness Letter Template

When you ask your body for forgiveness, it's not enough to say, "I'm sorry." Here are the components to a satisfying apology:

+ Take responsibility for your actions.
+ Acknowledge how your actions affected your body.
+ Try to understand how your body "felt."
+ Make amends. Have a plan so you will not hurt your body again.

- Say you're sorry.
- Ask for forgiveness.

In the body forgiveness template, I've added a section for a witness. By having a supportive witness that you trust, you get the advantage of account-ability and the experience of sharing your intentions with a caring person. Building a community of body love supporters is paramount to your recovery. I encourage you to write an apology letter to your body. If you are sincere, I am confident that your body will forgive you.

Here is an example to get you started:

Body Forgiveness Letter Template

Dear Body,

I am writing to acknowledge and take responsibility for all the times I

_____

_____

I know this affected you by

_____

_____

You must have felt

_____

_____

I commit to love and honor you by (Amends)

_____

_____

I am sorry. (Ask for forgiveness)

_____

_____

Signed: _____

Date: _____

Witnessed by: _____

Date: _____

If you are not ready to share your body forgiveness letter with anyone, keep the witness section blank until you find that person you trust to support you in your recovery. Body forgiveness letters are one tool that you can use from the Love Warrior Community to add to your Self-Love Diet. To read more body forgiveness letters on the Love Warrior Community website, to submit your own body forgiveness letter or to download the body forgiveness letter template, go to www.lovewarriorcommunity.com, hover over Create/ Explore on the LWC menu, then hover over Writing and click on Body Forgiveness Letters. (www.lovewarriorcommunity.com/body-forgiveness-letters/)

Quotes

Quotes can be powerful bursts of inspiration. They are like little nuggets of gold. With a few carefully crafted words, a single sentence or a concise paragraph, the author of a quote can convey a feeling, inspire action or help you see things from a different perspective.

Here are some quotes from the Love Warrior Community:

Revolution begins with one courageous soul, and can become a gorgeous contagion.

—Eve Ensler

Everyone can join in this revolution by starting with yourself. Stop self-condemnation, criticism and judgment. Start self-acceptance, gratitude and love.

—Michelle E. Minero

What quote will inspire you to love yourself today?

_____

_____

_____

Inspiring quotes are one tool that you can use from the Love Warrior Community to add to your Self-Love Diet. To read others' quotes on the Love Warrior Community website, to submit original quotes or your favorite quotes from others, visit www.lovewarriorcommunity.com, hover over Create/ Explore on the LWC menu, then hover over Writing and click on Quotes. (www.lovewarriorcommunity.com/quotes/)

Short Fiction

Have you ever read a short story that excited you, moved you or inspired you? A short story has the ability to capture your attention, tap into your emotions and convey deeper themes and symbolism through the art of storytelling. The creative process of writing a short story can work as a catharsis and a creative outlet.

Here is a short story from the Love Warrior Community that is said to come from Chinese, Indian and Universal folklore:

The Two Pots

A Water Bearer in China had two large pots, each hung on the ends of a pole, which he carried across his neck.

One of the pots had a crack in it while the other pot was perfect and always delivered a full portion of water. At the end of the long walk from the stream to the house, the cracked pot arrived only half full.

For a full two years, this went on daily, with the bearer delivering only one and a half pots of water to his house. Of course, the perfect pot was proud of its accomplishments, for which it was made. But the poor cracked pot was ashamed of its own imperfection, and miserable that it was able to accomplish only half of what it had been made to do.

After two years of what it perceived to be bitter failure, it spoke to the water bearer one day by the stream. "I am ashamed of myself, because this crack in my side caused my water to leak out all the way back to your home."

The bearer said to the pot, "Did you notice that there are flowers on your side of the path, but not on the other pot's side? That's because I have always known about your flaw, so I planted flower seeds on your side of the path, and every day while we walk back, you water them. For two years I have been able to pick these beautiful flowers to decorate the table. Without you being just the way you are, we would not have such beauty."

In what ways have you seen yourself as imperfect only to later realize that your "imperfection" was actually worthy of celebration?

_____

_____

_____

Short fiction is one tool that you can use from the Love Warrior Community to add to your Self-Love Diet. To read others' short fiction on the Love Warrior Community website, visit www.lovewarriorcommunity.com, hover over Create/Explore on the LWC menu, then hover over Writing and click on Short Fiction. To submit your original short fiction or your favorites from others, visit www.lovewarriorcommunity.com, hover over Submit, then hover over Submit Writing and click on Submit Short Fiction.

Positive Images

"A picture is worth a thousand words."

—Napoleon Bonaparte

What does self-love look like to you? If you were to submit an image of hope, self-acceptance, self-empowerment, motivation and love, what would we see? The positive images on the Love Warrior Community inspire. They range from images with inspiring quotes, to photographs that capture the essence of self-love, body positivity and empowerment to self-love portraits where you can see non-airbrushed pictures of real people. Different from writing, and other forms media, an image can resonate with you instantly.

You can take inspiration from each photo on the Love Warrior Community by simply looking at them, or you can respond to the prompt that follows each image as part of your Self-Love Diet.

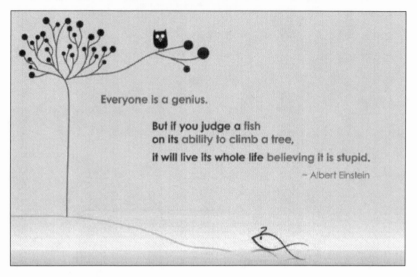

Everyone is a genius.

But if you judge a fish
on its ability to climb a tree,

it will live its whole life believing it is stupid.

– Albert Einstein

Inspirational Images

Have you compared yourself to others and come up short? What could you do differently?

_____

_____

_____

Love Warrior Photography

This section allows you to submit photos that represent self-love to you, as well as share the meaning those photos have for you on your self-love journey. You may find inspiring photography to submit, or you may also want to submit your own photos. By sharing your personal photography, you're sharing your unique perspective on self-love with us. Below is an example of a photo I took and how that photo is a representation of self-love.

I took the following picture of my daughter right before her guests arrived at her wedding shower in Maui. She had been living in Maui for only a year and although the location is gorgeous, it was a hard transition for her due to her challenging new career. I wasn't expecting the large number of close friends that came to celebrate her upcoming wedding. Each girlfriend had an intimate and close connection to my daughter. It was inspiring for me to recognize that my daughter does a good job of loving herself, which was evident in the number of friends she had created in a short period of time. One of the gifts of self-love is that by loving ourselves, we love others more easily as well.

Photo by Michelle E. Minero

Have you become aware of the impact that loving yourself has on others?

_____

_____

_____

Self-Love Portraits

Many people I work with have a difficult time looking at photos of themselves. They have a hard time because they are comparing themselves to a non-existent standard of perfection that is offered to us daily in the form of air-brushed models. Below you will see a few examples of people who have contributed self-love portraits to the Love Warrior Community. You may also contribute to the Self-Love Portrait Gallery. This is a *non-air bushed, real people only* portrait gallery. When you share a non-airbrushed picture of yourself, you are creating an antidote to the illusionary images that tell us what we should look like.

Photo by Kathleen Conti

Did you notice a difference in your emotions after looking at the Self-Love Portrait Gallery compared to how you feel after looking at pictures of women in magazine advertisements? What did you notice?

Positive images are one tool that you can use from the Love Warrior Community to add to your Self-Love Diet. To view the photo galleries on the Love Warrior Community website, visit www.lovewarriorcommunity.com, hover over Create/Explore on the LWC menu, then hover over Positive Images. A new drop down menu will appear with different galleries you can view, click on the one you want to see, or you can click on Positive Images to view each photo individually and for guidance on creating your own images. To submit images, visit www.lovewarriorcommunity.com, hover over Submit, then click on Submit Positive Images.*

Love Warrior Art

Creativity is a powerful healer. Its energy flows through you freely even if you don't think of yourself as artistic. You may express your creativity by setting a beautiful table, thinking outside of the box, planting a garden or decorating or fixing up your house. The artist lives inside all of us. Discover how the artist lives in you. So far we have paintings, masks and collages submitted to the Love Warrior Community. Expand your awareness of how you can create art to share the message of self-love.

Together we will craft a creative, loving and inspiring art community that will bring healing to ourselves, and the world, through the theme of self-love. When you submit artwork to the Love Warrior Community, you have the option to write about the inspiration behind the art and how it resonates with self-love. Here is an example of art that was inspired by my dream of women loving themselves and their bodies.

Dancing in the Light of the Moon, by Michelle E. Minero

This painting was inspired by a conversation I had with Anita Johnston

---

* The Body Positive, a non-profit organization in Marin County, California has a mission to deliver the message of body acceptance through workshops, books, videos and activists opportunities, go to: http://www.thebodypositive.org/ to find out more.

PhD, author of *Eating in the Light of the Moon*. She told me she was thinking of writing a second book with the title of *Dancing in the Light of the Moon*. The title caught my imagination and resulted in this painting. I dream of a day when all women will inhabit their bodies with joy and feel secure and free enough to dance naked in the light of the moon. Until then, I look at this painting as a glimpse of our future.

Have you experienced the joy and freedom of inhabiting your body with other women? If you haven't, how would your life be different if you did?

Art is one tool that you can use from the Love Warrior Community to add to your Self-Love Diet. To view the artwork on the Love Warrior Community website, visit www.lovewarriorcommunity.com, hover over Create/Explore on the LWC menu, then click on Art. To submit your original art or your favorite artwork from others (with permission), visit www.lovewarriorcommunity.com, hover over Submit, then click on Submit Art.

Love Warrior Videos

We watch movies, TV shows and commercials almost daily, engraining certain images and messages into our thoughts — that women are sex objects who have to maintain a certain look, a specific definition of beauty. What we see is wrong.

Jennifer Livingston, CBS' WKBT news anchor in Wisconsin is an inspiring example of the positive power of video. She received an email from a man who condemned her for her size, telling her that she was not a responsible role model for girls in particular because she was obese. He linked size with health, clearly ignorant of the data that proves fitness and health, not size is an important factor in health. Jennifer's response was inspiring and educational. She was able to use this man's criticism of her appearance as a tool to help school aged children and adolescents be aware of, and fight against this type of bullying. We seldom see this kind of message on TV. If you haven't seen it yet, please check it out at www.lovewarriorcommunity.com/jennifer-livingstons-inspiring-message-about-self-acceptance-and-love/ and pass it along to others. This kind of message regarding self acceptance is paramount to our younger generation growing up strong and confident in themselves.

Now you have an opportunity to watch, and add to, a library of videos that celebrate the diversity of humans. Share your favorite videos with the Love Warrior Community that empower you, that give you courage, that question the standard idea of beauty, that celebrate all body sizes. Go beyond the topic of body image, and share short movies, short documentaries, poetry slams, skits and lectures, any form of video that helps you on your journey of self-love.

Don't be limited to videos that have already been made. Create your own videos. I invite you to create a Love Warrior short film. What would it explore? How would the process of creating a Love Warrior video influence your Self-Love Diet?

Some of the videos you will find on the Love Warrior Community are: "Pretty" by Katie Makkai, "Love Your Tree" by Eve Ensler, "A Fat Rant" by Joy Nash, "The Power of Vulnerability" by Brene Brown and "Tips for Taking Back Your Power" by Connie Sobczak. Visit the Love Warrior Community's video page to see our entire collection of videos.

Videos are one tool that you can use from the Love Warrior Community to add to your Self-Love Diet. To view the videos on the Love Warrior Community website, visit www.lovewarriorcommunity.com, hover over Create/Explore on the LWC menu, then click on Video. To submit videos, visit www.lovewarriorcommunity.com, hover over Submit, then click on Submit Video.

Music

Music is a universal language; it breaks down cultural barriers and brings people together. Music can alter your mood, making you tense, sad, happy or relaxed. Music can uplift and inspire you, or through its lyrics, it can insidiously repeat negative messages into your mind.

I remember loving the catchy beat of Katie Perry's song "E.T." As I began to sing along, I noticed the following lyrics from Kanye West:

> "Tell me what's next?
> Alien sex.
> Imma disrobe you
> Then Imma probe you
> See I abducted you
> So I tell you what to do."

Katy Perry responded by singing:

> "Kiss me, ki-ki-kiss me
> Infect me with your love and
> Fill me with your poison
>
> Take me, ta-ta-take me
> Wanna be a victim
> Ready for abduction."

Once I realized I was singing about an alien who wanted to probe me and that I wanted to be a victim, the song lost some of its appeal.

There are a number of women who are confronting misogynistic lyrics and protesting the performers who sing them. Students in Beverly Guy-Sheftalls' women's study class at Spelman College organized a protest when they discovered that a popular rapper, Nelly, was planning to visit their campus. They took offense to his video "Tip Drill," where a man swipes a credit card through the buttocks of a woman.

The students at this women's college went on to create a group called WORTH (Women Offering Representations That Heal). Not all of the women on their campus agreed with this group. Many of the women on campus thought their actions were unnecessary and did not take offense to the music video or the lyrics that outraged the women who created WORTH.

"One of the biggest challenges we face is getting more women to understand that this music is harmful. It's harmful for young people in particular to consume and internalize these kinds of messages every day, especially when there are no counter messages and no filter," Guy-Sheftall said. "We have young people steeped in a culture of misogyny, violence and excessive materialism, and lots of education and raising of awareness needs to take place to counter that."

Carlos Morrison, an associate professor of Public Relations at Alabama State University commented on the founders of WORTH and their mission, "It's always been a small minority, never the masses, to bring about change."

You may be inspired to fight with the women of WORTH against music that you find degrading. You may also deicide to be a Love Warrior and use love as your weapon. This is the choice I've made on the Love Warrior Community music page.

By sharing songs that have positive lyrics that encourage self-love and body love, you can connect with others within the Love Warrior Community to share music's healing potential. Each time you submit a song that has inspired, encouraged and helped you to love yourself more, you are adding to the healing of others.

Some of the songs you will find on the Love Warrior Community are:

+ "Just The Way You Are" by Bruno Mars
+ "Closer" by Goapele,
+ "Details in the Fabric" by Jason Mraz
+ "Gentle with Myself" by Karen Drucker
+ "Crazy Beautiful" by Chasen
+ "Firework" by Katy Perry
+ "Video," "Private Party," and "Talk to Her" by India Arie
+ "Who Says" by Selena Gomez & The Scene
+ "Born This Way" by Lady Gaga
+ "Skyscraper" by Demi Lovato.

Music is one tool that you can use from the Love Warrior Community to add to your Self-Love Diet. To listen to the songs on the Love Warrior Community website, visit www.lovewarriorcommunity.com, hover over Create/Explore on the LWC menu, then click on Music. To submit songs, visit www.lovewarriorcommunity.com, hover over Submit, then click on Submit Music.

How would your life be different if you used the Love Warrior Community site to continue your self-love journey?

>> Action Plan <<

A) Visit the Love Warrior Community (www.lovewarriorcommunity.com) and find a page that reinforces your commitment to your self-love practice.

B) Write a blog post about your self-love practice and submit it to the Love Warrior Community's group blog (http://www.lovewarriorcommunity.com/contribute-to-group-blog/).

C) Subscribe to the Love Warrior Community to receive email notifications of new posts as a way to stay connected to others on a similar path and to continue your self-love practice. Visit www.lovewarriorcommunity.com and click on any of the pages. Once on a new page, on the right side bar you'll see LWC Newsletter. Enter your name and email address and click on Submit. Shortly after, you'll receive a confirmation email. Click on the link from the confirmation email, and you'll be on your way to receiving a weekly email to help support you on your self-love journey.

45

Safe Place Visualization Script

Instructions provided to create your own safe place

The ache for home lives in all of us, the safe place
where we can go as we are and not be questioned.

—Maya Angelou

The Safe Place visualization uses your senses to bring a sense of immediacy to your brain and therefore your body. By bringing in your visual, auditory, olfactory and sensate senses you "trick" your mind into feeling the sensations and coinciding emotions of being in your safe place. This is only a small bit of the full AMST (Affect Management Skill Training) skill set taught by John Omaha Ph.D. utilizing bi-lateral stimulation. You may want to get the full benefit of managing your emotions through this procedure by a therapist trained in the AMST protocol.

For the self-love purpose of self-soothing you will use the following guide to "upload" the above senses into the neuropathways of your brain. You can enhance this visualization by alternately tapping your feet while creating your safe place, or alternately tapping your shoulders with your hands while giving yourself a hug, while imagining each of the separate senses that will complete your safe place experience.

Begin by imaging a place that is beautiful and safe. This can be an actual place you have been where you have always felt secure. This is a place where you feel completely safe. Your safe place is just for you. Some people have invited

Jesus, Divine Mother, Babba Gi Krishna, and angels depending on their belief system. Feel free to bring in loving spiritual company if you feel the need.

My clients usually imagine a beautiful natural setting for their safe place. Usually it's the beach, a lake setting or a wooded area. From time to time people will imagine their bedroom. Whatever safe place you choose, make sure it has always been connected with safety and a sense of well being.

If an actual place where you have felt completely safe does not come to mind, you can create your own.

Let's begin.

Visual: Close your eyes, or have a soft focus. While you imagine your safe place alternately tap your feet, or your shoulders with your hands as you hug yourself, and envision the surroundings of your safe place. Use your "mind's eye" to notice the time of day, the weather, and all the visual images that accompany your safe place. Continue for approximately 10-20 seconds.

Write out the visual images of your safe place below:

Visual:

_____

_____

_____

Auditory: Close your eyes, or have a soft focus. While you imagine your safe place alternately tap your feet, or your shoulders with your hands as you hug yourself, and listen for the sounds of your safe place. Whether your safe place is outside in nature or inside, just notices the specific sounds that accompany your safe place. Continue for approximately 10-20 seconds.

Write out the sounds of your safe place below.

Auditory:

_____

_____

_____

Olfactory: Close your eyes, or have a soft focus. While you imagine your safe place alternately tap your feet, or your shoulders with your hands as you hug yourself, and smell the fragrances, odors, or scents of your safe place. Whether your safe place is in nature or inside, just notice the specific smells that accompany your safe place. Continue for approximately 10-20 seconds.

Write out the smells of your safe place below.

Olfactory:

_____

_____

_____

Sensate: Close your eyes, or have a soft focus. While you imagine your safe place alternately tap your feet, or your shoulders with your hands as you hug yourself, and feel the sensations of your safe place. Whether your safe place is in nature or inside, just notice the specific sensations of temperature and texture that accompany your safe place. Continue for approximately 10-20 seconds.

Write out the sensations of your safe place below.

Sensate:

_____

_____

_____

Now you have experienced and written about the senses you've imagined in your safe place. The next step is to actually feel the sensation of safety in your body. This is different from imagining the warmth of the sunshine on your face if your safe place is in the beach in the sunshine. This last part of the safe place soothing activity allows you to tell the difference between thinking you're safe, and feeling safe.

You will be bringing your attention to the sensations in your body that tell you you're feeling safe. My clients usually tell me they notice relaxation, calmness, or a heaviness in their bodies. Notice how your body tells you you're feeling safe.

Once your mind brings your attention to the sensations of safety in your body, it has brought you the gift of feeling safe in the moment. This is a great soothing tool that you will have for life.

Sensations of safety: Close your eyes, or have a soft focus. While you imagine your safe place and bring all of the senses together, visual, auditory, olfactory, and sensate, alternately tap your feet, or shoulders with your hands as you hug yourself, as you bring your attention to the sensations in your body that tell you that you are feeling safe. Continue for approximately 20-30 seconds.

Write out the sensations of safety in your body below.

Sensations of safety:

_____

_____

_____

> **How would your life be different if you could soothe yourself when you were feeling scared, anxious, or other overwhelming emotions?**

>> Action Plan <<

Write in your journal, focusing on the following questions:

A) Use the above Safe Place Visualization template to experience your Safe Place and resulting feelings of safety. Write out your experience.

B) Practice this Safe Place Visualization before you go to bed each night for a month and see what you notice.

C) Use your new skill of self-soothing whenever you need to comfort yourself, and calm your emotions.

46

Introduction to the
Body Love Visualization

Preliminary suggestions and information
prior to using the visualization are offered

The body is a sacred garment.

—Martha Graham

Visualization works best when you can close your eyes and imagine the images that come to you from the suggestions in the words of the visualization. In the next chapter I will give you the script for the Body Love Visualization. I invite you to listen to it on my website: www.theselflovediet.com. To listen to the Body Love Visualization, visit www.theselflovediet.com and click on Bonuses. If you hover over Bonuses a drop down menu will appear. Ignore the drop down menu and click on Bonuses. From the Bonuses page you will be able to listen to the Body Love Visualization from the website and you will also be able to download it. You may want to download it so you can listen to it at your convenience and relax into it. You can also read it out loud into a recorder and then play it back and listen to it, or you can use the buddy system and take turns with a friend reading the visualization to each other.

Before you listen to the Body Love Visualization, I'd like to review some information with you about this visualization.

Important preliminary work includes being aware of any trauma or grief associated with certain parts of your body. If you have a history of trauma, or don't have any previous memories of loving your body it might be important to seek professional help from a psychotherapist, who specializes in trauma.

Since bodies hold memories and sensations that may be uncomfortable, having an advocate can help your sense of safety, as well as amplify your experience through verbally processing the visualization in the here and now. This allows for an experience of body love that can now be added to your self-love practice.

If all went well in your infancy, you had a mother, or main caregiver that was attuned to your needs, and helped you learn to self-soothe from birth. You had experiences of body love and exploration. This healthy relationship with your body is your birthright.

This legacy is lost to body-hatred if you've succumbed to an eating disorder. The good news is you can rediscover this loved relationship.

Bringing back an image and experience of love is a step toward recovering that loving relationship with your body. Starting with your physiological body may be easier than the outer appearance of your body. When you can become appreciative of what your body does for you, you have something to fall back on when you are critical of your appearance.

Remember that your body was created to be an instrument not an ornament.

Even if you are reading this book because someone you love is struggling with food and body image problems, you will still have times of strain in your own relationship with your body. Perhaps you have struggled with issues related to your menses, pregnancies, or infertility. If you are male or female, perhaps you have been in an accident, or perhaps you were hospitalized to recover from an unexpected disease. You may not have been immune to abuse in your past. The natural occurrence of aging or menopause can put stress on your relationship with your body, and call for renegotiating your agreements and expectations.

In the following chapter, you will find the script for the Body Love Visualization. There are questions after the text that I encourage you to write about. Your answers will help you to expand your awareness of the presence of love in your body. Enjoy the experience of love in your body.

47

Body Love Visualization Script

The script to the visualization

"Within my body are all the sacred places of the world, and the most profound pilgrimage I can ever make is within my own body."

—Saraha

Welcome to the body love visualization. My name is Michelle Minero. My purpose is to love myself and to help others love themselves. By practicing this visualization, you will experience the presence of love in your body.

In preparation for this body love visualization, you will want to turn off your phone, fax or pager. You may want to put a "Do not disturb" sign on your door for the duration of this visualization. This is your time to be nurtured and to receive love.

You may want to create time for yourself after you listen to this visualization to write about your experience in your Self-Love Diet journal or in the space provided in your Self-Love Diet book.

As I guide you through the progression of moving love into and throughout your body, I will invite you to focus on different senses to allow for a diversity of modalities of experience. Please use my words as invitations only. Your image of love may carry with it, or be replaced by a sensation, energy, emotion, sound, thoughts, perhaps color, words, or even temperature. Just notice your experience without trying to control it or change it in any way.

If you find yourself having difficulty coming up with an image or sense of love, imagine a bright light and this can be your representation of love for today. Begin by getting comfortable. Give yourself permission to make changes in your position to ensure your comfort. I will start by ringing a bowl, followed by beginning the visualization.

(Bell is rung.)

Gently bring your focus inward. Notice your breath and the rhythm of your body as you inhale and as you exhale. Notice the movement of your chest as it rises and falls. As you inhale, feel the sensation of your breath along the back of your throat. As you exhale pay attention to the temperature of your breath as it leaves your body. Breathe in calm. Exhale tension. Continue following your breath as you breathe naturally. (Pause for three or more breaths.)

I invite you to bring your attention to your image or sense of love. Notice how your body becomes aware of its presence. Imagine this love within you and all around you. Imagine connecting with the loving energy above you. Some people imagine a golden light shining down upon them; others have described this loving energy as a warm vibration. Begin sensing this loving energy flowing from the heavens above into the top of your head, through and around your brain, saturating your brain with love. Imagine this love as it flows across your forehead, into your eyes, sinus cavities and into your ears, releasing love into the bones, muscles, tendons and cells of your face, jaw and neck.

Bring your awareness to this love flowing through your neck muscles, swirling around your shoulders, into your upper arms, through your elbows, into the muscles of your forearms, and into your wrists, hands and fingers.

Feel this loving energy as it flows back towards your forearms, through your elbows, into your biceps and triceps, into your shoulders, across your upper back and chest, flowing around and through your rib cage, lungs and heart. Perhaps you experience love as a sound pulsating as it moves through your heart and throughout your body. Notice the love flowing down your spine brining love to your central nervous system as it streams through the openings of each vertebra.

Become aware of your internal organs as love permeates them. Notice the soothing effect of love in your stomach as love permeates every cell.

Bring your attention now to your reproductive organs, pelvic girdle, hip joints, buttocks and sit bones. Notice any shift in temperature as you sense this loving energy flowing down your quadriceps, hamstrings and into the joints of your knees. Pay attention to the sensations of love as it continues to flow down your calves, shins and into your ankle joints, heel, arch and balls of your feet. See this love flowing through all the bones in your toes. Feel this energy grounding you to the earth. Some people describe this sensation as if there are roots coming from the bottom of their feet into the ground. Others describe the sensation of scrunching their toes into the sand at the ocean's shore. Your body is now connected to the earth below you, and to the sky above. Be mindful as this loving energy circulates through your body. Feel this sensation of love in your bloodstream. Notice the joy that accompanies this energy as it replenishes every cell in your body with love.

This energy of love is filling every cell to the depth of its nucleus with love. Love has its own vibration level, and impacts your mind, body, emotions and spirit. Imagine this love overflowing into your energetic body, surrounding you with love and light, connecting you to all that is. You may be able to feel the energetic vibration of love and perhaps even notice a color surrounding you and flowing within you.

Scan your body, lingering on those parts, images or sensations where you are most aware of the love, or the need for love. Stay with this experience, expand it, and let it become as true as it can be in this moment. There is a difference between imagining love in your body and feeling love in your body. When you can feel the sensation of love in your body, bring your thumb and index finger together. By bringing your thumb and finger together when you are most aware of the sensation of love in your body, you are connecting these sensations of love in your brain to your finger cue. These inner visualizations are as real to your brain as your experiences in the outer world. With daily practice, you will be able to eventually bring back this sensation of love to your body whenever you need it simply by bringing your thumb and finger together. With continued practice this love experience will come with more ease, and last longer.

Now, bring your attention back to your breath. Notice the movement of your chest as it rises and falls. As you inhale, feel the sensation of your breath along the back of your throat. As you exhale, pay attention to the temperature of your breath as it leaves your body. Breathe in calm. Exhale tension. Continue following your breath as you breathe naturally.

I will strike the bowl; when you can no longer hear the bell or feel the vibrations, take a deep breath, release your finger and thumb if you haven't already, open your eyes and come back into the room with an awareness of this love ever-present in you.

(Bell is rung.)

How would your life be different if you made a daily practice of this body love visualization?

>> Action Plan <<

A) What did you notice in your body?

B) What senses were active: Visual, Sensate, Thoughts, Emotions, Smells, or Sound?

C) What is it like to experience love in your body: Where did you feel it?

D) Is there anything else you want to write about this experience?

Final Thoughts

Creating and writing the Self-Love Diet has been a joyful, nerve wracking, enlivening, exhausting, isolating and deeply connecting journey with myself and others. Sort of like life. I am more confident and loving towards myself and my body than before writing this book. I know it's because I've been living and breathing self-love. Mini miracles continue to pop up in my life exactly when I need them. Faith in the process without knowing the outcome has been my constant companion.

My minimum prayer at the beginning of the book was that you would end up being more polite to yourself after ingesting the ideas of this book and putting some of the ideas into play. That is still my minimum wish for you; however, I want so much more for you. I want you to love yourself like never before. I want you to look at your body and experience the miracle of loving it, seeing its beauty and being grateful each day for what it does for you, and for what it allows you to do in the world.

In my imagination I see you waking up in the morning with thoughts of gratitude and anticipation for the day. I can feel your sensations as you are filled with awe as you spend time with the sunrise in the morning, spend time in nature and with the moon when it comes to visit you at night. I imagine you having a positive impact on people in your life, and I envision you feeling loved. If this seems impossible to you now, have faith in the process. You don't need to know how it will happen, stay in the "not knowing" and just take the next step, the next action and see what happens.

All of us on this journey together are connected. We are all beautifully imperfect just as we are meant to be. I send you love and pray that it will touch the love in your heart until your heart is full to overflowing. I pray that in those dark times that are a part of life, you will have learned that all feelings come and go, and that each emotion has something for you. And perhaps most importantly, I hope you will experience the fact that you are lovable no matter how you're feeling.

My dream is that self-love will be such an integral part of your life, and for the coming generations, that it will become a non-issue. This prayer for the future was what inspired me to look for evidence of self-love and body acceptance in the past; it was the inspiration that led me to write the short story, Dancing in the Light of the Moon. In Marianne Williamson's book, *The Gift of Change*, she writes: "Years from now, when we ourselves are no longer remembered, people will live on a peaceful planet, not knowing whom to bless, not knowing whom to thank. Children will ask their parents, 'Is it true that there was once a time when people had wars?' And the parents will say, 'Yes, there was such a time. But a very long time ago. Wars don't happen anymore.'"

By replacing the war with your body and yourself with love, you become one of the people whom the future generations can bless and thank.

I thank you for reading this book, and I invite you to share your Self-Love Practices with me, and whoever will listen. Together, we can change our lives and our world.

Blessings,

Michelle

Acknowledgments

Writing this book has been a journey of love. Birthing this book has filled all the nooks and crannies in my life to overflowing. I want to thank those people who have spent their precious hours with me to help me clarify my message, as well as those whose lives I was missing from during this process.

As I write this acknowledgement page, I know I will miss some people who helped me in the process of writing this book because there were so many of you. Please know that you are in my heart, and I am grateful for your encouragement and support. Writing this book has been a labor of love.

First, I want to thank all of my courageous clients. Thank you for your trust in our work together. It's your diligence and hard work that kept me writing so that others could learn from your stories, but most importantly, it's the miracles in recovery, the gratitude and the newfound sense of self that you shared with me that kept me writing. Your work has paved the path for others to live life free from the lies that cloud their ability to see themselves clearly. I hope your work will help others believe that they too are lovable, worthy, valuable, powerful and able to live the passionate lives of their dreams.

Eating Disorder Recovery Support Inc., (EDRS) board, thank you for your endless hours of service to the cause of preventing, educating, treating and ending eating disorders. Thanks to all of the presenters at our annual conferences who offer their expertise pro bono each year to fill our scholarship treatment fund. You all are Love Warriors whether you know it or not.

Thank you Haleh Kashani, Bridget Whitlow, Pam Carlton and Joan Thompson for reading my manuscript and offering your expertise to make it as helpful and clear as it could be. Special thanks to Ronnie Benjamin and

Barbara Birsinger for your consultation as I was developing the Conscious Body-Based Eating: Self-Love Diet Food and Eating Guidelines.

Gratitude to Cat Caracelo for your encouragement and advocacy for utilizing the creative process for healing. Doris Smeltzer, thank you for your passion in telling your story in hopes of preventing the suffering of losing a loved one to an eating disorder for others, and thank you for reading my manuscript and offering your sage advice.

Anita Johnston, your work has been an inspiration to me. Thank you for inspiring the painting of Dancing in the Light of the Moon. Carolyn Costin, thank you for your continual gifts to this field, your generous acceptance of reading my manuscript and for helping me promote the message of self-love. Appreciation goes to Judith Duerk for her encouragement and the refrain, "How would your life be different?"

Thank you Pauline Laurent for your coaching. When I first sat down to write this book, and couldn't stay focused, you became my advocate. Marlene Cullen, I thank you for offering your writing group. It was my first forge into the writing culture. Thanks also to Margo Gallagher, Susan Mattison and Wayne Street for reading my tentative first drafts and helping me become a writer. Margo, extra thanks for your continued support and advocacy throughout this whole process. Christine Walker, I thank you for offering me your time, writing lessons and advice. I send my gratitude to Tara Brown's writing group, Writer's Hollow, for going over my chapters and offering such thoughtful perspectives. Eric Adams, thank you for your timely encouragement.

Thanks goes to my sister, Maria Hawkins, for reading my manuscript and offering encouragement, and to my niece, Kaelyn Hawkins, for suggesting a song for the Love Warrior Community Music page that you thought would spread the message of body acceptance and self-love. To my cousin, Dorene Curtis, thanks for your lawyerly support in looking over that publishing contract, which turned out not to be such a good deal. To my cousin, Lillian Ortiz, thank you for your encouragement over the years, for reading my manuscript and for offering such a helpful perspective. The book is much better because of your input. Ramona Ho, thank you for suggesting I put an index in the book so it can be used as a textbook for your high school kids. And thanks to Laurence Blanchette for stepping in to make that index, and thank you for helping me toward the end to get this book out into the world. Steve Poplar, I am grateful for our weekly Thursday morning telephone calls. You have been one of my greatest encouragers, and a great listener. Over the years, I've clarified my message about the Self-Love Diet in part from our weekly chats.

When I think of support and encouragement, my women's circle is unparalleled. Thank you to Katie Haas, Nancy Schwartz, Rebekah Negro, Ronnie Benjamin and Wendy Lagerstrom for keeping my candle lit in our circle when I stayed home to finish this book.

There is a saying, "You can't judge a book by its cover." I'm so glad that quote is not true in this case. I thank you Victoria Webb for your beautiful photography, but more importantly for your beautiful soul. I did not get any takers when I asked for belly models for the cover of my book. Thanks for capturing the love that I now have for my belly on this book cover. Nancy, I want to thank you for coming over to my house and delivering my early Christmas present of the book *The Fearless Way*. You gifted me twice because its cover was so compelling it led me to Gary Newman. Gary, you showed up just in the nick of time. You were the perfect midwife for birthing my book. Thank you for your patience, help, creativity and attention to detail for the cover design, as well as the interior design of this book.

Last in line for my thanks, but first in my heart is my family. Albert Jr., thank you for sharing your knowledge and perspective on how I could best convey my message. Renée Ho, watching you write and publish your first book was an inspiration—thank you for lighting the way. I also thank you for honoring my writing, even when you could have used my help with Ninel. Matt Ho, thank you for Ninel, our first grandchild. Watching her eat when she was hungry, stop when she was satisfied and experience the joy she found in her body highlighted these birthrights. Kristina, thank you for helping me keep my perspective on what's important. Going with you to plan your wedding on the weekends got me away from the computer and back into life when I needed the balance.

To Emelina, you have been my constant companion and co-creator on this journey. Thank you for bringing the Love Warrior Community into reality. You are my social media guru, my editor, consistent blogger, and most importantly, my loving, enthusiastic, positive, fun daughter. I ask forgiveness for all the mornings when you were still trying to wake up and I already had a list of questions for you. And I thank you for your patience with me in the evenings when you were awake and brimming with ideas, and I was ready for bed and not as available as I could have been. Given our blue bird and night owl qualities, we did amazingly well. Your attention to detail, clarity of thought and passion for self-love made this book much better than it would have been without your expertise. Thank you.

To Al, the love of my life and greatest supporter, thanks for all the nights you sat in the family room and watched TV on your own, while I was writing. You consistently encouraged me to get my book out into the world, and your faith in me lifted me when I doubted myself. Thank you for being my loving partner in life. When I count my blessings in the morning, you are the first on my list.

Appendix

Conscious Body Based Eating
Self-Love Diet Food and Eating Guidelines

+ Eat when you are physically hungry.

+ Stop eating when you are satisfied.

+ Neutralize foods and choose foods that you enjoy.

+ Mindfully bring gratitude to all the people who grew, packaged, delivered, sold and perhaps cooked this food to you.

+ Set the table for your meals; treat yourself like an important guest.

+ Distinguish between body hunger and emotional hunger.

+ Learn the symbolic message of your food cravings when your body is not physically hungry and take non-food action.

An Incomplete List of Emotions

+ Fear Nervous Anger Love Tired Secure Respected

+ Weary Courageous Proud Scared Sad Playful Pain Hatred

+ Hopeful Despair Ashamed Happy Trust Blessed Grateful Disrespected

+ Appreciated Detached Pleasure Depressed Joy Disgust Bold Rebellious

+ Cautious Stressed Surprised Excited Confused Amused Mean

+ Patient Relaxed Confident Loved Pity Kind

+ Anticipation Calm Pitiful Jealous Indignation Envy Contempt Anxiety Embarrassed

+ Resentful Frustrated Enthusiastic Grief Delighted Authentic Vulnerable

+ Disappointed Overwhelmed Comfortable Fascinated Proud Stimulated

+ Certain Determined Shocked Worried Bored Terror Alert Distracted

+ Serenity Ecstasy Acceptance Rage Remorse Self-Loathing Important

BASIC HUNGER/SATIETY SCALE

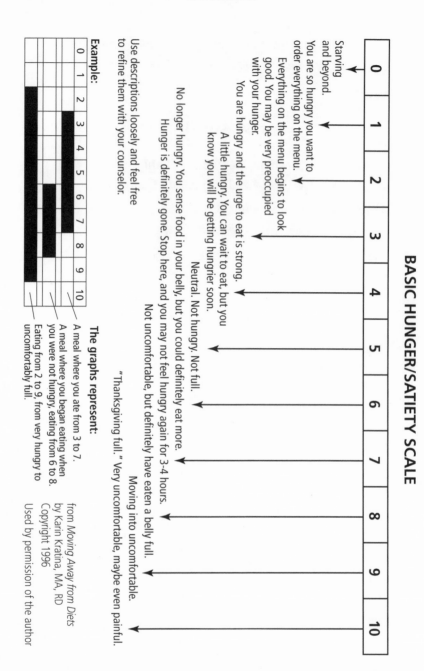

0	1	2	3	4	5	6	7	8	9	10

Starving
and beyond.

You are so hungry you want to
order everything on the menu.

Everything on the menu begins to look
good. You may be very preoccupied
with your hunger.

You are hungry and the urge to eat is strong.

A little hungry. You can wait to eat, but you
know you will be getting hungrier soon.

No longer hungry. You sense food in your belly, but you could definitely eat more.

Neutral. Not hungry. Not full.

Hunger is definitely gone. Stop here, and you may not feel hungry again for 3-4 hours.

Not uncomfortable, but definitely have eaten a belly full.

Moving into uncomfortable.

"Thanksgiving full." Very uncomfortable, maybe even painful.

Use descriptions loosely and feel free
to refine them with your counselor.

Example:

0	1	2	3	4	5	6	7	8	9	10

The graphs represent:

A meal where you ate from 3 to 7.

A meal where you began eating when
you were not hungry, eating from 6 to 8.

Eating from 2 to 9, from very hungry to
uncomfortably full.

from *Moving Away from Diets*
by Karin Kratina, MA, RD
Copyright 1996
Used by permission of the author

Karin Kratina, PhD, RD, LD/N created the Hunger Satiety Scale in her book
Moving Away From Diets: Healing Eating Problems and Exercise Resistance

Unexpected Gifts of Recovery in the Self-Love Diet

+ You wake up in the morning with a clear mind and positive expectations for the day. Food thoughts are no longer your clingy companions.

+ You enjoy food as an integral part of life without unwarranted emphasis.

+ You look in the mirror and see a person of value and innate beauty, and it's you!

+ You are grateful for your body and send it loving thoughts.

+ You experience harmonious, reciprocal relationships where you are free to speak your truth and be respected for it, even if you are not agreed with.

+ You are clear about your purpose in life and experience the joy of living a life with passion.

Body Love Letter Template

Dear Body,

When I think of you as an instrument instead of an ornament, these are the things I appreciate that you do for me:

_____

_____

_____

These are the things I love about your appearance:

_____

_____

_____

I commit to love and honor you by

_____

_____

_____

Signed: _____

Witnessed by: _____

You can keep your body love letter private, or you can have a trusted person witness it. Sharing your body love letter with someone else, when you are ready, can strengthen your resolve to love yourself and help keep your gratitude toward your body more mindful.

Body love letters are one tool that you can use from the Love Warrior Community to add to your Self-Love Diet. To read others' body love letters on the Love Warrior Community website, to submit your own body love letter or to download the body love letter template, visit www.lovewarriorcommunity.com, hover over Create/Explore on the LWC menu, then hover over Writing and click on Body Love Letters (http://www.lovewarriorcommunity.com/body-love-letters/).

Body Forgiveness Letter Template

Dear Body,

I am writing to acknowledge and take responsibility for all the times I

_____

_____

_____

I know this affected you by

_____

_____

_____

You must have felt

_____

_____

_____

I commit to love and honor you by (Amends)

_____

_____

_____

I am sorry, (Ask for forgiveness)

_____

_____

_____

Signed: _____

Date: _____

Witnessed by: _____

Date: _____

If you do not think you have a support person in your life who you trust with this information, keep the witness section blank until you find the person you trust. In the meantime you can receive this support and positive messages by going to www.lovewarriorcommunity.com

Mirror work, connecting with your soul:

Step 1: Look into your eyes in the mirror, not *at* your eyes or face.

Step 2: Continue to look into your eyes until you feel yourself *sink down* and connect with your authentic self, or soul.

Step 3: Say out loud, "I am lovable. I am worthy. My worth is not connected to the size of my body. I have a purpose."

Step 4: Take another moment silently looking into your eyes with love, committing the experience to memory as you start your day.

Deciphering your emotions

Tool #1: Use Your Mind

When you are aware of an emotion ask yourself: What is this feeling?

The acronym **HALT** can be used to help discern emotions.

H = Are you hurt? If you are hungry is it physical or emotional?

A = Are you angry? Are you anxious?

L = Are you lonely?

T = Are you tired?

Tool #2: Use Your Body

When you are aware of an emotion ask yourself:

- Where do I feel this emotion in my body?
- Is it in more than one place?
- What does it feel like?
- How big is it?
- Does this emotion have a color?
- Does it have a sound?
- If you still don't have the answers try the following;
- When is the first time I can remember feeling this sensation in my body?
- How does this feeling connect to what's going on in my life now?

Tool #3: Just Notice

Once you are aware of a thought or an emotion; use the tool of "just notice". Observe it. Pay attention to the sensations in your body that accompany the thought or emotion. If you begin to judge yourself as good or bad, stop. Neutralize your experience by thinking, "Isn't it interesting that I seem to judge things as good or bad."

Tool #4: Allow Yourself to Feel

There is no such thing as a good or a bad emotion. Some emotions are more comfortable than others, but emotions are just sensations in your body that give you information to help you deal with any given situation. Once you understand the difference between feeling your uncomfortable emotions and reacting impulsively to them, you will have freedom to experience your emotions safely.

Tool #5: Writing

Writing works to clarify emotions. First you have to stop and pay attention to the feeling so you can write about it. Once you have clarity, you can explore your sensations and emotions in more depth through the process of writing. One writing technique is called "stream of consciousness" writing. This method is a process of writing without regard to spelling, grammar, or punctuation. By getting uncomfortable feelings out of your body and onto the paper, you can discover the gift this emotion has for you.

Tool # 6: Talk to Someone

Talking to someone who is trustworthy, and a good listener, allows you to process your emotions verbally.

An Invitation to Look Within

When you're pointing the finger at someone else, look at the three fingers pointing at you and ask yourself these questions:

(Pointing finger by Adam Crowe)

1. The first finger tells you to ask yourself "What am I feeling?"

_____

_____

_____

2. The second finger informs you to ask yourself, "Why am I feeling this emotion?"

_____

_____

_____

3. The third finger reminds you to ask yourself, "What do I want?"

_____

_____

_____

Self-love Practices

Examples from people who have begun their Self-love work:

What does self-love do? Here is a list of suggestions from women in my support groups and workshops. You can use this list to begin your own Self-Love Diet.

- "If I'm tired, I'll rest or go to bed. I listen to my tiredness, and figure out what it's trying to tell me. It's usually telling me slow down my pace of life. I have a tendency to put a lot of activities into my days and nights."

- "I'm buying bath salts and I'm going to take a bath and light candles."

- "I decided to forgive myself for all the times I've done things to myself that were not loving."

- "I'm eating three meals a day even if I don't feel hungry because I know my body needs the nutrients."

- "I'm paying more attention to myself when I get nervous. I try to stop and figure out what's going on, and then I do what I can to change it. If there's nothing I can do to change it, I put it in a pink balloon and let it float up into the sky."

- "I commit to taking 3 deep breaths, before I answer the phone."

- "I've begun to stop mid day and meditate, stretch, or go for a walk."

- "I'm making time to get in nature a weekly priority."

- "I pray when there are things I can't "fix"."

- "I discovered that I believed I was a burden if I asked for help. Now I'll call a friend just to say "hi" and appreciate them for their friendship. It makes it easier for me to call them when I want to ask for their support, because I don't feel like I only call when I have a problem."

- "I've added hugs into my repertoire of behaviors! I now ask for a hug, or give a hug."

- "I'm checking in with my body to find out if I'm hungry before I eat. If I'm not physically hungry, I don't eat. I try to figure out what I really want, and then give it to myself. I'm learning food is not always what I really want, eating has just been a habit I've developed over the years."

- "I'm giving myself permission to say "no" to myself when I realize I've over committed to things, even if I want to do them all."

- "I write my concerns on slips of paper and put them in my God box and let him take care of it."

- "I wake up in the morning and decide to love myself each day."

- "Another loving practice is to do the things I've been procrastinating. I feel so much better after it's done, and I've found out it doesn't take half the time to do what I've spent years thinking about!"

- "Last week I was on the phone with my cousin and I took a big breath, and said "no" respectfully and assertively. It was hard to do, but it was the loving thing to do for myself. It was actually a loving thing for my cousin as well, because she won't worry that I'm saying "yes" when I really want to say "no"."

- "I'm getting monthly massages because I deserve it!"

- "I'm catching myself when I criticize my body and I apologize to myself."

- "I'm changing the word "exercise" to "moving in a fun way" so I don't get caught in the *have to exercise to lose weight* trap."

- "I've always been interested in Buddhism, so I'm going to classes even though my family is not interested."

- "I decided to go camping with my friends this summer which entails going swimming at the lake. I'm not going to wait until I lose weight to buy a bathing suit. I'm going to focus on having a good time, not about what I look like."

- "I am slowing down, and taking it easy."

- "I will learn something new."

- "I commit to giving more affection to myself and others."

- "I am working on trusting myself."

- "I will be an example of a woman with powerful self esteem and confidence for my children."

- "I commit to spend time at the ocean with myself."

Use the space below, or in your Self-Love Diet Journal, to add your own Self-Love Practices, or to write about your experiences with the above activities.

_____

_____

_____

_____

_____

_____

_____

_____

_____

_____

_____

Self-Love Commitments

These are commitments taken from participants in my workshop from the 2009 Eating Disorders Awareness Week Conference held at IONS in Petaluma, California.

One of the statements is made up; see if you can find the imposter.

A) "I will take time to rub lotion on my hands and feet each morning and evening. This will be my time to be with myself, and to care for my body lovingly."

B) "I commit to catching myself criticize my body. Once I catch myself, I will stop it, confront the thought, apologize to myself, and affirm that body part, acknowledging what it does for me with appreciation."

C) "I will commit to going to bed earlier at least once a week. I will remind myself that sleep is a loving thing to do for me and my body."

D) "I commit to meditate a minimum of 3 days a week in the morning before I leave for work."

E) "I commit to getting myself in nature at least once a month."

F) "I commit to eating when I'm hungry, stopping when I'm satisfied, and learning the difference between physical hunger and emotional hunger."

G) "I commit to love myself by going on a diet and sticking to it this time! It will increase my self esteem, and will help me to be more active because I'll be able to move with more ease."

If you picked G as the imposter of self-love, you were right! Congratulations! If you don't understand why that would not be a loving choice, go to Chapter 33: *Are You an Inny or Outty?* or Chapter 38: *Wars and Diets* to review the information.

Bibliography

Agbayani, Pastor Boots S., and Aesop. *The Two Pots*. Quezon City: Lampara House, 2008. Print.

All Walks Beyond the Catwalk. N.p., n.d. Web. 26 Nov. 2012. <http://www.allwalks.org/category/about-us/>.

Allison, Nan, and Carol Beck. *Full & Fulfilled: The Science of Eating to Your Soul's Satisfaction*. Nashville, TN: & B, 1998. Print.

America the Beautiful. Dir. Darryl Roberts. 2007.

Amritanandamayi, and Janine Canan. *Messages from Amma: In the Language of the Heart*. Berkeley, CA: Celestial Arts, 2004. Print.

Association for Size Diversity and Health. N.p., n.d. Web. <https://www.sizediversityandhealth.org/Index.asp>.

"Association of Professionals Treating Eating Disorders." *Association of Professionals Treating Eating Disorders*. N.p., n.d. Web. Nov. 2012. <http://www.aptedsf.org/>.

Auel, Jean M. *The Clan of the Cave Bear: Earth's Children*. New York: Crown, 1980. Print.

Bache, Christopher M. *The Living Classroom: Teaching and Collective Consciousness (Suny Series in Transpersonal and Humanistic Psychology)*. N.p.: State University of New York, 2008. Print.

Bacon, Linda, and Lucy Aphramor. "Weight Science: Evaluating the Evidence for a Paradigm Shift." *Nutrition Journal*. N.p., 2011. Web. 25 Nov. 2012. <http://www.nutritionj.com/content/10/1/9>.

Bacon, Linda. *Health at Every Size: The Surprising Truth about Your Weight*. Dallas, TX: BenBella, 2008. Print.

Ban, Breathnach Sarah. *Simple Abundance: A Daybook of Comfort and Joy*. New York, NY: Grand Central Pub., 2009. Print.

"Binge Eating Disorder/Compulsive Overeating." *Tree.com*. N.p., n.d. Web.

25 Nov. 2012. <http://www.tree.com/health/eating-disorders-binge-eating.aspx>.

Birsinger, Barbara. "The Behavior Decoding Method™ and The Quick Decoding Process." *Barbara Birsinger*. N.p., n.d. Web. 25 Nov. 2012. <http://www.BarbaraBirsinger.com/>.

"Body Forgiveness Letter: Thank You For Sticking With Me." Love Warrior Community. N.p., 6 Nov. 2011. Web. 30 Dec. 2012. <http://www.lovewarriorcommunity.com/body-forgiveness-letter-thank-you-for-sticking-with-me/>.

"Body Love Letter: Wear Sunscreen." Love Warrior Community. N.p., 4 Feb. 2012. Web. 30 Dec. 2012. <http://www.lovewarriorcommunity.com/body-love-letter-wear-sunscreen/>.

"Body Love Letter: What I Need." Love Warrior Community. N.p., 6 Nov. 2011. Web. 30 Dec. 2012. <http://www.lovewarriorcommunity.com/body-love-letter-what-i-need/>.

The Body Positive. N.p., n.d. Web. Nov. 2012. <http://www.thebodypositive.org/index.php>.

Bolen, Jean Shinoda. *Like a Tree: How Trees, Women, and Tree People Can save the Planet*. San Francisco, CA: Conari, 2011. Print.

Bolen, Jean Shinoda. *Urgent Message from Mother: Gather the Women, save the World*. York Beach, Me.: Conari, 2005. Print.

"Breathe Deeply to Activate Vagus Nerve." *Travel and Health*. N.p., n.d. Web. 25 Nov. 2012. <https://sites.google.com/site/stanleyguansite/health/health-tips/breathe-deeply-to-activate-vagus-nerve>.

Carlton, Pamela, and Deborah Ashin. *Take Charge of Your Child's Eating Disorder: A Physician's Step-by-step Guide to Defeating Anorexia and Bulimia*. New York: Marlowe &, 2007. Print.

Chiu, Alexis. "Eating Disorders Accompany Television to Fiji, Study Finds." *Dimensions Online*. N.p., 19 May 1999. Web. 25 Nov. 2012. <http://www.dimensionsmagazine.com/news/0,2107,50700-81467-578111-0,00.html>.

Costin, Carolyn. *100 Questions & Answers about Eating Disorders*. Sudbury, MA: Jones and Bartlett, 2007. Print.

Costin, Carolyn, and Gwen Schubert. Grabb. *8 Keys to Recovery from an Eating Disorder: Effective Strategies from Therapeutic Practice and Personal*

Experience. New York: W. W. Norton &, 2012. Print.

Council on Size and Weight Discrimination. N.p., n.d. Web. <http://www. cswd.org/>.

Crowe, Adam. Image of pointing finger. Digital image. *Adam Crowe*. N.p., Sept. 2008. Web. <http://www.flickr.com/photos/adam-crowe/2902680974/>.

David, Marc. *Nourishing Wisdom: A Mind/body Approach to Nutrition and Well-being*. New York: Bell Tower, 1991. Print.

David, Marc. *The Slow Down Diet: Eating for Pleasure, Energy, and Weight Loss*. Rochester, VT: Healing Arts, 2005. Print.

Diagnostic and Statistical Manual of Mental Disorders: DSM-IV-TR. 4th ed. Washington, DC: American Psychiatric Association, 2000. Print.

"Diet." *The Concise Oxford Dictionary*. Oxford: Oxford Univ. [u.a., 1992. N. pag. Print.

"Dieting Statistics with Prospective HCG Dieters." *HCG Diet Direct*. N.p., n.d. Web. 25 Nov. 2012. <http://www.hcgdietdirect.com/hcg-diet-news/hcg-dieting-statistics.html>.

"Durga." *Sanatan Society*. N.p., n.d. Web. 25 Nov. 2012. <http://www. sanatansociety.org/hindu_gods_and_goddesses/durga.htm>.

"Epidemic." *Dictionary.com*. N.p., n.d. Web.

"Genetic Risk Factors For Eating Disorders Discovered." *ScienceDaily*. ScienceDaily, 12 May 2007. Web. 25 Nov. 2012. <http://www.sciencedaily. com/releases/2007/05/070511150158.htm>.

Gilbert, Elizabeth. *Eat Pray Love*. London: Bloomsbury, 2007. Print.

Gladwell, Malcolm. *The Tipping Point: How Little Things Can Make a Big Difference*. Boston: Back Bay, 2002. Print.

Gürze Books. "Genetic Study of Anorexia Nervosa Fueled by NIMH Grant." *Eating Disorders* 13.6 (2002): n. pag. Print.

"HALT." *Alcoholics Anonymous*. N.p., n.d. Web. 25 Nov. 2012. <http:// www.aa.org/>.

Harb, Cindy. "Child Eating Disorders on the Rise." *CNN*. Cable News Network, 22 Aug. 2012. Web. 25 Nov. 2012. <http://www.cnn. com/2012/08/22/health/child-eating-disorders/index.html>.

"Health at Every Size." *Health at Every Size.* N.p., n.d. Web. 25 Nov. 2012. <http://www.haescommunity.org/>.

"History." *The Peace Alliance.* N.p., n.d. Web. 25 Nov. 2012. <http://www.thepeacealliance.org/who-we-are/history.html>.

Horon, Sonia. "Stella McCartney Exposes Leather Industry." *Global Animal.* N.p., 10 Feb. 2012. Web. <http://www.globalanimal.org/2012/02/10/stella-mccartney-exposes-leather-industry/66126/>.

Hyman, Bruce M., and Cherry Pedrick. *The OCD Workbook: Your Guide to Breaking Free from Obsessive-compulsive Disorder.* Oakland, CA: New Harbinger Publications, 2005. Print.

Janes, Beth. "8 Ways to a Happier You." *MSN Living.* N.p., n.d. Web. 27 Nov. 2012. <http://living.msn.com/life-inspired/8-ways-to-a-happier-you>.

Jang, Hwee-Yong. *The Gaia Project 2012: The Earth's Coming Great Changes.* St. Paul, MN: Llewellyn Publications, 2007. Print.

Japan Monkey Center. "Hundredth Monkey Effect." *Primates* 2, 5, 6 (n.d.): n. pag. Print.

Jesus. "Love Your Neighbor as Yourself." *Bible - New International Version.* N.p.: n.p., n.d. Mark 12:30-31. Print.

Jin Park, Bum, Yuko Tsunetsugu, Tamami Kasetani, Takahide Kagawa, and Yoshifumi Miyazaki. "The Physiological Effects of Shinrin-yoku (taking in the Forest Atmosphere or Forest Bathing): Evidence from Field Experiments in 24 Forests across Japan." *National Center for Biotechnology Information.* U.S. National Library of Medicine, 2 May 2009. Web. 25 Nov. 2012. <http://www.ncbi.nlm.nih.gov/>.

Johnson, Craig. "Genetics Research: Why Is It Important to the Field of Eating Disorders?" *Laureate Psychiatric Clinic and Hospital* (n.d.): n. pag. Web.

Johnston, Anita A. *Eating in the Light of the Moon: How Women Can Transform Their Relationships with Food through Myths, Metaphors & Storytelling.* Carlsbad, CA: Gürze, 2000. Print.

Kabatznick, Ronna. *The Zen of Eating: Ancient Answers to Modern Weight Problems.* New York, NY: Berkley Pub. Group, 1998. Print.

Karpinski, Gloria D. *Where Two Worlds Touch: Spiritual Rites of Passage.* New York: Ballantine, 1990. Print.

Kashdan, Todd. *Curious?: Discover the Missing Ingredient to a Fulfilling Life.* [New York]: William Morrow, 2009. Print.

Kelly, Joe. *Dads and Daughters: How to Inspire, Understand, and Support Your Daughter When She's Growing up so Fast.* New York: Broadway, 2002. Print.

Koenig, Karen R. *The Food & Feelings Workbook: A Full Course Meal on Emotional Health.* Carlsbad, CA: Gürze, 2007. Print.

Koenig, Karen R. "Healthy vs. "Normal" Eating." *Eating Disorders Resources for Recovery Since 1980.* Gurze Books, 2010. Web. 26 Nov. 2012. <http://www.bulimia.com/client/client_pages/heathly_normal_eating.cfm>.

Koenig, Karen R. *Nice Girls Finish Fat: Put Yourself First and Change Your Eating Forever.* New York: Simon & Schuster, 2009. Print.

Koenig, Karen R. *The Rules of "normal" Eating: A Commonsense Approach for Dieters, Overeaters, Undereaters, Emotional Eaters, and Everyone in Between!* Carlsbad, CA: Gurze, 2005. Print.

Koenig, Karen R. *What Every Therapist Needs to Know about Treating Eating and Weight Issues.* New York: W.W. Norton, 2008. Print.

Koop, C. Everett. "Former Surgeon General Wages War on Obesity." *CNN.* N.p., 29 Oct. 1996. Web. 25 Nov. 2012. <http://articles.cnn.com/1996-10-29/health/9610_29_nfm_obesity_1_guidelines-bmi-obesity-new?_s=PM:HEALTH>.

Kratina, Karen. "HAES and Eating Disorders: Using Internally-Regulated Eating as a Recovery Tool." *Health at Every Size* 19.1 (2005): n. pag. Print.

Kratina, Karin, Nancy King, and Dayle Hayes. "Moving Away From Diets: Healing Eating Problems and Exercise Resistance." *Nourishing Connections.* Helm Publishing and Continuing Education, n.d. Web. 25 Nov. 2012. <http://www.nourishingconnections.com/moving_away_diets2.htm>.

Lindbergh, Anne Morrow, and Carl H. Pforzheimer. *Gift from the Sea.* New York: Pantheon, 1955. Print.

"Love Warrior Community." *Love Warrior Community.* N.p., n.d. Web. 25 Nov. 2012. <http://www.lovewarriorcommunity.com/>.

Maine, Margo, Beth Hartman. McGilley, and Douglas W. Bunnell. *Treatment of Eating Disorders: Bridging the Research-practice Gap.* Amsterdam: Academic/Elsevier, 2010. Print.

Maine, Margo, William N. Davis, and Jane Shure. *Effective Clinical Practice in the Treatment of Eating Disorders: The Heart of the Matter*. New York: Brunner-Routledge, 2008. Print.

Mathieson, Jewel. *This Dance: A Poultice of Poems*. Sonoma, CA: Jewel Mathieson, 2004. Print.

Nadeau, Kathleen G., and Patricia O. Quinn. *Understanding Women with AD/HD*. Silver Spring, MD: Advantage, 2002. Print.

"National Eating Disorders Association." *National Eating Disorders Association*. N.p., 2005. Web. 25 Nov. 2012. <http://www.NationalEatingDisorders.org/>.

Normandi, Carol Emery., and Laurelee Roark. *Over It: A Teen's Guide to Getting beyond Obsessions with Food and Weight*. Novato, CA: New World Library, 2001. Print.

Normandi, Carol Emery., Laurelee Roark, Jane R. Hirschmann, and Carol H. Munter. *It's Not about Food: End Your Obsession with Food and Weight*. New York: Perigee Book, 2008. Print.

O Magazine 9.3 Mar. 2008: 120. Print.

"Office of the Director - National Institutes of Health (NIH)." *U.S National Library of Medicine*. U.S. National Library of Medicine, n.d. Web. 25 Nov. 2012. <http://www.nih.gov/icd/od/>.

Piver Dukarm, Carolyn. *Pieces of a Puzzle: The Link Between Eating Disorders and ADD*. N.p.: Advantage, 2006. Print.

Ramachandran, V. S. "Mirror Neurons and the Brain in a Vat." *Edge The Third Culture*. N.p., n.d. Web. 25 Nov. 2012. <http://www.edge.org/3rd_culture/ramachandran06/ramachandran06_index.html>.

Richards, P. Scott., Randy K. Hardman, and Michael E. Berrett. *Spiritual Approaches in the Treatment of Women with Eating Disorders*. Washington, DC: American Psychological Association, 2007. Print.

"The Role of Genetics in Eating Disorders." *Eating Disorders Help Guide*. N.p., n.d. Web. 25 Nov. 2012. <http://www.eatingdisordershelpguide.com/genetics.html>.

Ruud, Maddie. "What Is Body Dysmorphic Disorder?" *HubPages*. N.p., n.d. Web. 25 Nov. 2012. <http://maddieruud.hubpages.com/hub/Body-Dysmorphia>.

"Safe Place Protocol, Affect Management Skills Training, AMST and Affect Centered Therapy ACT." *John Omaha Enterprises, LLC - Affect Centered Therapy - About.* N.p., n.d. Web. 25 Nov. 2012. <http://www.johnomahaenterprises.com/about.html>.

Sarah, Breathnach. *Simple Abundance: A Daybook of Comfort and Joy.* New York: Grand Central, 2009. Print.

Schaefer, Jenni, and Thom Rutledge. *Life without Ed: How One Woman Declared Independence from Her Eating Disorder and How You Can Too.* New York: McGraw-Hill, 2004. Print.

Schaefer, Jenni. *Goodbye Ed, Hello Me: Recover from Your Eating Disorder and Fall in Love with Life.* New York: McGraw-Hill, 2009. Print.

Schwartz, Jeffrey, and Beverly Beyette. *Brain Lock: Free Yourself from Obessive-compulsive Behavior.* New York: Regan, 1997. Print.

Shaw, Sylvie. "Sacred Interconnections: Connecting to Nature's Spirit." *International Community for Ecopsychology.* N.p., Aug. 2003. Web. 25 Nov. 2012. <http://www.ecopsychology.org/>.

Sheldrake, Rupert, and Rupert Sheldrake. *Morphic Resonance: The Nature of Formative Causation.* Rochester, VT: Park Street, 2009. Print.

Sheldrake, Rupert. "Chapter 6." *The Presence of the Past: Morphic Resonance and the Habits of Nature.* London: Icon, 2011. 112. Print.

Smeltzer, Doris, Andrea Lynn Smeltzer, and Carolyn Costin. *Andrea's Voice-silenced by Bulimia: Her Story and Her Mother's Journey through Grief toward Understanding.* Carlsbad, CA: Gürze, 2006. Print.

Starhawk, and Donna Read. "Belili: About Marija Gimbutas." *Belili: About Marija Gimbutas.* Belili Productions, n.d. Web. 25 Nov. 2012. <http://www.belili.org/marija/aboutmarija.html>.

Thompson, J. Kevin, and Leslie J. Heinberg. "The Media's Influence on Body Image Disturbance and Eating Disorders: We've Reviled Them, Now Can We Rehabilitate Them?" *Journal of Social Issues* 55.2 (1999): 339-53. Print.

"Twelve Steps." *Overeaters Anonymous.* N.p., n.d. Web. 25 Nov. 2012. <http://www.oa.org/newcomers/twelve-steps/>.

Web log post. Inspirational Images. Ed. Vicky. N.p., 3 June 2012. Web.

"Weight Loss Market in U.S. Up 1.7% to $61 Billion." *PRWeb*. Vocus, Inc., 16 Apr. 2013. Web. 31 Oct. 2013.

"What Is Cognitive-Behavioral Therapy?" *National Association of Cognitive-Behavioral Therapists*. N.p., n.d. Web. 25 Nov. 2012. <http://www.nacbt.org/whatiscbt.htm>.

"What Is EMDR?" *EMDR Institute, Inc.* N.p., n.d. Web. 25 Nov. 2012. <http://www.emdr.com/francine-shapiro-phd.html>.

Williams, Dana. "Women's Rebellion: From Outrage to Action." *Super Consciousness*. N.p., Nov. 2007. Web. <http://www.superconsciousness.com/topics/society/rally-against-misogynistic-lyrics>.

Williamson, Marianne. *The Gift of Change: Spiritual Guidance for a Radically New Life*. San Francisco: HarperSanFrancisco, 2004. Print.

Zhao, Yafu, M.S., and William Encinosa, Ph.D. "Hospitalizations for Eating Disorders from 1999 to 2006." *Healthcare Costs and Utilization Project*. Agency for Healthcare Research and Quality, Apr. 2009. Web. 25 Nov. 2012. <http://www.hcup-us.ahrq.gov/reports/statbriefs/sb70.jsp>.

Index

Made in the USA
Charleston, SC
11 November 2013